MW01628563

BRIBED WITH OUR OWN MONEY

New Visions in Native American and Indigenous Studies

Bribed with Our Own Money

Federal Abuse of American Indian Funds in the Termination Era

David R. M. Beck

CO-PUBLISHED BY THE UNIVERSITY OF NEBRASKA PRESS

AND THE AMERICAN PHILOSOPHICAL SOCIETY

The University of Nebraska Press is part of a land-grant institution with campuses and programs on the past, present, and future homelands of the Pawnee, Ponca, Otoe-Missouria, Omaha, Dakota, Lakota, Kaw, Cheyenne, and Arapaho Peoples, as well as those of the relocated Ho-Chunk, Sac and Fox, and Iowa Peoples.

Library of Congress Cataloging-in-Publication Data
Names: Beck, David, 1956–, author.
Title: Bribed with our own money: federal abuse of American Indian Funds in the termination era / David R. M. Beck.
Description: [Lincoln]: University of Nebraska Press; American Philosophical Society, [2024] | Series: New visions in Native American and Indigenous studies | Includes bibliographical references and index.
Summary: "Bribed with Our Own Money analyzes the pernicious policy decisions made by both congressional and bureaucratic officials in their efforts to eliminate tribal polities from the U.S. legal and political system. Specifically, David R. M. Beck explores one specific aspect of the termination policy—the continuation of federal efforts to use money belonging to tribes to push a U.S. agenda that damaged both the tribes and individual tribal members and enriched outsiders"—Provided by publisher.
Identifiers: LCCN 2023034421
ISBN 9781496237750 (hardback)
ISBN 9781496239174 (epub)
ISBN 9781496239181 (pdf)
Subjects: LCSH: Indians of North America—Government relations—1934– | Indians of North America—Finance. | Indian termination policy. | BISAC: SOCIAL SCIENCE / Ethnic Studies / American / Native American Studies | LAW / Indigenous Law
Classification: LCC E93 .B36 2024 | DDC 323.1197—dc23/eng/20231108
LC record available at https://lccn.loc.gov/2023034421

Set in Charis by N. Putens.

This book is dedicated to
my cousin Neil Froemming,
a good and generous man.

CONTENTS

ILLUSTRATIONS

MAPS

TABLES

ACKNOWLEDGMENTS

We would not be able to do our work effectively without the work of our colleagues. The field of Native American and Indigenous history has matured significantly since I began in the field. I benefitted tremendously from works that have been published since I first began to ponder the extent to which bribery with Indigenous nations' own funds was a simple expedient in the Menominee case, or part of a broader policy. Especially the work of Laurie Arnold on the Colville, Warren Metcalf on the Utes, and Laurence Hauptman on the Seneca Nation provided valuable background and led me to sources for those chapters of this book.

I would like to extend a heartfelt thank you to the many people who have, over the years, encouraged and supported this project in a broad variety of ways—both intellectually and practically. These people include Pat Albers, Rebecca Alegria, George Barton, Jennifer Beck, Joel Beck, Jon Beck, Katy Beck, Paul Bohan, Brenda Brainard, Joe Brainard, Wade Davies, Carol Dodge, Michelle Fredericks DuBray, Neil Froemming, Dave Nahwahquah Grignon, LaDonna Harris, Laura Harris, Brian Hosmer, Fred Hoxie, Aura Wharton-Beck, and those no longer with us who helped define and shape the project in its early stages: Edgar Bowen, Michael Chapman, Ada Deer, Sid Dodge, Nancy O. Lurie, Beatrice Medicine, and Sol Tax. Thanks to Ellen Hurst for fine copyediting. Thanks to Dawn Voyles for helping navigate the intricacies of the acquisition of images.

Special thanks to Carol Higham for a careful reading and to Rich Clow for his line-by-line critique and the discussions about the book at the Double Front. Special thanks as well to Laurie Arnold for sharing so much of her research with me, and to her Gonzaga University students Mary Cate Babcock, Melissa Bazante, and Jonathan Hayes for their invaluable help. Special thanks also to Matt Bokovoy, Heather Stauffer, Ann Baker, and the entire crew at the University of Nebraska Press, who have been wonderful to work with over the years.

Portions of this work were presented in various venues, and I would like to thank all who commented on it in the following places: at a 2023 presentation at University of Illinois Urbana-Champaign Native American House; the 2022 Western History Association conference, San Antonio; a 2022 presentation at the University of Illinois Urbana-Champaign Department of History; 2021 presentations at St. Philip's College, San Antonio, and the University of Montana; the 2017 American Society for Ethnohistory conference, Winnipeg; and the 2001 American Society for Ethnohistory conference, Tucson.

Financial and other support from various sources helped make this work possible. Heartfelt thanks, therefore for the Charles Redd Fellowship Award in Western American History at the Charles Redd Center for Western Studies, Brigham Young University; the East-West Center in Manoa for a Visiting Scholar Position; the University of Illinois Department of History; the University of Montana Humanities Institute of the College of Humanities and Sciences; the University of Montana Native American Studies Department; and the University of Montana Office of the Vice President for Research and Creative Scholarship's University Grant Program. Thanks also for time away from teaching to write from the University of Illinois Urbana-Champaign Department of History and a University of Montana sabbatical. Support from the University of Montana Mansfield Library Interlibrary Loan office was essential to the completion of this book, as was the help of dedicated archivists at each of the repositories that I visited to conduct the research for this book.

My most heartfelt thanks go to my amazing children, Abaki and Iko'tsimiskimaki, and to my life partner, Rosalyn LaPier, whose encouragement and support continue to sustain me.

INTRODUCTION

Failure of Trust

> Like deadbeats dodging bill collectors, as a nation, we keep dodging responsibility for what has transpired, what was perpetrated, and that from which we have benefited.
>
> —North Dakota senator Byron Dorgan

In August 1954 the U.S. Congress delivered a devastating blow to the Menominee Indian Tribe of Wisconsin. After the Menominee finally prevailed in a timber mismanagement lawsuit brought against the United States in the 1930s, Congress appropriated funds to pay damages caused by federal clear-cutting of the tribal forest. Congress then forced the tribe to accept termination of federal trust responsibilities as a condition for receiving the millions of dollars that the Menominee were awarded in the lawsuit.[1] This ugly congressional coercion of the Menominee to support termination as a condition to receive their timber settlement prompted Menominee tribal member William Grignon to proclaim, "We were bribed with our own money!"[2]

During Senate hearings on the Menominee Termination Act, Arthur V. Watkins of Utah insisted that the Senate would not release Menominee judgment funds unless the tribe accepted termination. In a meeting on the Menominee reservation where many tribal members did not speak English, Watkins permitted no translation, causing tribal members to unwittingly vote for termination of their political relationship with the United States. Before a month passed the tribe met again and agreed to forego the timber-damage judgment money they won in the lawsuit in order to avoid termination. Federal officials ignored the second vote. They had successfully coerced the Menominee to pay for their own termination.[3]

My introduction to this ugly reality became the seed for this book when I began to question how common this congressional coercive tactic was and the extent to which using tribal moneys to try to force termination actually drove policy decisions. I started my study of Menominee history in the late 1980s as a graduate student. In the days before the ready availability of digitized newspaper collections, Nancy O. Lurie of the Milwaukee Public Museum generously opened her anthropology news clip files to me. There I found Grignon's incisive comment. Then in the early 1990s, while working in the Robert Rietz Papers at the Community Archives of NAES College (Native American Educational Services) in Chicago, I read a 1954 newsletter issued by Superintendent Ralph Shane of the Fort Berthold Agency in North Dakota. In it the commissioner of Indian Affairs urged the Three Affiliated Tribes to accept termination as a stipulation for receiving money due to them for lands taken in the tragic flooding of their reservation with the construction of the Garrison Dam.[4] This caused me to question and begin to explore how widespread this attempted bribery was.

While trying to understand the connection between these two cases, I reread Vine Deloria Jr.'s *Custer Died for Your Sins*. In his book Deloria commented that Senate Interior and Insular Affairs Committee staffer James Gamble attempted to insert a termination clause into nearly every judgement bill that he possibly could.[5] These funds were reparations to tribal nations either for federal mismanagement of or taking of tribal resources. Yet termination was foisted on the tribes as quid pro quo for the payments that were due to them. Those damage payments should have been unencumbered. At that point I began to consciously look for evidence of federal termination coercion.

It turns out that William Grignon and Vine Deloria Jr. were not the only ones who recognized this pattern. It was clear to people throughout

Indian country. In 2006 I interviewed a group of western Oregon tribal elders about their tribes' termination experience. Don Whereat told a similar story. The Confederated Tribes of Coos, Lower Umpqua, and Siuslaw Indians (CTCLUSI) were lumped with dozens of tribes, some of whom had actively supported termination, into a single termination bill. "The dirty little secret is, and nobody's uncovered the business from the government, is that they were tying termination to land claims. You know, . . . if you terminate you get your money. They have that carrot out there. That's why these tribes all voted for termination, was to get their land claims money."[6]

In the summer of 2004, while I was beginning my search of primary documents relating to the termination of the Coos, Lower Umpqua, and Siuslaw Indians, I traveled with my family to Provo, Utah, to research Senator Watkins's papers at Brigham Young University. Watkins played a key role in pushing termination legislation. But like many public servants, he had either cleansed his papers of records relating to termination or never kept them in the first place. There was little evidence in his papers to show even any involvement with the termination policy and era.

While there I discovered a letter that Assistant Secretary of the Interior Orme Lewis had written during the termination era. It stated in unequivocal terms the Interior department's policy: "When Indian tribes have a constant income" the Bureau of Indian Affairs (BIA) should work with them to shift management of their affairs to either the tribe or state or local counties.[7] (This delegation of oversight had been proposed in the 1930s and even before, and many states and counties had pushed back against it—not wanting to assume federal responsibilities.[8]) Lewis's pronouncement signaled that use of tribal moneys to accelerate termination was indeed Indian bureau policy but that it also was driven from above.[9] The question that remained was to what extent was bribery part of this policy?

This book is an effort to answer that question. It is not intended to provide a comprehensive history of termination. Instead, in the context of the long history of federal appropriation of tribal funds to impose U.S. policy initiatives, this story is grounded in a study of a handful of specific cases. In them Congress used tribal monies to try to force termination on individual tribes that depended on the United States to defend their guaranteed rights. In some cases the coercion ploy worked; in others it did not. The reasons for success or failure of federal subterfuge were as varied as the tribal nations involved.

Assistant Secretary Lewis's attitude, supported by Secretary of the Interior Douglas McKay, drove the hiring of commissioners of Indian Affairs, for example, who were more sympathetic to termination than to tribes. This reversed John Collier's efforts to increase tribal home rule or self-determination under the protection of the federal trust relationship. That short-lived policy of empowering tribal governments under federal protections virtually disappeared from the mindset within the department by the late 1940s. And congressmen, especially western congressmen, opposed to the continuation of American Indian polities as "domestic dependent nations" now had key allies within the administration to help them formulate and carry out policy initiatives to end the government-to-government relations between the United States and Indigenous nations.

As the Second World War ended, Congress decided that the federal government had become bloated, both by FDR's response to the Great Depression and by the war effort. Congressional plans to shrink the size of the federal bureaucracy dovetailed neatly with a long-standing federal policy toward Indian nations: assimilation into white America by ending tribal political standing. Spurred on by the 1949 Hoover Commission reports, the Republican Party supported making the federal bureaucracy more "efficient," while the Democratic Party proclaimed that it already was.[10] Across Congress there was a belief that New Deal programs had been emergency related, and with increased national prosperity the need for an enlarged government no longer existed.[11]

At the same time, both parties agreed that it was a federal responsibility to assimilate Indians into the larger American society. The Republican Party stated in its 1952 platform, "All Indians are citizens of the United States and no longer should be denied full enjoyment of their rights of citizenship." The 1952 Democratic Party platform signaled agreement: "The American Indian should be completely integrated into the social, economic and political life of the nation."[12]

The ideas in these party platforms presage the euphemisms that politicians and bureaucrats would use to describe termination—*freedom* and *emancipation*. Following World War Two U.S. policymakers began to feel pressure from several sides to increase racial equality. Internationally, U.S. allies from Africa and Asia were angered at the Jim Crow treatment and racial animosity they faced when they visited the United States. U.S. cold war enemies in the Soviet Union delighted in underlining the failure of democracy to provide equal treatment or even end racial violence against American citizens. President Harry Truman believed that one way to blunt Soviet propaganda was to support African American civil rights.[13]

On the home front African Americans returning from fighting a war against Hitler's fascism began to push for an end to racist U.S. laws and policies. Many initially did so in a multiracial coalition with labor activists. Their efforts were complicated in the 1950s with the rise of McCarthyism and anti-Communism. In effect, African American civil rights leaders decided to distance themselves from the left and labor to avoid being charged as seditionists under new federal guidelines. In the words of Mary Dudziak, in the 1940s and early 1950s "civil rights groups had to walk a fine line, making it clear that their reform efforts were meant to fill out the contours of American democracy, and not to challenge or undermine it."[14] Marsha Biondi put it this way: "Black leaders" decided "to distance the civil rights movement from the increasingly unpopular Communist orbit and to firmly cast Black aspirations in the language of American nationalism."[15] The language of freedom and emancipation for Indians used by members of congress fit snugly with this embodiment of Cold War civil rights.

In her Pulitzer Prize winning novel *The Night Watchman*, Louise Erdrich's character Thomas Wazhashk, the fictional tribal chairman of the Turtle Mountain Band of Chippewa of North Dakota, reflects on this language: "In the newspapers, the author of the proposal had constructed a cloud of lofty words around this bill—emancipation, freedom, equality, success—that disguised its truth: termination. Termination. Missing only the prefix. The ex."[16] Wazhashk's thoughts accurately reflect much of Indian country's responses to the policy. The ideas represented in the party platforms served to strengthen the resolve of Congress and political appointees on both sides of the aisle to "get out of the Indian business" in any way possible, including bribing tribes with their own money. They would do so in the name of freedom at a time when federal officials were posturing an image of an increasingly just nation.

In the 1940s and 1950s the agents of U.S. policy exploited Indigenous peoples and their lands and resources using the language of liberty and freedom. Ngũgĩ Thiong'o says, "The conqueror has always felt it imperative to control the mind of the conquered. The easiest route to that conquest is language. Colonization of a people's naming system is an integral part of an oppressing system."[17] And our interpretation and understanding of history reifies the colonizer's naming systems.

As a general rule, much of the populace unthinkingly embraces the colonizer's perspective. Too often, to white Americans, liberty is defined as freedom *from* others, not freedom *for* others.[18] This ethnocentric perspective perpetuates an often unrecognized belief that the United States is a nation grounded in white cultural systems and a place where nonwhite people are either peripheral to the national story or else becoming interconnected within it. There is no space for those whose story does not mesh with the nationalist narrative.

As a result, most American historians have long viewed the majority of the Indigenous past as marginal to U.S. history.[19] Unfortunately the histories of Indigenous peoples within the United States is still treated, to a large extent, as somehow separate from American history, rather than integral to it. So while the groundbreaking work being done by historians of Indigenous and American Indian history is changing the field and being recognized by historians of the West, of the environment, and of the Pacific, it has yet to make its way into broader national political and economic histories.

William Hitchcock, for example, in his sweeping reinterpretation *The Age of Eisenhower*, devotes two full chapters to race relations, which was one of the most pressing domestic issues facing the nation in the 1950s and beyond.[20] American Indians are absent from his work. He is not alone; aside from volumes specifically about Indigenous peoples, and their communities and nations, histories of this era are silent on the subject.

In fact, the academy at large pays little attention to the U.S. exploitation of Indigenous lands and resources to further the national interest. This is true of both domestic and American foreign policy studies. Despite the U.S. use of its strategic trust territories in Micronesia to position the nation as a nuclear power, for example, and its use of those islands for other military purposes, historians and political scientists have paid little attention to the impacts of those policies and actions on Indigenous peoples. The stories of Indigenous dispossession for the benefit of national growth and development rarely get told except in works that focus specifically on Indigenous peoples.[21] Indigenous lands and resources, both in the United States and in its territories and protectorates, were viewed by congressional, executive-branch, and military leaders as sacrifice zones.[22] Agricultural and industrial development, as well as the expansion of military presence and power, were viewed as sufficient excuses for the taking of Indigenous lands and rights, both on the continent and abroad, and for subsuming Indigenous people into an economic underclass.

A 1954 House report supporting termination reinforced this policy of sacrifice, couching it in the language of Indian progress and advancement. Arguing that the past should not define the present, the report said, "Today there is no possibility of recapturing the Indian way of life which characterized the great unfenced expanses of an undeveloped continent wherein tribes roamed at will and were impeded only by clashes with stronger and more numerous groups in bloody, intertribal warfare." Though this grossly misstated the Indigenous past in North America, it created the foundation of the argument for change. "The present day economic development of this country and its resources requires the cooperation of persons of Indian descent along with other citizens," the report continued.[23] This statement dismisses Indigenous heritage—whether cultural, political, or economic—as no longer distinct from the American mainstream. From this point of view, freedom or emancipation from the past would be considered a humane policy and a next logical step.

It is not surprising, then, that a unified Congress enacted the termination policy. For several reasons termination was pursued with very little opposition in the House or Senate. For one thing, Congress was very conservative in those years. Most Republican legislators, as well as most southern and western Democrat legislators, were conservative. Political scientist Barbara Sinclair has observed that the 83rd Senate—which passed the initial termination legislation (HCR 108)–was the most conservative senate of the 1950s.[24] Western legislators, whose home states contained Indian reservations, were more likely to gravitate to Indian affairs committees and subcommittees than their eastern counterparts. Interestingly, during these years legislators were more likely to vote with members of the opposing party than their own. Partisanship played only a minor role in lawmaking at the federal level.

Between 1946 and 1956 Congress and the presidency saw every possible configuration of the division of power. Democrats controlled the presidency while Republicans controlled Congress, Democrats controlled the presidency and both houses of Congress, Republicans controlled the presidency and Congress, and Republicans controlled the presidency while Democrats controlled Congress.[25] But through it all, Indian policy remained relatively constant.

A final factor played a key role in the unified support for termination policy—the role and function of congressional committees and subcommittees in the 1940s and 1950s. These "committees seldom split along partisan lines" before the mid-1970s.[26] Senators, for example, respected each other's autonomy and "expertise." They were expected to work in their areas of interest and expertise in committee. As a result, few bills that came out of committee were challenged on the floor. As Sinclair tells us, "The policy decisions reached by the committees tended to be broadly acceptable to the Senate membership. During the 1950s, the ideological spread of the Senate was relatively narrow by later standards; the membership was predominantly conservative and moderate. The committees, which were representative of that membership, found it fairly easy to produce broadly acceptable legislation."[27] They did not challenge their colleagues.

It would do us well to remember that Indian affairs held little interest for most members of Congress. In the postwar era of the 1940s and 1950s members of Congress spent much of their energy fighting and posturing on the Cold War abroad and hunting down Communists and Communist sympathizers at home. Many did it for the publicity it brought them. There was a rush to be part of the headlines that these efforts garnered. "In 1952," historian Ellen Schrecker tells us, "185 of the 221 Republicans in Congress applied for seats on the House Un-American Activities Committee."[28]

By contrast, in 1946 congressional Indian affairs committees were relegated to subcommittee status.[29] When the House established its Indian Affairs subcommittee in 1951, only twelve representatives of the 435 in the house signed up. This was the least popular even of the Interior and Insular Affairs subcommittees.[30] This gave a small number of members of Congress significant power in determining the legal future of Indigenous communities in the United States. Although not all of the bills emanating from this subcommittee passed, the full committee on Interior and Insular Affairs, and the full House itself, were loath to challenge the bills that the subcommittee put forward. The same was true in the senate.

One way to view the termination policy is as one more brutal attack in a centuries-long assault on Indigenous rights to their lands, their resources, their cultural heritage, and their self-determination. Another way to view it is within the context of the U.S. legal system that established a federal fiduciary responsibility to America's Indigenous nations. The termination efforts that intensified in the 1940s are reflective of a century and a half of actions contradictory to the protections the law theoretically instituted for U.S. dealings with Indian nations.

Comprehensive histories of the termination process, both for some tribes that were terminated and some that were not, have been told.[31] For many others, the full story has yet to be written. The approach of this book is different. Instead, it analyzes the pernicious policy decisions made by congressional and bureaucratic officials in their efforts to eliminate tribal polities from the U.S. legal and political system.

This approach creates the theme of the book, which is a study of one specific aspect of the termination policy—the continuation of federal efforts to use money belonging to tribes to push a U.S. agenda that

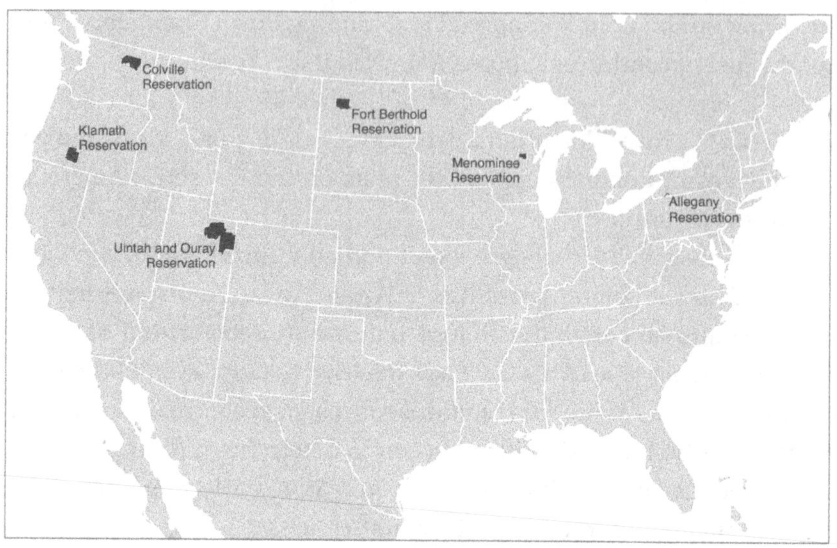

Map 1. Location of the six case study reservations. Courtesy Aileen Clarke.

damaged both the tribes and individual tribal members and enriched outsiders. In some instances Congress and the Indian bureau were successful in bribing tribes with their own money to accept termination. In other cases they were not.

The book presents case studies of six tribal nations subjected to bribery for the purposes of bringing about termination. Three of these nations, despite great pressure, succeeded in thwarting federal efforts. The Three Affiliated Tribes of North Dakota were among the first tribal nations targeted. The Seneca Nation of Indians of New York and the Colville Confederated Tribes in Washington were among the last. The Three Affiliated Tribes and the Seneca Nation both received large payouts for the loss of their best lands to flooding behind newly built dams. These compensation funds were the leverage that federal officials hoped to use to end their political status. The Colville case was more subtle, and their story has been well told by Laurie Arnold in *Bartering with the Bones of Their Dead*. In all three cases the tribal nations only succeeded in maintaining their relationship with the United States after years of bitter fighting.

Table 1. Tribal nations not terminated

	Greatest Threat of Termination
Colville	1953–72
Three Affiliated Tribes	1954
Seneca Nation	1964–67

In other cases, money bribery played a role in bringing the greatest twentieth-century political disaster to individual tribal nations—termination of their legal political relationship with the United States. Two showcase tribal nations known for their magnificent forest resource—the Menominee Indian Tribe of Wisconsin and the Klamath of Oregon—succumbed to the bribery, but for different reasons. The Mixed-Blood Utes case, like the Colville, reflects a more nuanced series of events. Their story is covered by R. Warren Metcalf in *Termination's Legacy*. In all three cases federal success caused lasting trauma to individual Indians and created dysfunction in tribal governance, economies, and social structures.

The book is divided into four parts. Part 1 of the book provides an overview of the evolution and enactment of the policies involved. It begins with a short chapter that illuminates the long history of the federal use of *tribal* funds to pursue *federal* goals and policies. It continues in the next two chapters with an overview of the policy initiatives and actions that shifted the focus on home rule to termination between the 1920s and the 1950s. In part these policies aimed at political disenfranchisement of tribes, in part they were an effort to change tribal relations to real estate, and in part they meant to pay off Indian claims once and for all to push the federal government out of the Indian business. Congress led the charge, with strong support from the executive branch. The BIA leadership, at the urging of the secretary of the Interior's office, enthusiastically took up the task.

The main narrative of the book is then presented in three parts. Each part includes two case studies grouped together thematically. Part 2 presents the first case studies under the theme of "Forests and Termination." The Menominee Indian Tribe of Wisconsin and the Klamath Tribes of western Oregon both held magnificent forest resources. Both struggled

Table 2. Terminations

	Law Passed	Termination in Effect
Menominee	1954	1961
Klamath	1954	1961
Mixed Blood Utes	1954	1956

Note: For a full list of terminated tribal nations see the table in the appendix.

in vain to gain control of those resources and their own governance. The Menominee gained a sudden influx of millions of dollars in their successful lawsuit charging federal mismanagement of their forest. The Klamath were promised tens of thousands of dollars in payments to individuals for their forest. As a result the two tribal nations were considered by both Congress and Indian bureau officials to be model cases for termination. And the bribery worked. In the initial waves of termination in 1954 they both saw laws passed that would eliminate their political relationship with the United States. The devastating impacts these laws wrought on these two nations made them cautionary tales for virtually all of Indian country, including the tribal nations that came under attack later.

Part 3, "Dams and Termination," illuminates the cases of two Indigenous nations half the country apart from each other. Their stories are also separated by a decade in time. In both cases, dams flooded significant portions of their reservation lands, and the compensation for the taken lands was tied to termination. The Three Affiliated Tribes of Fort Berthold in North Dakota saw their rich bottomlands along the Missouri River, which they had farmed for millennia, disappear under Lake Sakakawea. The building of the Garrison Dam in the 1940s destroyed many of their lifeways and led to a partial compensation bill in the 1950s. The Seneca Nation of Indians in New York also saw the most valuable lands on their Allegany Reservation inundated by flood waters with the opening of the Kinzua Dam in 1966. Both the Three Affiliated Tribes and the Seneca Nation thwarted congressional efforts to tie termination to the release of their funds, but only after energy-sapping battles that impacted their ability to revitalize their communities and recover from the losses.

Part 4, "Land and Termination," focuses on the "mixed-blood" Utes of Utah's Uintah and Ouray Reservation and the Colville Confederated Tribes of Washington. The Utes got caught up in the first wave of terminations in 1954. A successful and massive multimillion-dollar lawsuit over uncompensated, taken lands widened a split within the tribes based in part on the degree of Indian blood of individual tribal members. Those defined as "full blood" avoided termination by letting the federal government end its relationship with those of "mixed blood." At about the same time, a portion of the Colville tribes requested that federal officials terminate their political status. The resulting battle, which would be waged among various factions within the confederated tribes into the 1960s, had its basis in the desire by tribal members to have uncompensated, taken lands returned to them. The Colvilles avoided termination in the end. In both cases, the basis of bribery was uncompensated taken lands.

Though the termination and bribery policies were directed from above, they did not play out consistently on the ground. Tribal responses and local non-Indian politics both played a role in determining individual Native community outcomes. Diné scholar Andrew Curley cautions us that "more often than not colonial policy is makeshift, capricious, and discriminatory, built on evolving power relations that augment political and material difference over time."[32] Though the coercive use of tribal funds was a broad policy initiative, it played out in a wide variety of ways during the termination era when actually attempted within the context of specific tribal communities. The six tribal nations under consideration here were not the only ones to face down or succumb to this policy. But their stories do reveal the deep-seated nature and impacts of being bribed with their own money.

BRIBED WITH OUR OWN MONEY

PART 1

Policy

CHAPTER 1

Congressional Abuse of Tribal Moneys

> The treaty was not a grant of right to the Indians, but a reservation by the Indians of rights already possessed and not granted away by them.
>
> —Syllabus, *United States v. Winans*

Federal officials have a long history of using money that belongs to Indigenous nations to meet federal goals. In fact, they have done so since tribal nations began to receive payment for lands taken from them in treaties. These payments were meager to begin with, usually a small fraction of the land's monetary value. Federal officials used those funds to impose federal policy initiatives, often against the will of tribal leaders. The policies were designed to alienate Indigenous people from their lands and resources, and from their cultural heritage. This continued long beyond the treaty years.

In the late nineteenth and into the twentieth century, federal policy initiatives focused on destruction of Indigenous communities. Policymakers believed that they could force Indian people to meld into the American cultural milieu. They ignored the fact that Indigenous people desired to maintain their own national or tribal identities and cultural heritage. They also ignored the fact that white America had little interest in sharing its liberties and opportunities with people of color. And the policy of using money that rightfully belonged to Indigenous nations to bring about this destruction continued. By the time bribery was used in an effort to bring about termination, use of tribal moneys for federal policy initiatives as coercion and bribery were long-standing federal practices.

TRIBAL RIGHTS AND FEDERAL WRONGS

Treaties and the trust relationship form the twin pillars of the political and economic relationship between Indigenous nations and the United States. The trust relationship, a fiduciary responsibility that is grounded in Spanish legal theory, derives from both treaty obligations and congressional statutes. When the United States signed treaties with Indigenous nations, whether peace treaties or land cession treaties, the country agreed to protect the remaining lands and the rights of tribal nations and of Indian people. Some of those rights are known as reserved rights, which Indigenous nations held before signing treaties and never relinquished. Other rights are granted rights, which the United States promised in exchange for peace or for taking Indigenous lands and resources. Congress also has enshrined specific protections into law. The Supreme Court has ruled that both reserved and granted rights are protected under the federal fiduciary trust. Stephen Pevar, in *The Rights of Indians and Tribes*, tells us, however, that the U.S. trust responsibility "can be a shield to protect Indians or a sword to hurt them."[1]

Although Congress has ultimate authority over Indian legal status, the executive branch has the responsibility to carry out treaty and statute obligations to tribal nations. In the 1940s and 1950s nearly all this responsibility was carried out by the Indian bureau. "The history of the Office of Indian Affairs [OIA] is practically the history of the Indian policy of the United States," Laurence Schmeckebier wrote in 1927.[2] To a large degree he was correct, and this remained true into the 1970s. Of course Congress and the court system played key roles. But the OIA, which later became known as the Bureau of Indian Affairs, managed and often micromanaged the concerns and tribal funds of both Indigenous nations and individual American Indians.

Early in U.S. history the courts decided that the United States was responsible for administering Indian affairs, because Indians were deemed wards and therefore incompetent to do so themselves. This has been the basis of the paternalistic relationship that developed between the United States and both tribal nations and Indian individuals over time. The Marshall trilogy, three defining Supreme Court cases that Chief Justice John Marshall penned between 1823 and 1832, played key roles in shaping federal Indian policy. In these cases, among other things, Marshall defined Indians as "domestic dependent nations."[3] This recognized Indigenous nationhood but diminished the breadth of its powers at the same time. Marshall laid the foundation for the trust relationship here, establishing that the United States was responsible to act to protect the rights of tribal nations.

Legal opinions throughout the nineteenth century and into the twentieth regularly undermined tribal sovereignty.[4] Perhaps most significant in defining the basis of U.S. paternalism was the 1904 *Lone Wolf v. Hitchcock* Supreme Court decision. That case enshrined the basis of congressional plenary or absolute authority over Indian tribes by announcing that Congress could vote to break a treaty. It even authorized illegal actions by federal employees.[5]

One shady tactic officials regularly exercised was using tribal funds for federal purposes. These were funds that tribes received, either in exchange for land sales through treaties, or later as payment for resources such as minerals or timber, or for land use. Federal officials knew this was tribal money. In fact, they made clear distinctions between tribal funds and federal funds provided without contractual obligations. They referred to the latter as "gratuity."[6]

Unfortunately, the federal government has a long history of abusing tribal moneys. In 2011 Supreme Court Justice Antonin Scalia admitted that "The Government has often structured the trust relationship to pursue its own policy goals."[7] He could have added that the United States often used tribal, not federal, moneys in its effort to achieve those goals. This is clear from the language of treaties, from the actions of Indian agents and bureaucrats, and from congressional actions and court decisions.

The levers Congress used to exert federal authority included control of and restrictions on expenditures and withholding of both tribal and federal money. This control applied to individual American Indians as well as tribal nations. Indian moneys went into the U.S. treasury and could only be released through an act of Congress. But even when the funds were authorized, they often were released through bureaucrats within the OIA rather than to tribal nations or people directly.

Federal abuse of tribal funds dates to treaty moneys and later to funds generated from tribal resources. Many treaties were broken almost as soon as they were signed. Harvey Rosenthal tells us that between 1789 and 1840, when the United States acquired some 443 million acres of Indian lands, it paid approximately ten cents per acre. The going price for public domain lands averaged $1.25.[8]

Tribes knew that they had been cheated in the sale of lands and that they were often denied the little they were slated to receive in exchange as well. Whether in payment of goods or payment in cash, this was the tribe's own money that it had received for its land. Tribal leaders regularly protested to the local Indian agent, to the commissioner of Indian Affairs, and to the president of the United States. Occasionally they sued in the U.S. Court of Claims, though unlike white claimants against the federal government, they needed special authorization from Congress to do so.[9] This of course undermined tribal political power.

Treaty money paid to tribes in exchange for land was often used to achieve federal, rather than tribal, goals. Treaties regularly set aside money due to tribes in a combination of cash payments and payments in goods and services. These goods and services aligned directly with federal genocidal policies.[10] Policymakers and historians have generally referred to the cultural side of these policies as focusing on assimilation and civilization, although historians are increasingly willing to use the language of cultural genocide that is rather commonly used within Indigenous communities. Ever since Thomas Jefferson's presidency, and arguably before, the cornerstones of this policy were American style agriculture and education.[11]

In many cases these expenditures were either directly destructive of Indigenous economies or impacted only a limited number of individuals and families. Much of the money never made it to the reservations, being paid to white traders, businessmen, or agency employees. Such payments were regularly referred to by federal officials in terms of the United States spending money for tribal benefits, rather than the United

States spending the *tribe's* money on those perceived benefits. Unfortunately, that misconception has carried through the twentieth century and into the twenty-first.

The distribution of the meager amounts of cash were rife for exploitation. In 1963 Henry Fritz depicted the process in general as follows: "The term 'Indian Ring' described any corrupt group which designed to steal from the red man, and numerous such rings were scattered over the country wherever there was an opportunity to exploit Indian annuities. Three principal figures were usually included: the politician, the agent, and the contractor or trader. This triumvirate was interdependent."[12]

One way to think about the treaty payments that the tribes received in exchange for the sale of their land is in the land that was lost in relation to the services that were provided. The Menominee Indian Tribe of Wisconsin's treaty of 1848 provides an instructive, and somewhat typical, example.[13] The federal purpose of the treaty was to remove the Menominee entirely from Wisconsin Territory as it gained statehood.[14] The tribe wholeheartedly opposed this. The United States owed the Menominee interest money from their 1836 treaty, and by 1847 President James Polk decided that they should be compensated. But the OIA chose to leverage those funds as a bribe to force the tribe to remove to Ojibwe territory in what is now Minnesota. Wisconsin territorial governor Henry Dodge did not mince words. He wrote to Indian agent Albert Ellis, "I trust it will be in your power, or that of the Sub-Agent, to Satisfy the Indians that . . . should they treat for a cession of their lands, [the President] shall cause the fund to be promptly applied, in a manner most beneficial to their interests, as originally designed, in the Country to which they may remove."[15]

When bribery failed, the Menominee were threatened with deportation, officially called removal, without compensation.[16] Under this pressure, in 1848 they agreed to sell off all their remaining Wisconsin lands in exchange for lands in the Crow Wing River region in Minnesota Territory. However, they inserted a clause in the treaty permitting them to "explore and examine" those lands.[17] In 1854 the tribe was able to use this clause together with various political machinations to regain the approximately 230,000 acres of land that comprises their modern Wisconsin reservation.[18]

The 1848 treaty sold between four and 7.7 million acres of Menominee land, depending on whose numbers are believed. The official U.S. figures counted both four million and 5,230,240 acres. The set price in 1848 was a lowball figure of 18.9 cents per acre, the same as the tribe had been paid for its 1836 treaty cessions. A Senate committee stated that the land at the time was worth at least one dollar an acre. The amount of $350,000 was set aside for the purchase, which at one dollar per acre would have bought 350,000 acres of Menominee land.

At the allowed 18.9 cents per acre rate, the money that the Menominee received for their land would have purchased 1,851,852 acres. Actually, for the amount of land the tribe sold, as calculated by the U.S. General Land Office, they received less than seven cents an acre.[19] Or another way to look at this is as follows: the tribe received payment for just 35 percent of the lands that it sold in 1848 at the already low rate authorized for payment. Basing the calculation on the actual value of the land, the Menominee received payment for just 6.7 percent of the land that they lost. At one dollar an acre, the 7.7 million acres of land would be valued at more than 290 million in 2022 dollars.[20]

It is also useful to consider the relationship of the money received to the lands taken. A majority of the funds that were paid to the tribe under the 1848 treaty provided for ten annual payments of $20,000 in cash, to be divided among tribal members. More than eight and a half percent—$30,000—went to pay individual debts to traders. In other words nearly half a million acres of the tribe's land was lost to pay debts accrued by individual tribal members. The sum of $20,000 went to pay deportation expenses, and another $20,000 went to subsistence expenses in the first year after the treaty. The majority of this money, representing just less than six hundred thousand acres of land, went to Ewing, Chute and Company, a trading and lobbying firm based in Fort Wayne, Indiana. The company never provided the subsistence promised. Michael Witgen refers to such theft of treaty moneys as a collusion between officials and traders and calls it part of the "political economy of plunder."[21]

Another $40,000—again representing close to six hundred thousand acres of land, went to buy "mixed-blood" tribal members out of the tribe. In addition, $40,000 was paid to implement federal assimilation efforts

Table 3. 1848 Menominee Treaty funds calculated into acreage

Funds received/ Purpose	Percentage of Funds Received	Acreage Lost at 4 Million Acres (Commissioner Medill)	Acreage Lost at 5,230,240 Acres (General Land Office)	Acreage Lost at 7,718,560 Acres (Tribe & Senate Committee)
$200,000 cash	57.1	2,284,000	2,986,467	4,407,298
$40,000 "Mixed-blood" buyout	11.4	456,000	596,247	879,916
$40,000 Assimilation uses	11.4	456,000	596,247	879,916
$30,000 Individual debts	8.6	344,000	449,801	663,796
$20,000 Removal costs	5.7	228,000	298,124	439,958
$20,000 1st year subsistence	5.7	228,000	298,124	439,958

Note: This table shows the amount of acreage the Menominee lost for each of the specified expenditures in their 1848 treaty. The funds expended only actually purchased 1.85 million acres at the authorized price per acre. Commissioner of Indian Affairs William Medill claimed to have purchased 4 million acres. The General Land Office calculated the purchase at 5,230,240 acres. The tribe claimed the land base lost to be larger and the U.S. Senate found that as much as 7,718,560 acres were lost to the tribe in the deal. Because the percentages are rounded and add up to 99.9 percent, the acreage in the table is slightly lower than the actual acreage lost.

such as farming and milling.[22] (See table 3.) In all, these expenses of tribal money for U.S. purposes accounted for well over two million acres of lost land and the natural resources associated with it. Using the tribe's and the senate committee's calculations, the disparity between money for the tribe and dollars lost is even greater. (See table 4.)

Table 4. 1848 Menominee Treaty payment per acre

Number of Acres	4,000,000	5,230,240	7,718,560
Price per acre (authorized at 18.9¢)	8.8¢/acre	6.7¢/acre	4.5¢/acre
Acreage actually purchased at 18.9¢	1,851,852	1,851,852	1,851,852
Acreage lost for no compensation	2,148,148	3,378,388	5,866,708
Percentage of land not paid for	53.7%	64.6%	76%

Note: Table shows the actual price per acre paid for the land that the United States purchased from the Menominee in the 1848 treaty, depending on how many acres were actually sold. The authorized payment for the treaty was 18.9¢ per acre. The amount set aside for the purchase, $350,000, would pay for only about 1,851,852 acres. Commissioner of Indian Affairs William Medill believed he would purchase 3,022,800 acres but arriving on site, realized the amount would be closer to four million acres. The General Land Office calculated that the treaty actually purchased 5,230,240 acres. The tribe and a U.S. Senate committee determined that the tribe actually lost 7,718,560 acres in the deal. The senate committee held that the land value was at least $1 per acre at the time. In their 1854 treaty the Menominee tribe agreed to accept $242,000 for the land that they had been cheated out of in 1848.

Other treaties were more egregious. The 1854 treaty with the Chippewa of Lake Superior and the Mississippi, for example, set aside more than 18 percent of the money the tribes received for land sales to settle individual debts with traders and approximately 60 percent to pay for U.S. assimilation tools such as fixed houses and furniture (to keep people from following seasonal rounds, traplines, and rising fields), farming equipment (to change the basis of the tribal economy), and western education (to change the cultural foundation of Ojibwe children).[23] Nearly 80 percent of the land sold in this treaty went to pay these expenses to achieve federal goals; not for what the Ojibwe might have defined as in their interests.

The money expended in these treaties was not federal money. It was the money that the tribes received in exchange for their land. Tribal leaders knew this. When Chickasaw people were deported from their homes in the southeast in 1838 they told the officer moving them, “We are moved out of our own money." It was indeed their own money that paid for removal.[24] In the early twentieth century Blackfeet leaders in Montana, when told that their annuities would be withheld as punishment, told their agent, "Our rations are not a gratuity—they are bought with our own money."[25]

All of this abuse of tribal funds crippled these tribes' economies for generations to come. It also redirected cultural norms in ways that the people in those Indigenous communities are working to cope with to this day.

Treaty funds were also sometimes used in ways that did not even benefit the tribe that sold the lands. This was legal under the congressional plenary power doctrine. According to attorney Glen Wilkinson, the Court of Claims ruled in 1927 "that jurisdiction, both legal and equitable, 'arising under or growing out of any treaty or agreement' did not authorize setting aside a treaty alleged to have been made under duress or procured by threat."[26] In other words, illegally or unethically negotiated treaty agreements were considered good law. Although nearly all treaties directed tribal funds to be spent for federal goals, this was especially galling to tribes in treaties that federal officials negotiated in clearly underhanded ways. Tribal leaders readily recognized subterfuge and regularly protested what they viewed as federal misuse of their money.

In 1834, for example, the Menominee protested the use of education treaty funds to support an Episcopal mission school. Most Menominee people were not Christian at this time. The vast majority of those who were had become Catholic. In fact, the Episcopal school, which received all the Menominee education funds, served just two American Indian students. All the rest of its students were white. The tribe's principal chief, Oshkosh, told the local Indian agent that "if any portion of this money be paid to the Mission here, he would employ a lawyer, or as the Indian language expresses it, a Judge to go to Washington immediately, and protest against such proceedings, to the President."[27] Three years later the tribe unsuccessfully attempted to reject expenditure of all of their treaty education money. They were caught in a broader Protestant-Catholic battle being waged by religious leaders and federal officials.[28] Despite the religious conflict, the federal policy was clear—Christian religion and western style education were foundational to the assimilation project that the United States insisted on foisting on tribes. And tribes would pay for this cultural genocide with their own money.

Thirty years later, the northern and southern Osage tribes fell victim to a scheme in which federal officials used their money to pay for assimilation programs with multiple tribes. The Osage signed a treaty in 1865 that left no written record except the treaty document itself. The treaty stipulated that money the Osage received for their lands would go to the federal "civilization fund" "for the education and civilization of Indian tribes residing within the limits of the United States." The Court of Claims doubted whether Osage tribal members understood the full scope of the treaty when they signed it. In fact, they must not have, since they later sued. They argued that their money should not have been used to educate children of other tribes. The court ruled against them in an early decision that helped cement the idea that Congress holds plenary power, or absolute authority, in the disposition of or control over tribal funds. The outcome was devastating for tribal rights.[29]

In both these instances federal, not tribal, policies were funded with tribal money. This occurred in case after case across Indian country in the United States. Tribal funds were abused in a variety of other ways as well. When tribes tried to collect on money owed them, the courts often ruled that federal expenses in tribal upkeep be deducted from their claims.[30] This diminished the cost of the federal trust responsibility at the expense of tribal economies and cultural preservation. It also severely restricted tribal sovereignty. Even when tribes did have funds, they were held in the U.S. Treasury and released at the behest of Congress. Without a stable economic foundation, tribal nations simply had few avenues to exert authority. But they continuously tried to. They regularly worked "to insure that the voice of our people shall be heard in determining our own destiny," in the words of Chippewa businessman Scott Henry Peters.[31]

NEW POLICIES, OLD ACTIONS

As genocidal wars and deportation gave way to ethnocidal allotment and citizenship policies in the late nineteenth and early twentieth centuries, unethical use of tribal funds by federal officials continued. The

1887 General Allotment Act, or Dawes Act, authorized Congress to pass laws relating to specific tribes that would confiscate reservation lands to dole out parcels to individual heads of household for agricultural use. Surplus lands could then be sold to non-Indian farmers, ranchers, and speculators.

In a further blow to Indigenous control of resources, in 1873 the Supreme Court ruled that because tribal lands were held in trust and controlled by the federal government, "the Indians ha[d] only a right in occupancy of the lands," not the right to exploit the reservation's resources without federal permission. This meant that U.S. officials would oversee the extraction of resources, provided that the funds received were used for the benefit of the tribes.[32]

As the allotment policy was pursued, federal spending continued to push U.S., not tribal, needs. David Grann succinctly describes the experience of the Osage, which reflects that of many tribes: "The [federal] government owed the tribe annuity payments for the sale of its Kansas land but refused to distribute them until able bodied men . . . took up farming. Even then the government insisted on making the payments in the form of clothing and food rations." Osage leaders had to appear forcefully before the commissioner of Indian Affairs in Washington to end the ration system, a system that ironically caused continued dependence. In a display of self-rule the tribe opposed this and wished to gain control of its own funds.[33]

The Allotment Act itself stipulated the sale of surplus lands and required the funds to be placed in the U.S. Treasury. Getting funds out to a tribe could only be done with a Congressional appropriation.[34] So in addition to tribes being cheated on the value of the resources, the money that they did receive from land sales was controlled not by the tribes themselves but by federal officials. Both the secretary of the Interior and Congress held the tribal purse strings. These funds were often spent on "civilization" efforts that supported misguided U.S. assimilation policies, actions that tribes opposed.

This was especially damaging for tribes with timber or mineral resources. The Menominee and the Klamath saw both the value and extent of their timber resources dwindle through mismanagement.

Then their timber funds disappeared. Some went to pay the very federal employees who were mishandling their timber. When Congress established the Forest Division of the Office of Indian Affairs in 1910, it gave the secretary of the Interior the authority to sell tribal timber and ordered that the funds "be used for the benefit of the Indians of the reservation in such a manner as [the secretary] may direct." Unfortunately the 1910 law did not provide administrative costs.[35] So the income included a deduction that paid the salaries of OIA foresters.[36] The law exempted the Menominee from the rules, but they were already paying a broad variety of expenses from their profits under a 1908 law.[37] Timber tribes would fight this practice for decades.

But perhaps the most egregious cases involving theft of Indian moneys took place in Oklahoma.[38] There, the federal government abdicated its authority altogether. Although entry into statehood in 1907 had included a requirement that Indians remain under federal authority, Congress passed a law barely a year later that removed the trust relationship from land held by members of the Five Civilized Tribes and gave the responsibility over to county courts.[39] Since the trust responsibility lies with the federal government and plenary power resides in Congress, these courts were given a free pass to turn tribal and individual Indian resources over to their greedy white neighbors.

According to a 1924 report cowritten by Gertrude Bonnin and published by the Indian Rights Association, "The grafters were quick to realize the possibilities the Act of 1908 opened to them, and plans were soon working smoothly in their interest and to the great detriment of the Indians."[40] The report documented collusion between elected judges, other politicians, their friends, and undertakers who practiced outright theft of Indian property; abuse of a "guardianship" relation that was established; and even murder in venal efforts to steal Indian wealth and property. The authors of the report morosely observed "When oil is 'struck' on an Indian's property, it is usually considered prima facie evidence that he is incompetent, and in the appointment of a guardian for him his wishes in the matter are rarely considered."[41] The Indian bureau officials in the state could only look on helplessly as Indigenous children were married to white men, as doctored wills were presented in court, and as individual Indians were murdered for their riches. In some cases tens of thousands of dollars were stolen from Indian individuals and heirs. Historian Angie Debo risked her life studying the graft, which she traced to Oklahoma's top politicians. She was successful enough that all the books she wrote on Oklahoma Indian history were banned from the state's schools for much of her lifetime. As she succinctly said, "And they robbed the Indians."[42] The bribery and robbery was essentially sanctioned by Congress, which looked the other way.

The case of the Osage Indians has recently received broad attention due to the publication of Grann's *Killers of the Flower Moon* and the Martin Scorsese film based on the book. The Osage had been removed to Oklahoma by the time they were fleeced in the early twentieth century. Since the Osage had purchased their land, they were able to keep all of it in the hands of tribal members when it was allotted. And they were able to write their oil, gas, and mineral rights into their allotment act. When oil gushed from reservation wells, the money went to the tribe and was paid out to individuals. Nonetheless, even in what seemed the most favorable of circumstances for a tribe, the resulting thefts and murders were egregious enough to cause a national scandal that played a key role in the development of the Federal Bureau of Investigation. Federal officials were unable to stop the theft.[43] Congress cared little about its role as trustee in Oklahoma, and its neglect left an already weak OIA essentially powerless to protect the beneficiaries of federal trust.

As allotment abysmally failed to invigorate Indian economies—in part due to congressional restrictions on tribal moneys—individual Indians throughout the United States entered the cash economy in a variety of ways in the late nineteenth and early twentieth centuries. They did so both in order to escape the dire poverty of their reservation communities and as a way around the federal restrictions on the use of the funds that tribes and individuals held. They took up agricultural and freighting work, became entertainers, worked construction, became loggers, made material culture items for trading, entered the fishing trade, and more.[44] Ironically, federal officials and churches opposed this, arguing on the one hand that Indian people were not competent to manage money and on the other that earning cash money stifled Indian independence by making them dependent on the vagaries of seasonal work.[45] In many cases, though, Indian individuals decided that the most effective way to combat federal mismanagement of tribal money was to earn money on their own.

It is worth noting that not only were tribal funds used for American purposes but funds appropriated to benefit Indians often actually served to benefit non-Indians. Writing about the last two decades of the nineteenth century and the beginning of the twentieth, historian Harvey Rosenthal observed that when money "was appropriated for Indian affairs; this meant, in reality, for whites. Money went for white educators; for allotment, which in fact gave land to whites; and to maintain the 6,000 employees of the Indian Service," for example.[46]

All of this unethical use of tribal funds during the first century and a half of U.S. nationhood caused tribes to appeal for justice in the U.S. Court of Claims. Federal theft and chicanery were so prevalent that the court was swamped with tribal claims. In fact, the Indian cases became so predominant in the court that they had to be separated simply so that the claims court could continue its work. In 1946 Congress created the Indian Claims Commission to alleviate the pressure on the Court of Claims. In addition, and primarily, it was conceived as a place to end Indian claims against the United States once and for all in preparation for relinquishment of federal responsibility over tribal nations and individual Indians through termination.

In the meantime, beginning in the 1920s, tribal leaders across the country as well as federal policymakers began a push to increase tribal control of decision-making. This effort can best be described as seeking home rule. Tribal leaders had long been fed up with being shut out of leadership roles in their communities and deprived of spending their own dollars. They believed, with good reason, that federal money and resource mismanagement was responsible for the dire conditions on their reservations. Federal officials hoped that increased tribal leadership would bring a diminishment of federal responsibilities for the well-being of individual Indians. By the late 1920s parties on both sides were thus pushing for a policy change.

By the late 1940s and the 1950s these efforts led to an all-out crisis in Indian country. These decades saw a fierce assault on American Indian tribal sovereignty perpetrated by both the U.S. Congress and the Department of the Interior. Congress proposed numerous bills to weaken tribes, and several of them became law. Underlying these bills and laws was a congressional desire to relinquish the federal financial responsibility to Indigenous nations. This effort to eliminate tribal nations and federal fiduciary responsibility amounted to a repudiation of federal trust responsibilities. The evolution of the concept of home rule to a policy of termination occurred over about a quarter of a century, beginning in the late 1920s and culminating with the 1953 passage of House Concurrent Resolution (HCR) 108, the termination enabling act.

CHAPTER 2

Rights and Responsibilities

> The rhetoric of freedom and liberation for the Indians in the United States ultimately led to the desire to liberate Indians from their lands and resources.
>
> —Heather Daly, "American Indian Freedom Controversy"

> Instead of the Indian departing from the reservation and allowing the government role to wither, the government would withdraw and allow the Indian to wither.
>
> —Harvey Rosenthal, *Their Day in Court*

The anthropologist Sol Tax liked to say that the federal government's Indian policy has always focused on getting "out of the Indian business."[1] John Collier made a similar argument in 1944. He told congressional leaders that prior to reforms that resulted from the 1928 publication of the Meriam Report, federal Indian policy focused solely on "liquidating" the Indian estate.[2] Historian Rich Clow, parting from Collier's optimistic view of 1930s Indian policy, has said, "The modern termination era began in 1928." Like Tax he argued that this policy has not changed all that much since, despite the pendulum-like shifts in federal policy initiatives toward tribes.[3] The Montana Committee Against Termination went a step further in 1955 and argued that "termination dates from the Dawes Act of 1887."[4]

Sadly, race is an element that cannot be ignored in the trust relationship. Discussing race, Ibram X. Kendi argues that "the history of the racialized world is a three-way fight between assimilationists, segregationists, and antiracists." Indeed, federal Indian policy proposals before the 1960s almost exclusively fell into the assimilationist or segregationist categories. If antiracism is "based in the truth that racial groups are equals in all the ways they are different," then few people aside from American Indians worked to provide a culturally and politically recognized place for Indigenous Americans in the U.S. polity or social or economic milieus.[5]

Viewed from these perspectives, the federal policies that defined the treaty and allotment eras continued. The violation of trust continued as well. Both Congress and the Indian bureau failed to act in the best interests of Indigenous people or their nations. Twentieth century policies continued to include efforts to force American Indians to assimilate into mainstream society and to minimize federal responsibilities toward Indigenous nations. Both these initiatives would flow smoothly into the Collier administration's new policies of the 1930s. They got jump-started with the publication of the 1928 Meriam Report and a series of congressional hearings that would drag on for the next quarter century.

The Meriam Report, a document written at the request of Secretary of the Interior Hubert Work and officially titled *The Problem of Indian Administration*, found what American Indian community leaders and members already knew: that the federal policies enacted by Congress and carried out by the Office of Indian Affairs had failed to bring even basic decent living conditions to most reservation communities. Tribes chafed under the paternalistic and all-consuming control of incompetent bureaucrats.

The report laid bare the failures of congressional policy efforts to fulfill the U.S. trust responsibility to tribes. It recognized the abject failure of the allotment policy. "It almost seems as if the government assumed that some magic in individual ownership of property would in itself prove an educational civilizing factor, but unfortunately this policy has for the most part operated in the opposite direction," the authors observed. The report focused heavily on policy outcomes that impoverished individual tribal members, blaming their condition to a large extent on the "idleness" caused by unearned income.[6] Even though outsiders benefitted most from the lease and sale of tribal lands, the authors blamed Indians themselves for their poverty. Tribal leaders often viewed things differently. Many believed that mismanagement of their resources and of their funds by federal officials were the factors that had severely weakened Indigenous economies.

The Meriam Report did, however, recognize "the exclusion of Indians from the management of their own affairs" as one of the "two most serious deficiencies in Indian administration," according to legal scholar Felix Cohen.[7] By the 1920s Indigenous leaders across the United States were calling for more control over the management of their affairs. This perspective is reflected well in the motto printed on the letterhead of California's Mission Indian Federation: "Human Rights and Home Rule."[8]

At the same time federal officials, recognizing the economic failure of allotment, moved toward empowering tribes to take control of local decision-making. Indian claims attorney James Curry put it this way: "During the Hoover administration [1929–1933] it dawned upon the top men in government that the time had come to let the Indians run their own affairs to the largest possible extent."[9] This of course would have the advantage of diminishing federal responsibilities and costs. The trust obligation to protect tribal home rule would remain intact. But the extent to which it *should* remain intact, or whether it should at all, became the basis of conflict between federal officials and tribal leaders.

The Great Depression, the war effort, and the attendant growth of the federal budget and infrastructure provided fodder for congressional efforts to diminish expenses during those times and in the postwar years. Though expenditures on U.S. trust responsibilities to tribes have always been small, they also often have been targets for cuts by members of Congress eager to show voters that they can be thrifty with tax dollars. Indian self-determination was a goal of both tribes and federal officials, but they often viewed it in starkly different terms. Tribes were loath to let the United States abdicate its trust responsibilities, while U.S. policymakers too often simply wanted to be rid of historical obligations.

This conflict of definition came to a head over the quarter century from 1929 to 1954.

THE PUSH FOR HOME RULE, 1929–41

By the time allotment had ended, most treaty expenditures had run out. But that did not stop federal officials from using tribal funds for federal purposes.[10] Tribal funds held in the U.S. treasury were used "whenever Congress believes that the Indians should pay for the services rendered," according to historian Laurence Schmeckebier. In 1923 that amounted to more than two and a half million dollars, 18 percent of the congressional appropriations for Indian affairs that year. The bulk of the money was spent on "civilization" purposes. Such tribal funds included lease money and sale of resources, such as timber.[11]

Tribal disgruntlement with federal misuse of their funds only continued to grow. The Indian bureau took tentative steps to empower tribal governments after publication of the Meriam Report. However, control of tribal finances was a different story. Charles Rhoads, who served as commissioner of Indian Affairs from 1929 until Collier's appointment in 1933, began to reshape and professionalize the Indian Service. Rhoads accepted the appointment as commissioner with the promise from President Herbert Hoover that he would be able to use his position to advance the policy reforms outlined in the Meriam Report.[12] These focused primarily on education "in the broadest sense of that word." The purpose of child and adult education should be "the social and economic advancement of the Indians," the report opined. Immediate recommendations were all geared toward upgrading the training, positions, and work of bureau employees.[13] All of these changes cost money.

These changes also had the longer-term goal of elimination of the Indian Bureau. Rhoads said, "The general policy should be to increase the facilities for the care and development of the Indian for a short period of time with the general plan . . . of eliminating the Indian Bureau within a period of say twenty-five years."[14] Twenty-five years later the first termination bills would be passed.

Both Collier and the secretary of the Interior praised Rhoads for professionalizing the Indian bureau.[15] However, as Collier would later observe, the Indian bureau was crippled in its efforts to improve economic and social conditions in Indian country by the House appropriations committee, which restricted OIA funding primarily to children's education and hospitals. Collier reported that this "handicapped" "one basic element of our program and purpose, namely, tribal self-help and self-government."[16]

Tribes had grown increasingly frustrated at both the federal mismanagement of their resources and money and their own lack of control over it. They also chafed under the Indian bureau's control and use of tribal funds to cover the costs of federal personnel and administrative services, a long-standing policy. Tribes with extensive natural resources pushed especially hard for greater control of their assets in the 1920s and 1930s. They fought an uphill battle.

Collier wrote, and in 1934 Congress modified and passed, the Indian Reorganization Act (IRA). It was intended to facilitate greater tribal control of both governance and resources as well as to provide opportunities for substantive economic development. On its surface the IRA reflected a stark departure from previous policies by viewing tribal governments as partners in decision-making. Tribal nations could vote to accept the IRA and then vote whether to organize under it. If they did so, they could establish constitutions and then work with the Indian bureau on a government-to-government basis. The Indian bureau sent those tribes recommended constitutions based loosely on the U.S. tripartite organization of government. These documents, which ignore traditional governance methods, became ubiquitous in Indian country to the extent that they are referred to as boilerplate constitutions.[17]

In some cases the IRA succeeded. Luke Gilbert, Cheyenne River Sioux tribal chairman, told the House of Representatives Committee on Indian Affairs that the law had benefitted his tribe. The Cheyenne River Sioux organized under the law in 1934. Individual tribal members had been able to purchase cattle through a revolving-loan fund, and others could attend college using an educational loan fund established through the IRA. In the first six years, the tribe had been able to recover more than 440,000 acres of land that had been lost under the allotment policy. And finally, for the first time, the tribal council had control over the budget and was no longer paying administrative costs with tribal funds.[18]

Others viewed it differently. Seventy-seven tribes rejected the IRA altogether.[19] One, the Klamath Tribe of Oregon, rejected the IRA because they already had a functioning tribal government. In 1908 its members created an Executive Tribal Council, which became a six-person business committee in 1929. That same year the larger General Council authorized a constitution and bylaws. The already existing tribal government rejected the IRA.[20] The Klamaths wanted better control and management of their forest resources, but they did not see organization under the IRA as the best way to gain that. Unfortunately, even without accepting the IRA, the Klamaths continued to chafe under Collier's tenure, being forced to spend an increasing amount of timber dollars to pay federal salaries for services they believed tribal members could provide more reasonably.[21]

The Menominee Indian Tribe of Wisconsin accepted the IRA but refused to incorporate or organize a government under it.[22] They had already established a political system to govern their economic resources and were loath to give it up. They had worked hard, if without success, to gain control of their rich forest resources, since the 1870s. They wrote their first official tribal constitution in 1904, establishing a business committee to oversee the forest and logging management.[23] In 1908 they were beneficiaries of a federal law, commonly known as the LaFollette Act, which established long-lasting protection of the tribe's forest and its logging and sawmill businesses. It also required that Menominees would be in leadership positions in the industry.[24] All of this was merely theoretical.

The LaFollette Act also gave the secretary of the Interior responsibility for spending proceeds in support of the logging and lumber operations. The interest would be used "for the benefit of such Indians in such manner as the Secretary of the Interior shall prescribe." A 1934 law would give the tribe the right of "advance review and approval" of the budget. But Commissioner Collier failed to forward them the annual budget for review. All of this left the Indian bureau with discretionary power over spending of tribal funds.[25]

When federal officials failed to adhere to the law, the tribe sued. And when the Menominee were asked to incorporate under the IRA, its leaders politely but steadfastly refused, arguing that they had already established a governing system that met their needs.[26] Collier simply believed that he knew better than these tribal leaders what would be in their best interest. "Collier's failure to return home rule and to reduce Indian Service reservation roles led to tribal disenchantment" with both Collier and the IRA, according to historian Richmond Clow.[27]

In 1940 the Senate passed a bill that would have exempted numerous tribal nations from the IRA. It did so over the objections of Collier's OIA. The House did not pass the bill. But with some exceptions, the House hearings laid bare tribal opposition and legislative hostility to Collier's efforts at reorganization.[28] Tribal leaders from across the country bemoaned and called out federal failure. The Senate, in considering the bill, clearly attacked the separate status of Indian nations within the U.S. political system. Its accompanying report seemingly refuted John Marshall's seminal Supreme Court decisions. It said, "[The IRA] attempts to set up a state or a nation within a nation which is contrary to the intents and purposes of the American Republic." It went on to say, "In no way should they [Indians] be set up as a governing power within the United States of America."[29]

Nonetheless, during the war years, Collier desperately worked to save the policies he had developed as commissioner of Indian Affairs. He proposed a bill that would permit tribes to opt into or out of the IRA, and he proposed bills that would loosen restrictions in the appropriations process that hampered his administration's ability to be nimble. He also told Congress that Indian appropriations were woefully inadequate—funds set aside for Indian forest and range project work, for example, were made at one-third the level of funds for the same type of work that went to the forestry service within the Department of Agriculture. But by 1944 even he recognized that he was fighting a losing battle. He told house members that their "bills [were] designed to break down the system of Indian aid and protections and self-help." Senator John Murdock of Arizona observed, "These bills will die, but the idea will be perhaps brought up again."[30] He was right. The tide had begun to turn. Congress began to push in earnest for the bureau to move its policies away from strengthening support of tribal communities to terminating the federal trust relationship with them.

The failure of the Collier administration to provide the opportunity to bring effective home rule to most tribal communities, its use of tribal funds for federal goals, and its failure to improve tribal access to and benefit from Indian resources all directly paved the way for termination. The idea that tribes and the Indian bureau were working toward similar ends began to fray as federal officials increasingly viewed home rule as an opportunity to end federal responsibilities toward tribes. Tribal leaders, for the most part, continued to push for greater autonomy while remaining under the protection of the trust relationship. For many tribal leaders, all this boiled down to political control of tribal resources, especially money.

THE 1940S ASSAULTS ON TRIBAL SOVEREIGNTY

The 1940s saw a reversion to the pre-Hoover and Roosevelt years and strong efforts to reopen Indigenous lands to outside interests.[31] The first strong indication to tribes that termination was on the horizon came in 1947, during Harry S. Truman's presidency. Truman himself supported tribal treaty rights and hoped to improve economic conditions in Indian country. However, under the ill-conceived liberal view of the time, he believed assimilation to be the ultimate goal for the integration of Indian communities and people into the modern American economy.

Both Democratic and Republican politicians believed that both the reservation system and the Office of Indian Affairs were holding back tribal people. In the wake of the defeat of Naziism, and with the advent of the Cold War, they couched their language in terms of freedom and liberation. The 1946 midterm elections swept Republican majorities into the U.S. House and Senate. Republicans had a history of attacking Indian office policy under Collier's leadership. When he and Secretary of the Interior Harold Ickes resigned, the bureau lost its buffer against these attacks. In addition, Truman deferred to congressional leaders whose states encompassed significant portions of Indian country for development of policy initiatives.[32] Congress immediately expanded its focus on termination.

In 1946 Congress established the Indian Claims Commission to settle tribal nations' claims once and for all and pave the way for termination. Almost immediately after that, the Senate Civil Service Committee held hearings in January 1947 with the goal of shrinking the size of federal agencies. Assistant Commissioner of Indian Affairs William Zimmerman Jr. was called before the committee.[33] Zimmerman, who was second in charge at the bureau, was in the unfortunate position of serving as acting commissioner while William Brophy was on an extended sick leave from his post.[34] Brophy believed that termination was inevitable but hoped to find a way for tribal nations to become economically equipped to handle it.[35]

Zimmerman's views of what was best policy for the Indians' future clashed with that of the senators. He knew that the bureau had provided inadequate services to Indians historically because of inadequate funding. His response was to work with Congress to terminate the relationship with tribes that he believed had the resources to manage their own affairs. He said, "The fact is the Indian Service has never had sufficient appropriations to do a complete job on every reservation. We are coming to a time when we must make certain decisions; either we must withdraw entirely from certain areas, thereby making it possible to do a better job in the remainder of the Indian country, or we must continue over a longer term of years to do only a partial job."[36]

But Zimmerman's view of termination was more in line with that of many tribal leaders. To him a diminishment of federal oversight and even federal funding did not mean an abdication of federal trust responsibilities. He later discussed his role at those 1947 hearings with Menominee leaders. He told them, "Termination of federal service doesn't imply that there must be termination of trust. . . . In 1947 they were talking more of getting the Bureau out of certain activities rather than 'throwing the Indians to the wolves.'"[37]

Nonetheless, by July 1947 Senator Hugh Butler, who chaired the Senate's Committee on Public Lands, said, Zimmerman's testimony showed that "ten tribes are ready now to be released from Federal supervision." So he introduced several bills that called "to remove restrictions on the property and moneys belonging to the individual enrolled members" of the tribes, and "to provide for the liquidation of tribal property and distribution of the proceeds thereof" as well as "to confer complete citizenship on such Indians."[38]

Secretary of the Interior Julius Krug opposed "eliminat[ing] any functions" of the Indian Service "for which adequate substitutes [were] not available." He believed that those congressmen who wanted to eliminate or reduce federal services were motivated "primarily upon a desire to reduce federal expenditures, and secondarily, upon the theory that the Indians should be 'liberated.'"[39] At the same time, Congress devalued its role in Indian Affairs. In 1947, as part of a congressional reorganization, the House Committee on Indian Affairs was disbanded, and Indian affairs became a subcommittee of the Committee on Public Lands.[40] This moved the focus of Indian affairs from governance to real estate, at least symbolically.

Not everyone supported Krug's view. Representatives of western states, for example, began calling for elimination of reservation lands as tax-free spaces in 1948. At a meeting of the Interstate Association of Public Lands held in Pocatello Idaho, representatives of eleven states expressed frustration that they could not collect taxes on Indian lands. They also argued that reservation status "does not encourage the Indians to the state of independence that should be the goal."[41] They were not concerned with maintaining the future of the trust relationship.

Congressional leaders simply wanted to abolish the Indian bureau. By 1947 they were introducing bills that would do just that. One Northwest Coast tribal leader wrote to the chair of the house Indian affairs subcommittee, Henry Jackson, when he got wind of such legislation. His comments reflect the views of many tribal leaders: "We are thinking about our tribal rights under the treaty such as in the case of the Swinomish, our fishing rights on tribal grounds and oyster beds et. We ofcourse [sic] want to retain these," he told Jackson. The congressman responded, "I am afraid that the net result of such legislation might be that the Indian's ancestral rights might be seriously imperiled."[42]

The Association on American Indian Affairs immediately protested this move toward termination. Its vice president, Alice Rossin, reminded congress that the "obligations of the United States government to the Indians were established as payment for the ceding of, and extinguishment of, Indian title to practically all the land we now occupy as a nation." She emphasized the trust relationship which developed from this and which was meant to continue "in perpetuity." In a foreshadowing of what would partially play out in the 1950s and 1960s, she warned senators, "To abolish the Indian Bureau and supposedly 'set the Indian free' would only invite grave national tragedy and grant Indians . . . freedom for further exploitation, and freedom for greater dependency, all in defiance of our treaty obligations."[43]

Felix Cohen put it even more bluntly: "'Emancipating the Indian' has become the catchword of those who would like to free the modern Red Man from his property. Freeing the Indian from the Indian Bureau has become a high-sounding circumlocution for depriving Indians of promised Federal protection and opening their lands to all forms of encroachment." He argued that corporate developers were bent on stealing the Indian estate, in both Alaska and the United States proper. He described this theft as "the national interest in impoverishing the Indians." He added, "Of course, no assault on Indian lands can succeed if it is formulated as a bare-faced plunder. To be successful on a large scale, plunder must always wear the mask of national interest and high moral purpose."[44] This mask would facilitate congressional efforts to violate its trust responsibilities.

Congress was set on its path, however. Senator Edward J. Thye of Minnesota thought that Zimmerman's approach was the antithesis of what the Civil Service committee desired. "Mr. Zimmerman did bring us a recommendation, but where he proposed to step out of one field, he wished to expand in another, so that there was no curtailment."[45] Zimmerman did indeed view his plan as a method to move financial resources to the programs and tribes that needed them most. Congress's position, however, was quite clear: the purpose of the efforts was to diminish the number of employees in the Indian bureau (and other branches of government) and to cut costs.

In the end the Department of the Interior listed four qualifications for tribes to be withdrawn from federal supervision. Those included degree of assimilation into the local white community, economic viability, "willingness of the tribe to dispense with Federal aid and guidance," and provision of public services by states and local government agencies. Tribes were categorized three ways: those immediately ready for termination, those that would need some time to prepare, and those that would not be ready in the foreseeable future.[46] Zimmerman was told to draw up a list putting all tribes into one of these three categories.

American policymakers viewed the list of qualifications for termination and the tiered list for actual terminations as grounded in a kind of scientific reality that reflected their perception of logic. In reality the lists were arbitrary, based in cultural misunderstandings of the complexities of politics, economics, and social structures within Indigenous nations. Still, they could provide a handy guide to kill the trust relationship, congressional leaders hoped.

In May 1948 Zimmerman tasked Indian bureau regional directors with developing long-range plans that would lead to "the eventual discharge of the Federal government's obligation" to tribes, "legal, moral, or otherwise, and the discontinuance of Federal supervision and control at the earliest possible date compatible with the government's trusteeship responsibility."[47]

At around the same time, as part of a decentralization program within the Department of the Interior, the Indian bureau was reorganized, with the establishment of Area Offices.[48] These were intended to localize control and bring it closer to Indian agencies. These offices were tasked with developing six-year plans to lead to termination of federal responsibilities toward tribes. Some area offices were more successful than others—the Area Office in Portland managed to usher two bills terminating sixty-one tribes in total to passage within a week of the six-year goal.[49] But even those that were less efficient worked enthusiastically toward that goal. The Phoenix Area Office for example reported in 1953 that Indian opposition to termination had significantly weakened due to the efforts of bureau personnel to effectively communicate to tribal members across the region the purposes of it.[50]

In 1949 John Collier warned the public of a series of bills coming before Congress that would dismantle tribal sovereignty. In a sharply worded essay in *The Nation* he listed several bills that, in his opinion, intended "the ending of all effective federal responsibility in Indian matters."[51] By 1951 the "long-range objective of the Bureau of Indian Affairs [was] 'the step by step transfer of Bureau functions to the Indians themselves or to appropriate agencies of local, State, or Federal Government.'"[52]

Congress was swiftly moving in the same direction. In 1950 Democratic congresswoman Reva Beck Bosone introduced House Joint Resolution 490, commonly referred to as the Bosone Bill. The purpose would have been to study tribal groups "to determine their qualifications to manage their own affairs without supervision and control by the Federal Government."[53]

A critical question this raised was the extent to which tribal leaders could participate in decision-making. Bosone proclaimed, "It certainly is not the purpose of the bill, to release tribes, bands and groups of Indians who do not give their consent and who are not prepared."[54] But consent is a tricky standard. Historically, Indigenous leaders had been coerced and fooled into accepting treaties, land and resource loss, and inimical federal policy initiatives time and again. What on the surface may appear to have been decisions informed by tribal consent were often, in reality, underhanded efforts to undermine tribal decision-making.

Harold Ickes recognized this. In 1949 he warned Senator Clinton Anderson, "I have come . . . to be suspicious of bills affecting the Indians, even . . . when the Indians have apparently given their formal consent." He added, "Badly informed Indians have consented to their own economic disadvantage [in the past]."[55]

BIA central office employee G. Warren Spaulding argued, "It is absolutely necessary to work with the Indians and tribes on the program—that little could be accomplished without their acceptance, at least in part, and that we will need to gain Indian or tirbal [sic] cooperation toward that end." He believed that BIA employees on reservations could persuade Indians and local state and county political leaders to accept the termination policy. But he admitted, "This is a big job."[56] Later when Congress wrote termination bills, consultation would replace the idea of consent, and even consultation with Indians would be meager.

The movement toward termination gained speed in May 1950, when Dillon S. Myer was confirmed as commissioner of Indian Affairs. Upon taking the job, he later wrote, "I made it quite clear to the Secretary that I felt very strongly that the Bureau of Indian Affairs should get out of business as quickly as possible but that the job must be done 'with honor.'"[57] Legal scholar Felix Cohen marks this as a time when the BIA, under Myer's leadership, significantly expanded centralized control, eliminated oversight processes, and weakened local reservation-based authority.[58]

Both Collier and former Secretary of the Interior Harold Ickes expressed disgust at the inexorable movement of Congress toward termination.[59] In 1950 Ickes wrote Senator Edward Leahy out of frustration over an unnecessary battle over termination:

> I confess that I grow weary of pleading for justice for a handful of people for whom we ought to insist pridefully that we intend to do justice. Perhaps it might be just as well to throw them to the ravening dogs with one final grand gesture of pretended magnanimity. Then we could salve our consciences with the reflection that, after all, we had given these aboriginal Americans the freedom that all of us crave, even although as to them the freedom that we would be bestowing would be the freedom to starve, to be outcasts, to be landless Indians begging a crust from those who have grown strong and rich upon the wealth which the lands of the ancestors of the Indians abounded.[60]

Paschal George, a seventy-year-old tribal council member from the Couer d'Alene reservation in Idaho, echoed Ickes's comments in a meeting with Myer. He was concerned with the loss of land that would occur with termination. "I am thinking of the younger generation, what are we going to do with them? We have to do something. We don't want them to be any more dependent upon the government, nor do we want them in the gutters of the streets. Where Indians have sold their land, you will find their people in gutters, and dependent upon their folks. We want education. . . . I don't want my people to lose any more land." He added, in regard to land, "If the white people get it all, what are we going to live on?"[61]

The National Congress of American Indians (NCAI) contacted Myer even before he accepted the appointment as commissioner. Rosebud tribal member Robert Bennett, a regional secretary of the organization, sent him a copy of their "Indian Plan." One of its major goals was "adequate provision for protection of individual and tribal estate, including mineral and water rights." The plan urged tribal leaders to remember both their responsibilities and their "vested interests."[62] The status of these crucial protections would become the basis of much conflict between tribes, the bureau, and Congress in the coming years. The protests of Indians—and of Collier, Ickes, Cohen, and others—had little effect. Both the bureau and Congress pushed rapidly ahead to plan for termination, which often ignored Indians' "vested" rights, rights that the trustee would discard to achieve its own goal of getting out of the Indian business.

THE EARLY 1950S AND CONTINUED ASSAULTS

In 1950 Senator Arthur Watkins complained that the BIA had spent too much time studying Indian problems over the past hundred years. Instead, he said, "I have come to the conclusion that what is needed now is action on recommendations that have already been made, and not new investigations." If Congress would act quickly on the 1947 Zimmerman recommendations, he continued, "The better it will be for the Indians and for all the rest of us. For one thing, the demands on the Treasury will be greatly lessened."[63]

In 1950 the BIA budget accounted for slightly more than one-tenth of one percent of the annual federal budget.[64] There were far greater "demands on the Treasury" than Indian affairs in 1950. But this line of reasoning provided an argument to move forward with termination legislation and to diminish the federal trust responsibility to Indigenous nations in the United States.

By 1951 bills were already introduced in Congress to terminate the federal relationship with tribes in California and western Oregon. Association on American Indian Affairs (AAIA) executive director Alexander Lesser protested the California bill, arguing that the purpose was no more than to get the federal government out of the Indian business. He wrote to the White House, "The California bill is a brutal liquidation program which has as its sole purpose the liquidation of federal [trust] obligations and responsibilities without regard to the welfare of the people affected."[65]

Liquidation would mean severing the trust relationship between tribes and the United States and the loss of trust status for Indian lands, which provided some protection for those lands. It is important to recognize that liquidation was not new policy, nor new terminology. In his 1943 OIA appropriation statement, Collier wrote that the federal government had “compelled the Indians into poverty.” It had done so through the allotment policy that preceded his time in office. “The Indians, as official policy declared, were being ‘liquidated’, and their landed estate was being liquidated,” he wrote.[66] Both federal trust responsibilities and protection of tribal lands and resources were liquidated, opening the door to further erosion of tribal assets.

In 1951 tribal leaders pushed unsuccessfully for language providing them with more home rule authority to be added to the appropriations bill. Unfortunately, Indian Reorganization Act constitutions failed to provide tribal decision-making control without approval of the secretary of the Interior. Tribal leaders had hoped Congress would permit them to access their own funds without having to specifically request Congress for permission. John Rainer, executive secretary of NCAI, spoke for many tribal leaders when he told fellow NCAI leaders, “Congress has been bitterly criticizing the Indian Office for not working itself out of a job as quickly as it should, but it appears to us that congress itself refuses to hand over its control of funds belonging to the Indians.”[67]

Instead of pushing Congress to empower tribes and to fix the problems inherent in the IRA constitutions, though, the bureau doubled down on its push for termination. In the fall of 1951 the BIA established a new “Program Division.” It was created to “work with Indian tribal groups aimed at helping them to improve their economic status and to achieve ultimate independence from Bureau supervision.”[68] Myer confirmed that he was pushing for termination in a memo to all bureau employees in August 1952. However, he also implied that the directive came from Congress. “I think it may be fairly said that current Congressional actions with regard to the Bureau of Indian Affairs and Indian appropriations indicate future appropriations will be limited largely to financing items which will facilitate withdrawal,” he wrote.[69] Clearly, forced termination was part of the bureau’s planning process and breaking the trust relationship was the best way to achieve Congress’s dishonorable ends. Myer went on to say that the Bureau would seek cooperation with and agreement from tribes in developing termination plans. But, he said, “In the absence of such agreement . . . we must proceed, even though Indian cooperation may be lacking in certain cases.”[70]

NCAI had difficulty getting hold of Myer's memo, but when it did, executive director Frank George immediately contacted tribal council chairmen. He warned them in no uncertain terms that the future of the federal trust relationship was in imminent danger. He also pushed back against Myer's implication that Congress was behind the effort. He told the chairman that if congressional funding focused on termination, "it [would] be because the Commissioner want[ed] it that way." George argued that congressmen and senators generally wanted to legislate in the best interest of Indians, but that they relied on the BIA for direction in terms of specific policy. He flatly stated, "If Congress will consider only a program leading to abandonment of the Federal Government's guardianship responsibilities, it will be because the Indian Bureau does not offer them a better program."[71]

Myer responded to George's letter with a memo to all tribal council members. In it he said, "The time has come for constructive and cooperative planning with the many individual tribes here." He hoped they would be able to reach mutual agreements with the bureau. However, he continued, "Should all reasonable efforts fail to develop a joint program, then it would be incumbent upon me to present the facts to Congress and make suitable legislative recommendations." He added that if tribes disagreed with his recommendations, they were free to contact Congress themselves.[72] He did not dispute George's contention that the bureau would act without agreement from tribal leaders but in fact reinforced it.

Just the previous year Myer had written in the *Journal of Negro Education*, "No element of compulsion is contemplated in connection with the approach to the Indian problem." This statement was printed in bold type in a reprint of the article produced by the Chilocco Indian Agricultural School Print Shop.[73] Myer was either disingenuous in the article or had already changed his mind. Either way, he blatantly jettisoned the federal trust responsibility and shut off opportunities for tribal consent.

This was quickly recognized by religious organizations. The American Baptist Convention passed a resolution in May 1954 saying that though they supported ending Indian dependence on the federal government, they wished for "Congress [to] adopt further legislation only after considering the desires and needs of the specific tribes." The Council for

Social Action of the Congregational Christian Churches went further in their protest, urging that "negotiation in good faith between the Federal Government officials and freely chosen representatives of the tribes or bands affected, in formulating all policies relating to termination, [be] followed by consent of the groups involved before these policies are put into operation."[74]

In speaking with the western governors, Myer clearly outlined his plans for termination. He told them, "Ever since I became Commissioner of Indian Affairs, I have emphasized time and again that the Bureau of Indian Affairs has no desire to continue providing the Indians with any service which can be rendered just as efficiently and cheaply by some other agency or organization."[75] Western states increasingly pushed for a definitive termination plan. The Governors' Interstate Indian Council, in advance of the meeting where Myer spoke, advised the governors to recommend "a definite termination date" by which "certain tribes would receive full status of citizenship and responsibility earlier than others depending on existing conditions and local situations."[76]

At the same time, Congress wished to limit tribes' abilities to speak about this loss of the trust protection. In 1951 a House subcommittee recommended that tribal attorneys could only work in very narrow circumstances and could not, for example, advise on public statements made by the tribe. Though this did not become law, it was a congressional effort to give the BIA near-complete control of Indian statements to the public, seemingly the antithesis of shifting control from the federal government to tribes. Former commissioner of Indian Affairs John Collier pointed out that this would treat Indians differently from other American citizens. "If, as the Subcommittee wishes, the Indians are to gain in the ability to deal with white men and their customs, they should certainly be accorded the rights of any other citizens groups, that of freely consulting attorneys of their own choice who are employed to serve their interests and theirs alone."[77] It is little wonder that tribal nations chafed under the BIA's and Congress's draconian efforts to control their governments and their people.

American Indian Development (AID), "a field program of the National Congress of American Indians . . . devoted to self-help projects and leadership training in Indian communities," dourly observed, "Indians are in the unhappy position of possibly being held liable for the sins of their benefactors." AID argued that "because the Federal trustee has not succeeded in preparing Indians for a place in American life, they may be penalized by actions in Congress which will pauperize them." Casting the commissioner of Indian Affairs as "a majority stock holder," AID observed that Indians had "been put in the role of minority share owner who must vote his stock as directed."[78]

For the most part Myer opposed breaking up Indian lands but thought that they should be controlled by some sort of tribal organization. This attitude had been effectively conveyed down the chain of command. At a meeting on resources held by the Phoenix Area Office in January 1953, the director of the program division told bureau employees that resource "transfer may be made to individual Indians, to Indian tribes, to tribal corporate organizations, to other agencies of Government, or possibly to private trusts." In any case, "This transfer of responsibility and authority to others should seek to achieve termination of the Federal Government's trust responsibility."[79]

Myer firmly believed that the federal government should end its trust relationship with tribes. He told the Confederated Salish and Kootenai tribal council, "There is a trustee relationship that has grown up over a period of 100 years or more and it shouldn't take 100 years to dissolve this relationship but it will take a certain length of time to find out the problems to be solved and then to go to work to solve them."[80] Yet he wanted to move quickly. In August 1952 he said the bureau was "working with a number of bands and groups and they hoped to get as many drafts of [termination] legislation before Congress in December as possible."[81]

Upon leaving office in March 1953, Myer observed that only twenty to twenty-five of the more than two hundred tribal groups had the resources to establish a viable corporate business program. He also expressed his consternation that tribes were not enthusiastic about termination. He blamed this on tribal elders. On his departure, he told the secretary of the Interior, "There are also many of the older Indians who feel insecure about the matter. I was a bit surprised to find that the feeling was so nearly unanimous and that there are only a few groups so far who have been willing to agree with the government on immediate withdrawal or, for that matter, on discussing a definite plan for withdrawal some time in the future." He laid a significant portion of the blame at the feet of Felix Cohen, James Curry, the Association on American Indian Affairs, and NCAI.[82] Despite the opposition of tribes, the bureau, assisted by Congress, forged ahead with its plans.

In 1953 Senators George Malone and Hugh Butler sponsored a bill to "end Federal trust and liquidate all tribal organizations and dispose of their assets within 3 years." The bill failed. However, it prompted the Association on American Indian Affairs to observe, "Liquidation of Indian community life and the Indian estate cannot be too abrupt for some."[83] The AAIA might have added that the tribal estate had long been steadily diminished both through land and resource loss and through misguided use of tribal funds.

Arizona Senator Barry Goldwater took a slightly different tack, introducing a bill to diminish the size of tribes by specifying a national rule for tribal membership based on blood quantum. Known as the "half breed bill," it stipulated that anyone with less than one-half Indian blood would be "ineligible for Federal service and [would] remove their property from trust status."[84] This was a direct attack on tribal constitutions and their control of the definition of citizenship or membership. Though unsuccessful, this bill indicated the direction Congress intended to go.

Indeed, in August 1953 Congress passed HCR 108, which called for termination plans for tribes in ten states to be submitted to Congress within five months. Oliver La Farge, president of the Association on American Indian Affairs, immediately wrote a response. In it he charged that "there was no inclination" on the part of Congress "to wait to find out the wishes of the Indians," despite the fact that a house subcommittee was traveling through Indian country holding hearings on the issue.[85]

In 1953, under the new Eisenhower administration, Glenn Emmons replaced Myer as commissioner of Indian Affairs. He took office in August. In March Assistant Secretary of the Interior Orme Lewis had met with Senator Arthur Watkins as he took over chairmanship of the Senate Indian Affairs Subcommittee. Following the meeting, and during the transition between Myer and Emmons, Lewis wrote to Watkins, "Federal responsibility for administering the affairs of individual Indian tribes should be terminated as rapidly as the circumstances of each tribe will permit."[86] Watkins, who touted himself the "leading Senate figure in promoting '*freedom' policy for Indians*," believed that a major roadblock to this was the Indian rights organizations that had "badly misled" Indians about their real interests.[87] He did not believe that Indians themselves knew what was in their best interest, except on those rare occasions when they agreed with him. He took Lewis's suggestion to heart.[88]

Alexander Lesser reported that the AAIA believed that Emmons did not support the termination bills. He also said that the initial batch of ten bills were sent to Congress without Interior department support.[89] Lewis, however, strongly supported termination.

NCAI president Joseph Garry expressed concern, and perhaps scorn, for the termination bills that had been rushed through Congress. According to a 1954 Navajo newspaper account, "He said the legislation is just another way of taking land and minerals away from Indians. He continued the 'free the Indians,' bills will do any thing but free them." O'odham leader Thomas Segundo "pleaded that Congress and the Department of the Interior should have a better understanding of Indians."[90]

At the same time, Commissioner of Indian Affairs Emmons liberalized the rules for moving individual Indian lands from trust to fee-patent status.[91] Through this process the bureau significantly and rapidly increased the release of trust allotments to outright individual ownership. In many cases, these properties were then sold to non-Indians or lost for failure to pay taxes. In 1953 and 1954, 6 percent of Indian allotted lands, amounting to more than half a million acres in 1954 alone, were lost from trustee control in this way.[92] The bureau failed to provide money to tribes to purchase this land, using the justification that it was "the purpose of Congress to terminate all federal services to Indian tribes as soon as possible."[93] In fact, between 1947 and 1957 tribes and individual Indians lost more than two million acres of land, most of it sold to non-Indians.[94]

Ernest Wilkinson, the most successful Indian claims attorney of the era, represented the Klamath, Menominee, Ute, and Turtle Mountain Chippewa tribes in their victorious cases against the United States.[95]

All four tribes were among the first to be targeted for termination. The Menominee and Klamath termination bills became law, and the Ute tribe was divided as tribal members of mixed ancestry were terminated while others were not. The Turtle Mountain Chippewa were fortunate to avoid termination.

With "the few tribes that had acquired large sums in judgment monies awarded by the U.S. Court of Claims," Senator Watkins saw an opportunity to force or attempt to force termination using claims money to bribe them to accept termination.[96] He recognized that federal policy had long failed tribal communities, and he believed that the solution was for Indians to assimilate into American society. His policy initiatives were also grounded in his Mormon religion. American Indians are featured in the *Book of Mormon* as an impure people who have become "dark and loathsome."[97] To fix the "terrible mistakes" made "in the past," Watkins wrote, "It seems to me that the time has come for us to . . . help the Indians stand on their own feet and become a white and delightsome people as the Book of Mormon prophecied they would become."[98]

In his role as chair of the Senate subcommittee on Indian affairs, Watkins could hold up distribution of the funds from claims case awards. He could refuse to forward a bill authorizing payment of the funds out of committee, and he did so unless tribes agreed to develop termination plans. Some refused, but others made such plans, usually with little knowledge of what this would portend.

Interior department and BIA officials, and individuals in Congress, were hell-bent on getting out of the Indian business by ending the federal trust relationship with tribal nations and opening up access to Indigenous lands and resources. Watkins felt a particular political urgency, fearing that if Democrats won the presidency his plans would be disrupted. In January 1954 he told attorney Glen Wilkinson and a Menominee tribal delegation "that President Eisenhower's term would end January 1957 and he (Watkins) wanted this legislation 'wrapped up' prior to that time." He added, "If the Democrats get back in, 'you might sneak out of it.'"[99]

Some few members of Congress recognized that BIA officials used underhanded tactics to foist termination on tribes.[100] Montana Representative Lee Metcalf told some two hundred tribal leaders at the 1958

NCAI annual convention "that the Bureau of Indian Affairs had used 'duress, blackmail and pressure' to get Indians to agree to terminating Federal control and supervision." He said, "I object to . . . the specious reasoning that [Indians] become 'first-class citizens' only if we break the promises we made them and take away their benefits." By then congressional opinion was turning against the policy of termination. There was increasing recognition that it caused tribal nations and their citizens or members even more misery than they had been in before the new laws were enacted. According to the *New York Times*, Representative Metcalf "said the Administration . . . had 'terminated Indians' even faster than Congressional action would have done."[101] Metcalf called for the federal government to support tribes, not only economically but also in development of their human resources, as opposed to terminating tribal relationships with the United States.[102]

Metcalf's recognition that federal "blackmail" was involved in the policymaking speaks volumes regarding the extent to which Congress would go to violate good-faith dealings with Indigenous nations. Tribal leaders recognized the underhanded and coercive federal tactics from the moment that they were introduced. After all, they had a long history with federal bad-faith use of their moneys and misrepresentation in doing so. Too few federal officials understood that. The new battleground over abuse of tribal funds in the mid-twentieth century had moved from treaty moneys and allotment to judgment funds and money provided in compensation for newly taken land and resources. These battles would be fought in the Court of Claims and the Indian Claims Commission, as well as Congress and the BIA.

CHAPTER 3

Judgment and Compensatory Moneys

> What the white man chose to forget, the Indian chose to remember, and bided his time. When the fever of conquest subsided, that same legal conscience that necessitated the treaties was used to enforce them.
>
> —Harvey D. Rosenthal, *Their Day in Court*

By the middle of the twentieth century the United States as trustee possessing oversight of tribal funds had laid waste to most tribal economies. For some Indigenous nations the destruction had lasted for decades; for those farther east, centuries. Most often unwillingly, tribal nations had traded the bulk of their land and some of the resources associated with it for money that the federal government controlled and for questionably useful goods and services. What little money tribes acquired, the trustee regularly abused or withheld from them. Tribes were cheated out of or significantly undercompensated for the resources that they did retain. Theft of and underpayment for tribal resources was not merely a feature of past history; it continued unabated. Reservation resources, and those off-reservation resources guaranteed to tribes in treaties, represented what was left of the Indigenous patrimony. It also represented the economic foundations that tribal nations could use to build their futures. When the value in this was lost tribal communities suffered deeply.

Almost from the instant treaties were signed tribal leaders pushed back against the ways they were swindled by their trustee. Whether being paid too little for the lands they sold, not being paid at all for lands taken, or being cheated when the federal government failed to meet obligations agreed upon in the treaties, Indians fought for reparations. They protested to the local Indian agents and the commissioners of Indian affairs, they lobbied Congress, and they wrote the president. They also sued the trustee in court.

The tortuous process of tribes attempting to bring claims against the federal government was both expensive and drawn out. Though Congress established the United States Court of Claims in 1855, it excluded Indians from its jurisdiction just eight years later.[1] In the 1940s, arguing for a change in policy, U.S. representative and later senator from Washington Henry Jackson incisively described the 1863 change to the law as "punitive in purpose, . . . a method of striking at certain tribes which had turned against the Federal Government. This law . . . barred the Court of Claims to Indian tribes seeking redress against the United States for treaty violations. Since that date no Indian tribe [had] been able to present a claim for judicial determination without a special act of Congress." He described the 1863 law as "discriminatory action taken in the heat of armed conflict, an action which took from the Indian the right to have his day in court."[2] The law may have been aimed at those Indigenous nations that had allied themselves with the South in the Civil War, but it ultimately impacted all tribes.

In 1881 tribes began to sue in the Court of Claims, but they needed a congressional act approving it. From then until the mid-1940s more than two hundred tribal claims received congressional approval to be brought against the United States. Only thirty-five cases successfully "won awards."[3] The geographer Imre Sutton describes the complications of the process well in *Irredeemable America*. To win a case, tribes had to prove original title. Because original title is "based on proof of exclusive use and occupancy," it is a more stringent definition of rights than recognized title. "Original title necessitated careful reconstruction of ethnographic and historical data that demanded the expertise of scholars."[4] The Indian Claims Commission (ICC) historian Harvey Rosenthal described the complexity of the process: "The case presentation involved the expertise of anthropologists, ethnologists, historians, land appraisers, and specialized attorneys. . . . The experts had to establish which tribe lived where and when. This done, they were called upon to value the land at the 'time of taking.'"[5] This would take years, and thousands or even millions of dollars in expenses.

When a case was won, the process was not complete. Next, Congress had to appropriate funds that were awarded to tribes. American Indian Court of Claims cases took an average of fifteen years from passage of the authorizing jurisdictional act until the court finally rendered a decision.[6] The process was so painstakingly complex that in 1946 Congress established a separate Indian Claims Commission. On rare occasions tribes succeeded in gaining a significant judgment through the Court of Claims, the ICC, and Congress. By the middle of the twentieth century several tribes won hefty judgments.

At the same time Congress also began appropriating funds for direct taking of reservation lands. For example, when rivers were dammed and flooded, tribal nations would be compensated for the low-lying (and fertile) bottomlands along their shores. Tribal nations hoped to use these windfall funds both to alleviate poverty for individual tribal members or citizens and to develop sustainable economies. As James Olson and Raymond Wilson observed, politicians from both sides of the aisle viewed claims awards as an opportunity to bring about termination and rapid assimilation for American Indians. To conservatives, compensation followed by termination "promised an erosion of federal power," while "liberals appreciated it because compensation relieved their guilt-ridden consciousness about past shabby treatment of Native Americans."[7]

Whether through judgment funds or moneys for new land takings, though, Congress as trustee defined how the appropriated dollars would be spent by the tribes. Then it was up to the Indian bureau to administer the funds. By the 1950s these one-time infusions of cash created the opportunity to coerce and bribe tribal nations to accept termination. Using these three sources of sudden and significant money—from the Court of Claims, the ICC, or a compensatory fund—Congress, in collusion with the BIA, would attempt to trade past and present wrongs for tribal termination and destruction of the trust relationship.

COURT OF CLAIMS

The opening of the United States Court of Claims to Indian tribes in 1881 began a slow trickle of cases, some that tribes had been trying to bring before Congress for decades. In the next forty-two years the court would hear just thirty-nine Indian claims cases. That changed dramatically in 1924 after passage of the Indian citizenship act and as goodwill toward Indians increased after their role in the first world war. In just the next three years thirty-seven more cases would be brought to the court.[8]

Even so, it remained difficult for tribal nations to get a jurisdictional act passed that would permit them to sue the United States. The experience of the Consolidated Ute Tribes, in what would eventually become a successful, nearly $32 million judgment, is illustrative. After the fact their attorney, Ernest Wilkinson, described the process.

Wilkinson explained that in both the House and the Senate, the bills were brought through the consent calendar rather than by majority vote. In the Ute case, the congressman from the district where the Utes lived repeatedly promised to bring the bill up but failed to do so. Finally, Wilkinson went to see the man on another day that it was to be called only to find him in the hospital with appendicitis. So instead he asked another congressman to bring the bill on behalf of his colleague, and after the three-year effort, it passed. "When the author of the bill returned from the hospital he was furious at his colleague because, apparently, despite his promises to me, he wanted to have the appearance of being a friend of the Indians by introducing the legislation but remain also the friend of certain whites by seeing that the legislation never passed."[9]

Then the bill had to pass the Senate. Utah Senator William King, "a personal friend" of Wilkinson, opposed the bill "yet he kept professing that he was in favor of it." Wilkinson believed that King would not object to the bill, "but that probably when this bill was about to be called he would satisfy his conscience by leaving the floor of the Senate." This would be problematic. So Watkins asked Elbert Thomas, King's junior colleague from Utah, that if this were to occur, Thomas could explain that the bill had King's support—which King had told Wilkinson that it did. That is just what occurred, and the bill passed the Senate.[10]

But then, Wilkinson said, "Even after the bill was passed there were serious difficulties in getting the bill signed by the President," Franklin Roosevelt. FDR had just the previous week vetoed a similar bill, and in this case too, both his attorney general and the director of the budget recommended a veto. Wilkinson then persuaded Secretary of the Interior Harold Ickes to send a message to Roosevelt protesting that he had not been consulted in the matter but that this was a worthy bill. It is not clear what happened next, but FDR did sign the bill.[11] All of that was just the beginning of a process that would last seventeen years before a judgment was made.

The rapid increase in cases created fear in Congress of the cost to the nation. It also fed the myth that contemporary Indians were either trying to scam the federal government or that tribal nations simply did not deserve to be compensated for long-ago wrongs. According to Rosenthal, three major factors inhibited tribal nations' success in pursuing their claims. First was federal mistrust of claims attorneys, who in the words of New York representative Robert Bacon ran a "regular racket." There was a belief that Indians would not pursue claims on their own. Rosenthal observed that "it seemed that no amount of testimony or evidence could drive home the simple fact that the Indian was himself aware that he had been cheated and could demand redress without the external prodding of 'shyster lawyers.'"[12]

Second, Rosenthal says, Congress feared the cost of paying interest on claims that dated back decades and worked to ensure that it rarely happened. And third, and very costly to tribal nations, federal and even tribal expenditures over the years were deducted from payments in cases where tribes were successful. This was done through a process known as offsets or setoffs.[13]

According to attorney Glen Wilkinson, "most jurisdictional acts" permitting a tribe to sue in the Court of Claims "directed the court to set-off against any award the gratuitous expenditures made by the United States for the benefit of the tribe." This meant that any money the federal government expended for the tribe could be deducted from the judgment award. In all but two cases decided in tribes' favor between 1929 and 1935, these offsets exceeded the amount the tribe was to receive in the judgment; so the tribe got nothing.[14] Indians were the only appellants in the Court of Claims to which this restriction was applied.[15]

In cases where expenditures for tribes came from money the tribes brought in, either through treaty land sales or resource extraction, the tribes' own expenditures were deducted from the award. Given these circumstances, the Blackfeet can be considered fortunate in their 1935 award. The court found that they had not been compensated for any of the twelve million acres of land the federal government had taken from them in 1874, and they were awarded $6,130,874.88. But their offsets were valued at $5,508,409.31, and so they were left with only $622,465.57.[16] They only received 10.2 percent of the judgment they were awarded. And ten percent of that went to their attorneys.[17] At least they got something.

That was not the end of the Blackfeet travail however. One of the offsets was for buildings that housed BIA officials. The bureau continued to use the buildings and apparently rented some of them out. In a 1951 dispute with the bureau over management of affairs on the reservation, the tribe issued a press release. It said, in part, "The Indians think that since the Blackfeet Tribe has paid for the buildings they belong to the Blackfeet."[18] In this case, the tribe was first cheated out of payment for twelve million acres of land and then lost approximately 90 percent of its compensation for the loss to offsets—and then continued to lose resources when the buildings it had purchased with the offsets remained in control of the federal government.

Some thirty-six thousand California Indians fared slightly better in a 1944 judgment in a case involving land lost when eighteen treaties from 1851 and 1852 went unratified. They were awarded more than $17 million. After offsets for "support, education, health, civilization" their net award was slightly more than $5 million. They only lost 70 percent of their award to offsets.[19] And as with treaty money, the bulk of those offsets were paid to support federal, not tribal, policy initiatives.

Other tribes were not so fortunate. Nineteen Northwest Coast tribes suing together won a judgment, for example, against which the full amount was offset by government expenditures, "the net result being that the Indians received nothing in the form of a cash judgment."[20] The Osage tribe lost a judgment in the court of claims based on the offset of U.S. funds spent educating "Indians" from their treaty land compensation. This included education of not only Osage children but children of other tribes as well.[21] In this case, the Osage paid for the education of children from other tribes with the funds from the land taken from them by treaty.

These Court of Claims cases basically proved that the trustee, the United States, could protect itself better than it could protect its beneficiaries, Indigenous people, and nations. The claims process was stacked against tribal nations in myriad ways. Attorneys who worked for tribes worked to improve the process for tribal nations in the creation of the Indian Claims Commission, an entity Congress established for other purposes.

INDIAN CLAIMS COMMISSION

The backlog of cases in the Court of Claims, combined with congressional and executive-branch desires to end the federal relationship with tribes, caused the congress to establish a separate body to hear Indian claims in 1946.[22] Historian Donald Fixico has argued that the infamous 1947 Zimmerman memo defining which tribes were ready for termination and the Indian Claims Commission formed the two foundations on which the termination policy was built. "As the immediate postwar years came to a close, the Indian Claims Commission and the Zimmerman Plan became guiding factors that brought about termination in Indian affairs."[23]

As early as 1910 bureaucrats recognized the need to separate Indian claims from the Court of Claims. In 1928 the Meriam Report included establishment of such a commission in its recommendations. By the 1930s, proposals including bills that ultimately failed in Congress called for separating Indian claims from the Court of Claims through a commission rather than through a court system. A commission would be investigatory and advisory to Congress rather than adjudicatory.[24]

In 1928 the authors of the Meriam Report warned that federal efforts to assimilate Indians would be unsuccessful until claims were settled. "The Indians look forward to getting vast sums from these claims," the report said. "They will hardly knuckle down to work while they still hope the government will pay what they believe is due them." The report also intimated that "mixed-blood" Indians would give up their affiliations with their tribal nations once the claims were paid out and they received their own shares of the money.[25]

Both of these arguments were wrong. Indians worked in a broad variety of ways during the early to mid-twentieth century, as a growing body of literature clearly shows.[26] And most people of mixed heritage who were closely connected to their tribal communities were not interested in breaking ties with them. However, individual Indians and tribal governments were keen to see their claims resolved.

American Indian leaders had advocated for a separate adjudication system to settle their claims against the federal government for several decades prior to the establishment of the Indian Claims Commission. First the Society of American Indians and then the National Congress of American Indians proposed separating Indian claims from other claims against the federal government. As they conceived it, and as Harold Ickes advocated, such a claims court would have had much broader scope and impact. But after Ickes's resignation as secretary of the Interior in early 1946 the Indian bureau lost its shield from congressional overreach.[27] And after the 1946 election, American Indian tribes faced a far less sympathetic Congress. By then the Indian Claims Commission had been established. When he signed the bill creating the ICC in August 1946 President Harry Truman said, "We stand ready to correct any mistakes we have made." He said that the United States had always meant to deal fairly with tribal nations, but that inevitably, in the course of "the largest real estate transaction in history," the United States "made some mistakes and occasionally failed to live up to the precise terms of our treaties and agreements."[28] This understatement reflected either the belief or the political spin of the new secretary of the Interior, Julius Krug, who wrote Truman's statement.[29]

In addition to correcting past wrongs, Truman said that the work of the commission would lead to a new, brighter future for Indigenous Americans. "With the final settlement of all outstanding claims which this measure ensures, Indians can take their place without special handicap or special advantage in the economic life of our nation and share

Fig. 1. President Harry S. Truman signs the Indian Claims Commission bill, in Washington DC, August 13, 1946. Behind him are Sen. Joseph C. O'Mahoney, D-WY; Julius Murray of the Uintah Ute tribe, Fort Duchesne; and acting Interior Secretary Oscar Chapman. AP Photo/William J. Smith.

fully in its progress."[30] This statement reflected the bipartisan view that, once claims were settled, the past would no longer guide the future for Native people or federal policy. As Harvey Rosenthal observed, "As often is the case with such landmarks in Indian administration this one was primarily designed to serve the government and not the Indian."[31] It would do so by eliminating old grievances and opening the door to future terminations.

American Indians did not want to live in the past, but they did want past injustices rectified. They also wanted the trust relationship to be preserved and past agreements to continue to be honored. For the most part, they viewed treaties and federal trust responsibilities as an important feature of their future. Indigenous leaders viewed those as essential to successful nation building. But by the late 1940s both congressional members and bureaucrats viewed the righting of past wrongs as key to leaving those twin pillars of Indian policy firmly in the past.

Representative Henry Jackson introduced the bill that would become the Indian Claims Commission Act. It authorized five different types of claims, including for fraudulent treaties, land takings without payment, and failure to provide "fair and honorable dealings." It also severely limited offsets. For example, removal expenses, agency expenses, education, and administration expenses were among those excluded from offsets.[32] Ernest Wilkinson's firm wrote the provisions into the act that eliminated these federal offsets.[33]

Upon the passage of the act establishing the ICC, the secretary of the Interior's office wrote to the main sponsors in the House and Senate, Henry Jackson of Washington and Joseph O'Mahoney of Wyoming. The letters celebrated "a fair and final determination of grievances which have so long obstructed the progress of our Indian tribes and the work of this Department with them." The secretary himself optimistically told Jackson that the commission would "wind up this phase of our Indian problem."[34] Ironically, despite the goals that this be a vehicle to determine all claims once and for all, the act also authorized the Court of Claims to hear future claims that would arise.[35]

Jackson, the primary sponsor of the bill, privately explained his less-than-honorable purposes in sponsoring the legislation. "My thinking was that if the Indians would get their claims settled once and for all, possibly then they would start out from there to become self-supporting and self-sufficient citizens. So many of the Indians go on all their lives expecting someday to get their claims settled by the Federal government that it seemed to me that it destroyed their initiative."[36]

Jackson was more circumspect in his public statements about the legislation. "Will Congress now act to correct discriminatory action for which the Congress is itself responsible?" he asked, referring to the 1863 law barring Indians from the Court of Claims without congressional authorization. "The heaviest cost cannot be measured in terms of dollars. The effect of continuous frustration on the Indians has deteriorated their morale, retarded their economic efforts, increased the cost of administration, and pushed the achievement of complete rehabilitation farther into the future."[37]

Jackson added that claims fell into three categories: the land sales themselves, management of the funds from those sales, and U.S. management of trust resources the tribes retained after the treaties. Though "mistakes, misinterpretation and misunderstanding" should be expected to be considerable, since Indians for the most part did not speak or read English when the treaties were made, nonetheless, "the volume of claims arising from them is small when compared with the volume of disputes arising out of modern real estate and business transactions."[38] Jackson blamed "mistakes" on Indian unfamiliarity with the English language rather than white avarice combined with bureaucratic ineptitude, or a continuation of Witgen's political economy of plunder. Jackson and other federal officials also viewed those problems as being in the past, rather than ongoing.

In public Jackson argued that the legislation would both be fair to Indians, ending years of discrimination, and a benefit to the federal government. "Whatever the amount to which the Indian tribes are justly entitled, the sooner it is paid the better it will be for the Federal government, from a financial point of view as well as from the standpoint of national honor."[39]

Claims were filed slowly until a majority of them (530 of the total of 852) came in during the final month and a half before the 1951 deadline. Many were held back so long because attorneys wanted to see how the earlier cases were decided before finishing their paperwork. These 852 claims were consolidated into some 600 claims to be considered in 370 dockets.[40] They moved through the system slowly.

Indian bureau officials believed that Indians remained incompetent to manage their own affairs. As a consequence they continued to view attorneys hired by tribes as simply avaricious. They worked, in fact, to bar Indigenous nations from selecting the attorneys who would work for them in claims advocacy. This prompted a 1951 editorial in the *American Indian* to observe that the BIA's proposed regulations to limit tribes' abilities to hire their own attorneys "seem to imply that lawyers are so inherently evil and Indian tribes so gullible and incompetent that a hierarchy of officials is needed to cross every 't' and dot every 'I' in legal papers drawn up between them."[41] And so tribal nations were handicapped as Commissioner of Indian Affairs Dillon Myer used his prerogative to deny tribes the right to hire attorneys of their choice dozens of times.[42]

Individual Indians often misunderstood the claims procedure. After generations waited for their tribes to be compensated, individuals often believed that when legislation passed or when claims were being settled, they would immediately receive individual payments. One woman from California wrote to Henry Jackson, who chaired the Indian Affairs Committee in the House, in May 1946. She asked whether the Indian Claims Commission Act had been passed. "If so where can I file for my settlement of claims? I have my roll number."[43] This was more typical than not.

Edgar Bowen, elder chief of the Confederated Tribes of Coos, Lower Umpqua, and Siuslaw Indians told a similar story. Bowen recalled a meeting he attended as a child in about 1939. Whenever a federal agent visited the tribes in Empire, Oregon, tribal members hoped to be paid the money they were owed from their 1855 treaty. Unfortunately, Congress had never ratified the treaty and the tribes had lost all their land. They were never paid for it, but they brought claims cases to both the Court of Claims and the Indian Claims Commission and lost in both places. So tribal members held out the hope that they would be paid.[44]

When a federal official visited the tribes in 1939, the older people expected payment. Bowen told the story this way:

> So they had this big guy who live over across the bay . . . his name was John Kentuck. You could see him, he was . . . big. So the [federal official] comes in, little scrawny guy comes, about jockey [size]. And he was from Washington DC. So John Kentuck brought his sack. Heard the man was a-comin'. So when the meeting went on, Kentuck said, "Hell, where's our money." And he had his sack, he actually had a sack. [The official] didn't have money, so . . . John goes out the side of the building on the old wooden walk . . . grabbed that little guy right by the shirt and just run him up against the wall. Scared me you can imagine, I was a kid you know. . . . He was a federal man from Washington.[45]

As the ICC toiled away it seems fair to say that many if not most federal officials were unaware of its existence. Attorney General Robert Kennedy, when he began that job, had never heard of it. "There's no danger of having to give the country back to the Indians," he told readers of *Life* magazine in March 1962, "but we do still have to pay them for most of it, and one of the things I was not told when I became Attorney General is that it's up to 23 lawyers hidden deep in the Department of Justice to find out how much we owe."[46]

Initially the law that created the Indian Claims Commission stated that it needed to complete its work by 1956, but several extensions eventually made 1978 the final date for resolution of claims. In the end some 274 awards would amount to more than $800 million. By 1953 when HCR 108 (the bill authorizing terminations) became law, just five awards totaling around $6.5 million had been made.[47] Cases that had begun in the Court of Claims prior to 1946 continued to be adjudicated in that venue as well. The law that created the ICC did not permit return of lands that were taken illegally, "a disappointment to many Indians" who "would prefer ownership of it to money damages," according to attorney Robert Barker. It merely provided monetary compensation for stolen real estate.[48] And that compensation could be withheld by congress in an attempt to force Indigenous nations and tribal communities to accept termination.

CONGRESSIONAL APPROPRIATIONS AND COMPENSATORY FUNDS

Judgment funds were not the only revenue source bringing a windfall of money to some tribes. In addition to claims moneys, tribes were awarded funds for land takings, such as those that occurred when their reservations were flooded by dams that backed up rivers. These floods destroyed land (often the most fertile) and property of tribal citizens and effectively shrunk the size of reservations. Historian Michael Lawson has described the demographic upheaval experienced by individual Indian people who lost their homes as "involuntary resettlement."[49] Following a pattern established in the treaty-making and allotment years, the compensation that Indigenous nations received for these land takings was generally below value, and the lands that individuals received in return were generally inferior. Nonetheless, the process could still provide a significant sum of money.

When a tribe won a claims judgment, that was just the first step in the process. Congress controlled the actual payment and use of funds, whether from judgments or other sources. Congress as trustee would have to appropriate the funding before the tribe had the opportunity to get its money. But even that was a preliminary step. Congress would then pass another bill to actually distribute the money. It was on these latter pieces of administrative bills or laws that Congress put restrictions. Tribal nations had to get approval from the commissioner of Indian Affairs for how they would spend the money. This usually led to back-and-forth discussions that would take weeks or months or years before the tribe received its funds, as the trustee worked to ensure that its interests were protected. The trustee—the federal government—should have been working to protect tribal interests.

Uintah and Ouray Ute tribal member Julius Murray summed up the frustration that many Indian people felt at a 1950 tribal council meeting where a per capita request was being discussed. This would have provided payments from tribal funds to individual tribal members.

> I would like to ask a question. Why is it when dealing with these people it is the policy to say we got to hold this we got to hold that, you can't buy this, you can't buy that, that kind of stuff is out moded, it makes the people look like they are incompetent, why not give it to them and let them do as they want to, they are free-born Americans, can't they do as they please? Give them confidence, encourage them to handle their own affairs, say this is your responsibility, give them respect and they will give you respect.[50]

He was arguing against micromanagement of tribal funds and the paternalism inherent in the trust relationship.

Hubert Humphrey had tried to ease the paternalism problem in April 1949 with a tribal funds bill. "Under this bill," he said, "no departmental approval is required where the tribe wishes to spend current income." He did not believe that tribes needed secretary of the Interior approval to spend all of their own money. His proposal was modest. The tribes would still need secretarial approval to spend money that they already had in the treasury. The latter was a measure to appease hardliners. Humphrey viewed it as "a fair compromise."[51] The bill failed to pass Congress, however. Humphrey's attempt to provide a modicum of home rule was met with terminationists' efforts to maintain paternalistic control over tribal decision-making.

After Collier left the bureau, he argued that the federal trustees had an obligation to make Indians economically self-sufficient.[52] But both congressional leaders and bureaucrats focused on assimilation rather than helping to build robust tribal economies. They viewed money as both a tool to end the trust relationship with tribal nations and an opportunity to provide a modicum of stability for individual tribal members entering the mainstream American economic system. A one-time payment of money that tribes and individuals had little control over would not constitute self-sufficiency, but that was no longer a federal goal. By the 1950s those one-time payments were considered a way to terminate the political existence of tribal nations.

Judgment and compensatory funds could provide a one-time infusion of money into tribal coffers, and sometimes to individual tribal members. Congressional representatives and BIA officials surely knew that this did not ensure financial stability, let alone provide for a sustainable economic future for tribal nations or individuals. Nonetheless, Congress used the money as evidence supporting its efforts toward termination, which after all was the purpose of the work of the Indian Claims Commission. Ugly as this duplicitous representation of tribal funds was, the dishonesty shown here paled in comparison with the maleficent use of those funds to attempt to force tribal nations to accept termination of their trust relationship with the United States. It can be argued that the purpose of the ICC was to raise money to be used for bribery to those ends.

PART 2

Forests and Termination

CHAPTER 4

The Menominee Indian Tribe of Wisconsin

> The consent of the Indians is a necessary element in fair dealing. . . . That consent should not be obtained by pressure amounting to duress, such as was used last year, in the cases of Menominee and Klamath, when it was made clear to those Indians that they would be permitted to withdraw their own funds from the United States Treasury only if that withdrawal was coupled with Federal 'Termination.'
>
> —Association on American Indian Affairs, 1955

Indigenous people managed ancient forests to provide themselves with an abundance of resources for millennia.[1] By the late 1800s tribal forests became wellsprings of economic hope for tribal nations whose economies had been shattered when they lost a majority of their land and resources to an acquisitive white population. But unfortunately, congressional laws and Indian bureau policies increasingly restricted the ways that Indian communities could utilize their forest resources. In fact, all three branches of the federal government stymied prospects for resource development in reservation communities. An 1873 Supreme Court case ruled that Indians only had rights of occupancy on their reservations and that resources—such as trees—belonged to the United States. That was not reversed until 1938.[2] So while tribal forests could be logged for the benefit of Indigenous nations and people, that could only be done under strict federal rules.

This caused a series of problems for tribal nations. Federal forestry practices often worked against what would have been best practices for tribal forests. The law generally required tribes to pay for federal management and oversight of reservation logging. Federal employees assigned to Indian country often lacked even basic knowledge of forestry, let alone the role that cultural and local ecological knowledge could play in forest use. This meant that in many cases Indian loggers were better equipped to manage cutting on their lands than those assigned to oversee their work—but they lacked the authority to do so. And many federal officials viewed tribal timber as a temporary resource that should be cleared to make the way for farmsteads.

All of this meant that a tremendous opportunity to develop Indigenous economic independence, and to strengthen tribal communities, was squandered by federal mismanagement and neglect. Despite that, forest exploitation brought a modicum of economic relief to some devastated Indigenous economies. This conflict over mishandling of the resource, potential benefits to reservation communities, federal policy initiatives that worked in contradiction to Indian desires and needs, and the opportunity for Native communities to decide their own future path played out in reservation communities across the continent. The Menominee Indian Tribe of Wisconsin was one such community where the conflict would unfold in ways that would shape much of their twentieth-century world and lead directly to their termination.

The Menominee historically utilized between eight and twelve million acres of what is now Wisconsin, Minnesota, and Michigan's Upper Peninsula, a region they inhabited for thousands of years before white Americans invaded their country.[3] But beginning in the early nineteenth century they saw their land base shrink through a series of treaties that underpaid them for their lands and resources, or that on occasion took those lands without compensation.

In the 1848 treaty, signed at the time Wisconsin won statehood, the Menominee agreed to leave Wisconsin altogether for the Crow Wing River, on Ojibwe lands in what would soon become Minnesota Territory. However, Menominee leaders inserted a clause in the treaty giving them the right of refusal to move to that land after an inspection. They invoked

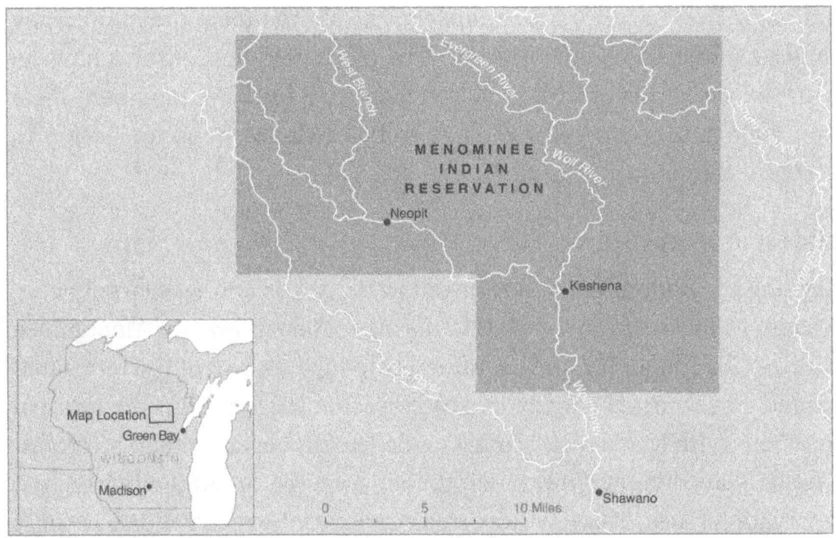

Map 2. Menominee Indian Reservation, Wisconsin. Courtesy Aileen Clarke.

that right and, after gaining support from the new state legislature in Wisconsin and their white neighbors, signed another treaty with the United States in 1854 that established their modern reservation. Two years later one-sixth of this land base was lopped off and provided to the Stockbridge and Munsee Nations, leaving the Menominee with ten townships of rich forest land split by rivers and streams, with lakes dotted throughout.

In the decades after the reservation was established, as the lands outside of the reservation were clear-cut and the woods replaced by farms, outsiders who coveted the Menominee forest began to steal trees. After 1871 the Menominee fought in various ways to retain control of their forest resource. They seemingly won this battle in 1908 with passage of the LaFollette Act, which was intended to both preserve the forest and give the Menominee the authority to manage it. However, the tribe remained under federal control, and so did its forest. By the 1920s both the Indian bureau in the Department of the Interior and the forest service in the Department of Agriculture had been fighting with each other for two decades to control the Menominee forest (and those of other Indigenous nations). These agencies mismanaged the Menominee forest, breaking the law under the LaFollette Act. The tribe sued and, after a lengthy court battle, proved victorious. Congress then used the judgment from that victory in its successful effort to bribe the Menominee nation to accept termination.

THE FIGHT OVER THE FOREST

Logging on Menominee lands began in the 1830s and was largely conducted by poachers for almost four decades. Then in 1871 the Menominee successfully fought off outside attempts to take control of the forest and gained a measure of control over reservation logging.[4] But the modern problems with Menominee forest management began in 1890 after passage of a law defining how much timber could be cut annually from the reservation forest. This law restricted cutting on the reservation to twenty million board feet per year in order to avoid overharvesting. The bill also intended that the Menominee themselves gain more benefit from cutting their trees than they had in the past.

The 1890 law controlled logging on the reservation for eighteen years. In the first year alone federal officials permitted overharvesting by more than 2.7 million board feet. This problem continued throughout the eighteen years the law was in effect.[5] Then, when a windstorm blew down a portion of the Menominee forest in 1905, U.S. Department of Agriculture (USDA) Forest Service officials under the direction of Gifford Pinchot bungled the recovery and sale of the blown-down trees, many of which were left to rot in the forest.[6] This mismanagement after the 1905 blowdown wreaked havoc on the reservation.

This led to passage of the 1908 LaFollette Act, which was intended to protect the forest over the long run. The law was titled, in part, "An Act To authorize . . . the preservation of the forests on the Menominee Indian Reservation in the State of Wisconsin."[7] According to Wisconsin senator Robert LaFollette, the dual purposes of the bill were to provide the Menominee with the opportunity to manage their forest and to provide for the "preservation and perpetuation of the forest." He added that under this law, "the harvest of the crop of forest products should be made in such a way that the forest [would] perpetuate itself." Secretary of the

Interior James Garfield also argued that the bill would "yield a larger return to the Indians as well as continue the growth of the forests."[8] In theory this would be a significant step in the direction of Menominee financial independence. This in turn would increase their opportunity for home rule, or Menominee governance under the protections of the federal trust relationship.

Unfortunately, the Forest Service and the Indian bureau ignored congressional intent, and "during the years from 1908 until 1924 the Menominee reached the nadir of their ability to govern themselves."[9] The hopes for greater control of their resources vanished almost as soon as the LaFollette bill became law as federal officials took control of nearly every aspect of Menominee life. This included the USDA asserting heavy-handed control of the forest, the logging operations, and the building and operation of an overly large capacity mill in the newly established town of Neopit. At the other extreme, the local Indian agent required tribal members to get written permission even to gather dead firewood.

By this time the Menominee had attempted to take control of their affairs, having twice written constitutions and established a business committee. When they attempted to reestablish this committee in 1910, the OIA flatly refused to let them.[10] The tribe could only look on helplessly as clear-cutting of the forest became the federal management system. The Indian agents assigned to oversee the Menominee had no forest experience. The Menominee had a lot but were powerless to put it to use. Instead, the USDA Forest Service insisted on cutting the forest to meet the mill's overlarge capacity—it could process nearly twice the amount of lumber allowed under the LaFollette Act. Pinchot, Chief of the U.S. Forest Service, was a strong advocate of clear-cutting, and that was the simplest method to get enough timber to run the Neopit mill at full capacity.[11]

Compounding these problems, the foresters assigned to the Menominee reservation admitted that their logging experience was based in clear-cutting. They were ignorant of the intentions of the 1908 law. Their goal, which meshed with the agency superintendents' plans to clear the forest for farming, focused solely on short-term profit.[12]

In 1912 tribal leaders, including former business committee members, asked agent Angus Nicholson to appoint Reginald Oshkosh, himself a

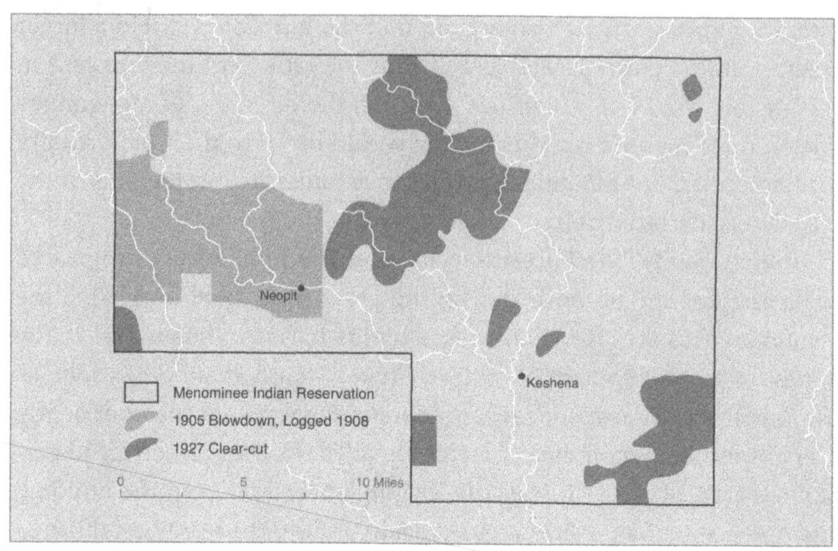

Map 3. Mismanaged forest area, Menominee Indian Reservation. Courtesy Aileen Clarke.

former business committee member who had been educated in government schools, to manage the forest. Nicholson refused. Then the tribe sent a delegation to Washington to push for Oshkosh's appointment. They were unsuccessful. Several tribal members, including Mitchell Oshkenaniew, then hired attorneys who brought mismanagement claims to Congress. This all led to an investigation by the Board of Indian Commissioners, a nongovernmental organization that was established to provide "the supervision of the Indian Bureau and the protection of Indian rights." Edward E. Ayer, a Chicago businessman and member of the board, published its findings in 1914.[13]

Ayer's report focused more on allotment and farming than on the forest work. He viewed logging as a means to denude the forest so that Menominees could farm the land as their white neighbors did.[14] Nicholson also supported allotment and farming over forest work. In 1915 the Menominee General Council, which consisted of the tribe's adults, exhibited its frustration with Nicholson's policy views and incompetence by twice passing a resolution asking him to resign. One of several

Department of the Interior inspectors sent to review the situation urged that "Nicholson be promptly transferred to some position not requiring the supervision or handling of Indians, or requiring knowledge of lumber operations."[15] Nicholson remained on the job for nearly three more years until his work fighting a forest fire hastened his death.[16]

An ongoing battle between foresters employed by the OIA and those working for the Forest Service was part of the cause for Menominee protests of federal mismanagement of their forest. In 1918 the Forest Service employees were removed from their duties on the reservation—but due to poor communication between the departments of agriculture and interior were not even aware of their dismissal until 1924.[17] They continued to work on the reservation, and the Menominee continued to pay employees of both agencies as well as other reservation expenses from their own timber revenue funds throughout.[18]

Nicholson's successor focused even more passionately on clear-cutting the forest to provide land for farming allotments.[19] From 1908 through 1925 federal officials authorized clear cutting of more than 22,500 acres of reservation forest land.[20] By 1934 the Menominee had suffered a loss of half a billion board feet of their timber since passage of the LaFollette Act, from clear-cutting, poor cleanup of the woods, which stopped healthy trees from regrowing, and other causes that lay at the hands of federal officials. In those twenty-six years, under the law, they should have harvested hardly more than one-tenth that amount.[21] But OIA officials believed that farming was the best path to the Menominee future, even if it meant Menominee individuals would lose their lands to "sturdy and thrifty" white interlopers. Their efforts to bring this about continued even after the 1928 Meriam Report pronounced that allotment would be disastrous to the Menominee.[22]

Menominee leaders, frustrated with federal actions, sought ways to take control of their forest economy and resources. They hired attorneys to fight for them on two fronts. The tribe proposed incorporation of their forest and mill so that they could gain management control. And they initiated claims for past federal mismanagement of their forest, their lumber mill, and other affairs dating almost continuously from the beginning of the treaty years. They used the same arguments to support both initiatives.

The Menominee voted to incorporate their forest in 1929. In 1930, with the help of their attorney Richard Dwight of the New York firm of Hughes, Schurman & Dwight, the tribe convinced Wisconsin congressman Edward Brown to bring two bills to Congress—one to permit them to hire attorneys and the other to permit them to bring a suit in the U.S. Court of Claims. Dwight worked pro bono for the tribe until Congress approved their hiring him.

Then in May the law firm drafted a bill to incorporate the tribe in order "to enable them to take, hold, control and administer, manage, operate and dispose of the assets and property of the tribe." The bill asked Congress to assign the tribe trusteeship for a minimum of fifty years. OIA officials opposed these efforts and argued that they had not mismanaged the tribe's resources. To an extent they were correct. They had merely supported USDA Forest Service mismanagement of their forest to pursue the goal of turning the forest into farmland. Still, Indian Service forester J.P. Kinney also supported clear-cutting.[23] None of these bills became law. But they represent the extreme frustration the Menominee felt at the federal failure to uphold its trust responsibilities.[24]

As I have previously written, "Incorporation and the tribal claim against the government were two faces of the same issue: federal control of Menominee resources had cost the tribe dearly and continued to do so. The Menominee attempted one method after the next to gain some semblance of control."[25] The Menominee also expended significant energy successfully fighting off outside efforts to gain control of their resources. These efforts included a private company that hoped to build electric generating dams on the reservation and a congressional bill that passed the house, but not the senate, that would have turned six of the reservation's ten townships into a national park.[26]

The Menominee abandoned the idea of incorporation when federal officials insisted that it be defined in a way that would undermine federal trust responsibilities. Finally, in 1935, Congress passed a bill permitting the Menominee to sue for a long list of damages in the Court of Claims, including "cutting such timber so as to prevent forest perpetuation" by the United States, thereby ignoring the LaFollette Act.[27] Reginald Oshkosh spoke for many when he said, "A lot of our old people now have passed away, those who have worked hard in order to save our properties, especially the timber. We can see now what the old people used to tell us, that some day the people would see how we have sacrificed many things in order to save our resources, i.e., the timber particularly."[28]

The thirteen claims eventually filed were an effort to stop mismanagement, to financially redress past wrongs, and to provide the tribe the opportunity to manage the forest in the way tribal members saw fit. The United States managed the forest for overall profit and individual benefit and to pay the salaries of federal employees. This meant they overharvested, clear-cut, and often hired non-Indians to do the work. Most Menominees, on the other hand, viewed the forest as a way to provide benefit for the community as a whole, and for generations not yet born.[29] With their long experience with the forest and as loggers the Menominee would have made very different decisions in forest management, had they been permitted to do so.

At the same time as the Menominee were authorized to bring their lawsuits, Commissioner of Indian Affairs John Collier initiated efforts to empower tribal communities, albeit in a limited way. In 1934 Collier appointed Ralph Fredenberg as the Menominee Indian agent, the first Menominee in that position. Unfortunately, at the same time, the power of decision-making on the reservation was moved from the agent to the head of the mill, who was white. Fredenberg recognized the weakness of his position, saying "I have proposed to them a number of times that they give me full charge and that something constructive could be worked out."

Collier then urged the Menominee to organize under the Indian Reorganization Act (IRA). They voted to accept the IRA, but they also voted against incorporating under it. They refused to accept an IRA constitution. OIA officials insisted that they preferred to work with a tribal government organized under IRA rules; the Menominee insisted they would retain the governing system they had reestablished in the 1920s, which would provide them with greater control of their governance than an IRA constitution would. Even into the 1940s the OIA refused to accept a constitution written by the Menominee. This severely hampered tribal efforts at self-government.[30] And so the glimmer of hope

Fig. 2. Menominee truck logging. The Menominee believed that the best use of their forest resource was to provide employment for as many tribal members as possible. Small truck logging helped accomplish that. Courtesy Menominee Tribal Historic Preservation Office.

that the Menominee would gain some control over the management of their resources vanished.

Both Congress and OIA officials in Washington increasingly viewed the trust responsibility as something to eliminate, while the Menominee viewed it as something to provide a solid foundation to support them in managing their own affairs. In 1946 agency superintendent Daniel Murphy argued that the tribe's advisory council worked against federal interests and should be ignored. Assistant Commissioner of Indian Affairs William Zimmerman Jr. responded that the opposite was true—the council needed to pay close attention to tribal business affairs "so that the Tribe [would] be able, in the not too distant future, to take over and manage its own affairs."[31] The next year, on orders from Congress, Zimmerman created his infamous list of tribal nations ready for termination, naming the Menominee as self-supporting and therefore among the tribes most ready for termination.

The mill and the forest did indeed provide significant economic support for the tribe, even considering federal mismanagement. Profits from logging helped pay for the hospital and for support for elders and indigent tribal members. "Nearly all Menominee men worked in one way or another for the lumbering industry at some point during the year." Occasionally the tribe was able to make per capita payments to individual tribal members to help with their daily needs and bills.[32] If managed correctly though, the logging and lumber businesses would have provided better support for the Menominee.

Profits also paid the salaries of nearly all federal employees on the reservation dating back to at least 1908. In 1947 Zimmerman was called to testify before a senate committee studying federal employees. The purpose of the hearings was to find ways to bring down federal costs and eliminate federal employees. When asked how many federal jobs could be eliminated if the Menominee were terminated, he merely told the committee that the Menominee Reservation provided jobs for fifty-eight employees.[33] He failed to mention that all of these employees were paid from tribal timber funds—and that elimination of their jobs would not save the federal treasury any money.[34]

Zimmerman brought a draft Menominee incorporation plan to the hearing. In his proposal Menominee land would be held in trust by the tribe and would be "inalienable and nontaxable" for fifty years.[35] Tribal leaders, however, opposed bureau and congressional efforts to withdraw federal fiduciary responsibilities from the tribe. Advisory Council chairman Gordon Dickie summed up Menominee views in a 1949 letter to terminationist Utah senator Arthur Watkins: "We are proud of the progress made by our people but wish to reiterate that we have not . . . reached the point of assuming full responsibility for our own affairs."[36] The Menominee recognized that without federal protections of their sovereignty and their nontaxable status, their future was endangered. Nonetheless Watkins fervently pursued termination for the Menominee.

Meanwhile, the Menominee claims cases slowly worked their way through the court system. Their attorneys filed thirteen claims in the

Fig. 3. Menominee leaders with their congressman and attorney. *Left to right*: Gordon Dickie Sr., John "Manny" Boyd, Congressman Melvin Laird, and Attorney Wilkinson. Courtesy Menominee Tribal Historic Preservation Office.

U.S. Court of Claims on December 1, 1938. These met with numerous procedural delays all the way until the court assigned a commissioner who reported his findings in 1949. By then, more than eight thousand pages of testimony had been presented.[37] The tribe's attorney succinctly reiterated the cause of the suit in the opening line of argument after the findings were sent to the court. "This suit is brought by the Menominee Tribe of Indians to recover damages for the unlawful and destructive cutting of their timber lands in violation of the Act of March 28, 1908."[38]

The findings themselves pointed out that the clear-cutting "embraced an entire disregard of forest welfare, forest conditions, the continuation or perpetuation of the forest. It was also practiced in utter disregard of a sustained yield."[39] In other words, Forest Service officials in collusion with OIA staff had clearly broken the 1908 LaFollette Act. In 1951 the tribe finally won an $8.5 million judgment in the long-standing lawsuits against the United States for mismanagement of their timber resource.[40] This provided the opening that Watkins needed to bribe the Menominee with their own money.

TERMINATION

Members of Congress and leading Indian bureau officials not only believed the Menominee were ready to be freed from federal wardship; they also strongly resented the tribe's successful lawsuit. In fact, federal officials supporting termination argued that if the Menominee were smart enough to sue the government, they were smart enough to run their own affairs, and they feared the tribe might sue them for mismanagement again in the future if the federal government did not put an end to its trust responsibilities.[41] Senators actually knew that the Menominee paid for federal salaries and sawmill expenses but believed that prepared them for termination.[42]

After the settlement award from the successful lawsuit, the Menominee voted to provide each member of the tribe a one-time payment of fifteen hundred dollars and to use the rest of the money, after attorneys fees, for various tribal social services.[43] Since the original enabling legislation for the claims suit did not allow any claims received by the tribe to be paid out to individuals in what are called per capita payments, Congressman Melvin Laird, on behalf of the tribe, introduced legislation in 1952 to allow these payments.[44]

Terminationist commissioner of Indian Affairs Dillon Myer opposed the bill, insisting that it explicitly be tied to termination. The first in a list of "key matters" that the bureau believed needed to be resolved before any funding could be distributed reads, "Determination of the type of organization and business management which is necessary to carry on tribal business without Bureau supervision." He wrote, "[Though] much progress has been made [in working toward termination], additional work needs to be done." He observed, "We believe that some plans can be worked out over the period of a very few months." Those plans clearly involved holding up tribal funds until the Menominee agreed to termination. Myer concluded by saying, "We further believe there should be no further impairment of the capital reserves held in trust for the tribe until such a program has been completed."[45]

Assistant Secretary of the Interior Orme Lewis concurred, telling Senator Watkins that he had rebuffed tribal delegates in their efforts for a per capita payment. His language was more direct than that of the commissioner. "As the proposal was not directed towards the termination of Federal trusteeship responsibilities, the tribal delegation was informed that the Bureau would have to respond adversely if requested by Congress for a report."[46]

On May 8, 1952, a Menominee delegation consisting of Al Dodge, Jim Frechette, Gordon Dickie, and others met with Commissioner of Indian Affairs Dillon Myer, Minneapolis Area Director Don. C. Foster and BIA program officers in Washington DC about hospital and school construction issues. As the discussion turned to oversight of the mill, "the Commissioner stated that the Bureau was willing to turn the whole operation over to the tribe so that they could manage it to their satisfaction," according to Program Officer John B. Keliiaa, who attended the meeting.

The tribal delegates immediately responded with caution, but the BIA officials urged them to consider the commissioner's suggestions. Al Dodge stated point blank that the federal government still held responsibility for tribal operations. According to Keliiaa, "The Commissioner stated that we do have the responsibility, but we are not sure we should have. In the meantime, we want the tribe to get the experience of acting as a board of directors." Bureau officials left the meeting under the impression that the Menominee were willing to work with the Bureau "in commencing studies designed to free the Federal Government of responsibility for supervision of the Menominee Reservation and the Menominee Indians."[47] Nonetheless, even at this point the tribe's attorneys believed that a per capita bill might pass without termination being attached to it. They also knew the Menominee opposed termination of their status as a federally recognized tribe.[48]

If there was any doubt of the commissioner's intentions after this meeting, it should have dissipated in June after Keliiaa visited the reservation as part of a BIA delegation to urge the Menominee to accept the inevitability of termination, or "withdrawal of federal supervision" as they called it. On June 3 Keliiaa flew to Milwaukee and commenced a trip to the reservation with two other bureau employees. Over the next three weeks, they attended council meetings, held community meetings in Zoar and South Branch, and met with individual tribal members urging them to plan for termination. Menominee tribal leader Gordon Dickie announced that he was planning to run for Congress, but abruptly changed his mind when he realized federal intentions, and recognized the fight in which the tribe would be involved.[49]

Menominees resisted the withdrawal of federal supervision, but Keliiaa and the others ignored them, saying, "They will probably be much more interested in the whole programming effort after they have given more thought to the matter." The bureau officials spoke in terms of withdrawal; the Menominee spoke in terms of self-government under federal protection of their tribal status. Their definitions were worlds apart since self-government in the minds of Menominees would occur under the protection of the federal trust relationship. Keliiaa commented after the meeting at South Branch, "I think that the comment of one of the members to th[e] effect that they were somewhat stunned is an apt characterization of the meeting, if slightly exaggerated."[50] The Menominee Advisory Council was reluctant to begin a program of withdrawal, which Keliiaa mistakenly believed was due to tribal political concerns rather than opposition to the "program," as he referred to termination.[51]

Meanwhile tribal leaders had traveled to Washington. One, Al Dodge, bypassed the BIA and went directly to the Interior department's Bureau of the Budget to lobby for the per capita bill. "The money we were asking for belonged to the Menominee Indians and not the United States Government," he said. He also argued that the federal government would save a million dollars in interest over five years if it would authorize the per capita payment. He was able to get the house version of the bill passed, but it died in the senate.[52]

On June 5, at a meeting in the office of Orme Lewis, "the Tribe was threatened that the $1500 per capita payments would be withheld unless they 'consented' to termination."[53] Tribal leaders were handicapped by the bureau's secrecy in decision-making. According to William Zimmerman Jr., "Bureau officials, including the Superintendent, frequently failed to inform tribal officials when plans were being considered and adopted by the Bureau."[54]

Fig. 4. Menominee tribal delegation. *Left to right*: Mr. Al Dodge, aka the Senator or King Fish, Mr. Antoine Waupochick Sr., Mr. John Fossum, Mr. Gordon Dickie Sr., and Mr. Simon Worden. They are conducting Menominee business in Washington DC. Courtesy Menominee Tribal Historic Preservation Office.

When the House passed legislation to release per capita money to the Menominee in 1953, Senator Arthur V. Watkins of Utah, the Senate's primary proponent of termination, rewrote the Senate version entirely, making payment contingent on the Menominee accepting termination. Watkins's legislation was called a bill "to provide for a per capita distribution of Menominee tribal funds and authorize the withdrawal of the Menominee Tribe from Federal jurisdiction."[55] When tribal members in Washington protested, the story made national news. Rex Curry, chair of Utah's Uintah and Ouray tribal council—a tribe that was dealing with its own termination issues—told council members he had read about the mess in the paper. When the Menominee were told they would have to "agree to be rel[e]ased from the Government aid" if they accepted the per capita, "the Indians decided against it."[56]

At this point Watkins agreed to visit the reservation.[57] At a tribal general council meeting on June 20, 1953, Watkins informed the tribe as a whole that if they did not agree to termination, the government would not release the claims money. Gordon Keshena protested, arguing, "You cannot ask the people to go on their own and govern themselves now when for all those years they have not been permitted to do anything for themselves."[58] His argument was a good one. The heavy-handed Indian bureau oversight of reservation affairs since the 1850s had severely crippled development of tribal leadership capacity. Maintenance of the trust relationship would be essential for successful oversight of Menominee governance and business.

Nonetheless, Watkins insisted that termination be tied to the per capita payment. He told the Menominee that if the federal government retained responsibility to the tribe, there was a good chance the Indian bureau and Congress "may make some more mistakes and get sued again."[59] This was to become a common argument for terminating the federal trust responsibility to the Menominee. A Mr. Worden, a tribal member protested: "Our good friend, Senator Watkins, comes along and says, 'You people go on your own or you don't get any $1500.' I may be mistaken, but I think he is selling my rights with my own money."[60] Ada Deer, in testimony before the Senate on behalf of a number of tribal members, later declared, "Senator Watkins did *not* believe that *our* consent to termination was necessary for its enactment. Yet he knew that his cause would be helped if he could persuade us to agree to termination."[61] Tribal members understood what was happening to them. They knew Watkins was withholding their own money in order to get them to accept a termination that they did not want.

With barely 10 percent of eligible voters participating, Menominees voted to accept Watkins's resolution, 169–5. To this day much confusion surrounds that meeting. Though Watkins knew that many of the Menominees at the meeting spoke only Menominee, or had little understanding of English, he refused to allow the proceedings to be fully translated by an interpreter. Several Menominees voted with the understanding they were voting to accept the per capita payout.[62] Only after the meeting did they realize that termination had indeed been tied to the vote. The nearby Shawano newspaper captured the outside world's view of events, however, with a headline reading "Menominees' Full Freedom Assured at General Council."[63]

Unfortunately for the Menominee, the tribe's attorneys immediately began to propose revisions to the legislation based on the June 20 acceptance of the premise of termination.[64] Though most of these revisions would be ignored, the argument in Washington essentially revolved around the minutiae of details regarding timing of termination from this point forward. Federal officials no longer considered whether termination was appropriate for the tribe. They were only concerned with the mechanics of how and when to do it.

Less than a month later, on July 17, the tribe held another council, rejecting the earlier vote by 197–0. They agreed to give up their $8.5 million claim settlement if it meant they had to accept termination. Nonetheless, Watkins used the earlier vote to convince the Senate to pass the Menominee termination bill, conveniently not mentioning that he had pressured the tribe into supporting it or that the Menominee had later reversed their decision.[65] And Members of Congress were assured that the tribe had been consulted and given consent to termination.[66] Even the Menominee's attorney, Glen Wilkinson, reporting on his work for the tribe between June 20 and August 1, 1953, made no mention of the July 17 council meeting or vote.[67] Tribal leaders did reference it in a July 18 memorandum, in a desperate bid to stop the bill from proceeding in the Senate.[68]

Gordon Dickie described the situation succinctly: "In 1953 is when Arthur Watkins, Senator from Utah, pushed termination. And one thing that I've always taken exception to is the accusation or allegation that the Menominee tribe sold out for the per capita payment. That is not true. Absolutely false. Because I presided at the meeting in July of 1953 when they voted 197 to 0 to drop the per capita payment rather than accept Watkins' proposal on termination. But Watkins went ahead and pushed it anyway."[69]

Watkins had plenty of support in the House. An exchange between Representatives Wesley D'Ewart of Montana and William A. Dawson of Utah on the same day that HCR 108 became law, August 1, echoes

Watkins's position and is revealing. D'Ewart argued that the Menominee were both wealthy and capable of managing their own affairs. "When a tribe of Indians sues the United States for not properly managing their affairs and gets a judgment for $8,500,000 is it not about time that we yielded to the Indians and let them manage their own affairs before we get them into more trouble?"

Dawson responded that after their success, "you could hardly blame the Indians for wanting to wait another 5 or 10 years to sue again so that they could get another $8,500,000." D'Ewart enthusiastically agreed. "That may well happen," he said. "Here is an opportunity to get rid of this trusteeship, return it to the Indians who are so competent that they won this lawsuit for 8½ million."[70] By now congressional fervor was so high that the Menominee stood little chance of reversing the momentum. Indeed, the Menominee would be the first tribe terminated under HCR 108.[71]

Echoing William Grignon, Menominee tribal member Sylvia Wilbur said at the 1961 American Indian Chicago Conference, "There would have been no termination if we hadn't been bribed."[72] Lee Metcalf, a Montana congressional representative, reinforced that sentiment to NCAI leaders, according to the *New York Times*, "charg[ing] that the bureau had withheld funds due to the Menominee . . . until the tribe had agreed to go along with its [termination] policy." In fact, Metcalf said, "The consent was obtained by refusal to permit the tribes to withdraw and use their own funds until the termination bills had received the tribe's consent."[73] Metcalf was angry at having been duped into believing the Menominee had asked for termination by the time he made this statement. Both NCAI and the Indian Rights Association supported Menominee termination, mistakenly believing that the tribe had requested it.[74] Congress passed the Menominee termination law in 1954, and termination went into effect in 1961.[75]

Termination would unleash the most tragic twentieth-century conditions for the Menominee. It brought economic destruction, taxes, social disintegration, health problems, and educational losses, and it disestablished both the reservation and the tribal government. In the process it created the poorest county in Wisconsin. The tribe fought back in a variety of ways.[76] The Menominee were able to hold onto their forest throughout termination by establishing a corporation. Although they did not have ultimate control of the corporation, this was a resource that they were able to later fight for and gain control over. Tribal member George Kenote and attorney Glen Wilkinson explained why the Menominee chose not to break up the valuable forest resource: "Wisconsin Indians who have sold timber rights on other reservations have become the State's severest health and welfare problems. We are trying to avoid that at Menominee."[77]

Help came in 1968 when the U.S. Supreme Court ruled that Menominee individuals still retained their treaty rights, since Congress had not abrogated them.[78] Then a grassroots movement of tribal members, both on and off the reservation, led by Ada Deer, James Washinawatok, and others, forced Congress to reverse termination in 1973 with a restoration law that reestablished reservation boundaries and recognized tribal sovereignty.[79]

In the process the Menominee gained far more self-rule and control of their governance and forest resources than they had had since before the treaty years. They did so under the protection of federal trust. This was what they had worked toward throughout the late-nineteenth and most of the twentieth centuries—federal protection of their sovereignty under the auspices of the U.S. trust responsibility.

The other tribe slated for early termination because of its rich forest resource, the Klamath of Oregon, faced both similar and different challenges and fared differently as well. Looking to the future, attorney Glen Wilkinson wistfully said, "I do wish some method could be found which would assure continued operation of the Menominee and Klamath forests on a program of sustained yield."[80] The Menominee would manage to do this, but the Klamath would not. Representative Lee Metcalf of Montana observed in 1956, "The price for Administration consent to a per capita distribution of tribal assets to the Menonimees was termination. The same was true of the Klamaths."[81] Federal bribery and failed federal trust both played a role in the Klamath story.

CHAPTER 5

The Klamath Tribes of Oregon

> The same old Bureaucrats in the Indian Bureau who have been wandering those halls for years carrying out their ancient policies [are still] refusing to permit the Indians to handle their own affairs.
>
> —Wade Crawford to Dwight Eisenhower, March 5, 1953

> Is there any reason why I shouldn't now do my best to conserve the reservation for the future generations, my grandchildren, keep the same rights and same privileges we have exercised over the years?
>
> —Boyd Jackson, Proceedings of General Council Meeting, December 17, 1953

Like the Menominee, the Klamath had long battles with federal bureaucrats and members of Congress over control of their rich forest resource. Unlike the Menominee, however, the Klamath were deeply split over whether they should be released from federal oversight. This division was mostly among tribal members who lived on the reservation. It dated from their anger over the failure of federal officials to uphold their trust responsibilities in the early twentieth century. The conflict centered around the tribal forest. The Klamath had virtually no say in either their logging business or what happened to the money they theoretically derived from it.

By the 1920s and 1930s a battle over the lack of home rule erupted that would divide tribal leaders over the next several decades and extend even beyond the termination fight. Congress and the Indian bureau exploited this division in their relentless efforts to coerce the Klamath to relinquish their political relationship with the United States.

The attorney for the Public Lands Committee of the Association of Oregon Counties, Forrest Cooper, wrote in December 1953, "It is here in the Pacific Northwest where the first opportunity exists to divorce the federal government from numerous Indian tribes."[1] The majority of the tribes terminated in the 1950s and 1960s hailed from Oregon and were among the very first subjected to termination laws.[2] This occurred to a significant extent for two reasons. First, Secretary of the Interior Douglas McKay came to that office from the governorship of Oregon, where he had begun an effort to prepare the state's tribes for termination in 1950. At a meeting of the Oregon Governor's Advisory Committee on Indian Affairs, McKay had said, "We must face facts. The time is coming when all Indian reservations will be dissolved . . . with or without consent" of Indians.[3] He hoped that Oregon could set a national example for termination efforts.

Historian Stephen Dow Beckham wrote, "The Indians in Mr. McKay's home state would be a showcase for the example of the legislative treating of the American Indian."[4] After taking over the Interior department, McKay himself told an Oklahoma Indian youth, "I am in sympathy with starting out on a program such as I handled in the State of Oregon where we tried to improve the situation of the Indian and allow him to be a citizen."[5]

Second, as fortune would have it for good or ill, the Portland Area Office was run by an efficient administrator, E. Morgan Pryse. On August 10, 1948, he issued a call to agency superintendents to develop six-year termination plans for Oregon tribes.[6] Remarkably, due to this planning and Secretary McKay's backing, two termination bills became law six years and three days later, on August 13, 1954—one terminating sixty-one tribes and bands in western Oregon and the other specifically terminating the Klamath.[7]

Unlike politicians in places like North Dakota and Montana, who opposed termination based on the costs to their state budgets, Oregon officials took the view that it would be economically advantageous. Cooper, the Public Lands attorney, wrote, "Our federal taxpayers have an annual stake of about $85,000,000.00 in ways and means of abolishing just one Indian Reservation. If we can do the job once and do it right we then have a precedent for plucking the ones that remain."[8] It is not clear what Cooper meant by the dollar number he used, which was higher than the BIA's total annual budget. But all of this created an environment in which the Klamath termination was supported at the state and national level.

Tribal members and federal officials fought over how the Klamath future would be managed. The rich Klamath forest resource was central to this battle. Tribal members were split on whether the future should or should not include federal oversight and protections, and even on whether the tribes should stay together. Some argued for home rule, an expansion of tribal sovereignty protected by the federal trust. Others argued for the federal government to withdraw but for the tribes to remain together. Still others wanted a division of the forest and payout of its value to individuals. And some changed their stances over the decades leading to termination as two factions evolved. Federal officials were able to use this intratribal conflict and the value of the timber as leverage to force termination on the Klamath.

THE FIGHT OVER HOME RULE

The Klamath Reservation was established in an 1864 treaty in which the Klamath ceded most of their twenty million acres of homelands, while retaining a two-million-acre reservation in southern Oregon. The reservation became home to three tribal groups, the Klamath, the Modoc, and the Yahooskin Paiute. The Modocs and Yahooskin Bands were removed from their own nearby homelands to the new reservation.[9]

After the reservation was allotted (confiscated from the tribes as a whole and broken up into individually controlled parcels) between 1895 and 1910, the tribes retained some 860,000 acres of exceptional pine forest.[10] Allotments were made on marshlands and some forest land, leaving most of the forest intact. Overall nearly a million acres of the tribes' forest was left untouched in the allotments.[11] The remaining forest

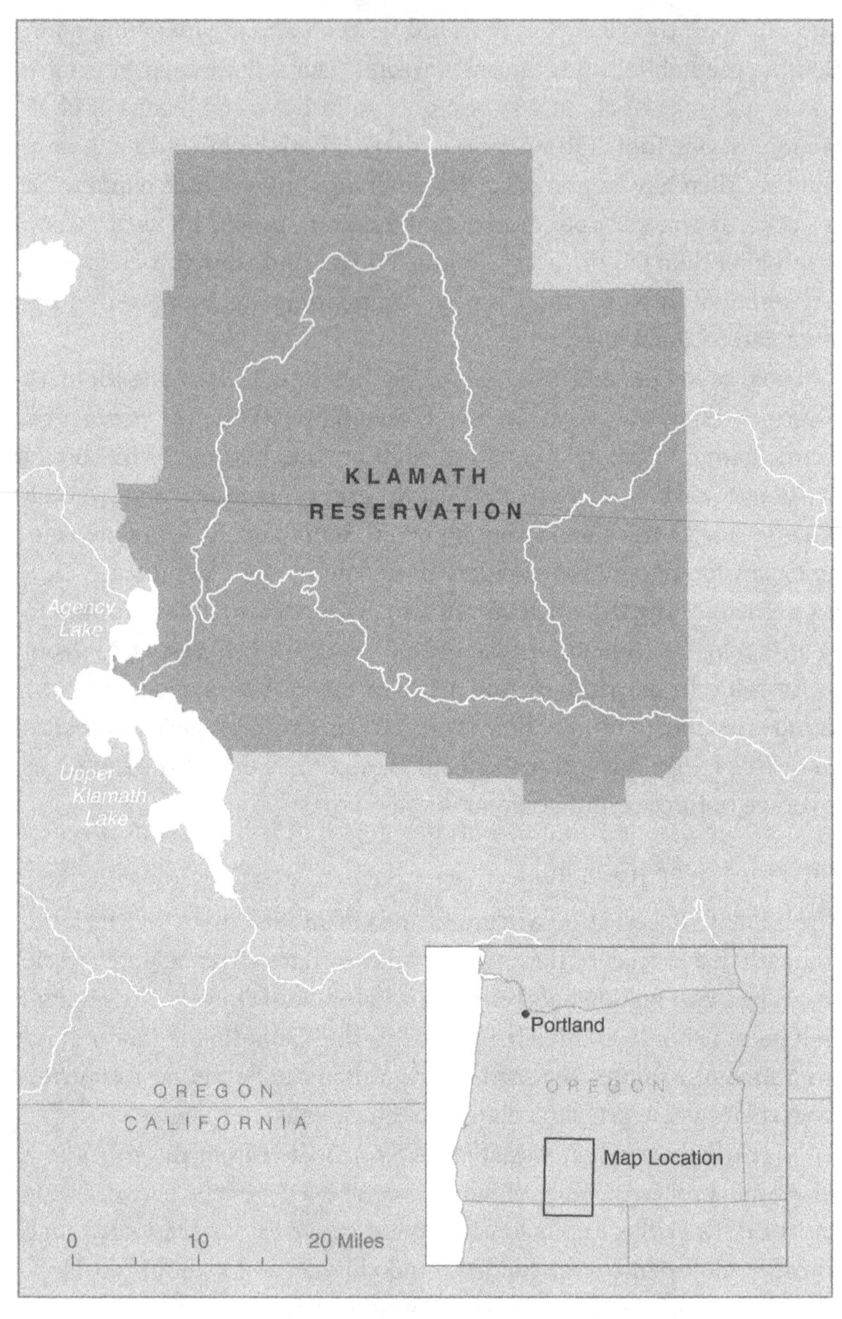

Map 4. Klamath Reservation, Oregon, 1954. Courtesy Aileen Clark.

held enough commercial timber that sixty million board feet could be harvested annually on a sustained yield basis.[12] That computes to three times the amount that the Menominee could safely harvest.

An errant survey of the reservation boundaries led to some 621,824 acres, including 87,000 acres of rich forest land to be illegally taken and owned "by white people [who began] extensive logging operations and farming." The tribes received "an 'unconscionable' consideration" in payment for the taken lands, less than four cents on the dollar in value for the 87,000 timber acres. In 1914 the Klamath tribal council asked the secretary of the Interior to make payments promised by the federal government for the land. Hoping to be able to allow individuals to better benefit from tribal resources they also asked him to push Congress to pass a law "providing for allotting of timbered lands to all the members of the Klamath tribes of Indians."[13]

It did not happen. The push to allot forest lands failed, and so the Klamath increasingly sought control over their forest decisions. Congress again stood in the way, passing a 1910 law that gave the secretary of the Interior the right to establish the rules for selling timber on nearly all tribal lands, which included the Klamath. (This did not apply to the Menominee, whose forest management had already been defined in the 1908 LaFollette Act.)[14] In 1916, Klamath council member Joe Ball angrily said in a meeting on a proposal to throw open the reservation to whites: "It has been the cry of this Council to become citizens and get out from under the jurisdiction of our Government, to be given responsibility, supervision, and the privilege of managing our own affairs."[15] Though Klamath tribal members who had taken allotments were U.S. citizens, they lacked what they considered citizenship rights over forest management.

The next year the tribes sent Clayton Kirk to Washington "to find out to what extent we, as individual members of the tribe, have any rights in regard to the management and control of our reservation, and to what extent our voices should be heeded in the management of our affairs." Kirk also insisted that "in the sale and disposition of the timber, the voice of the tribe should be heard."[16]

These conflicts in relation to forest resources grew significantly in the 1920s. As tribal members and federal officials increasingly recognized some Klamath people's competency to manage their resources, the Klamath pushed for a decrease in federal control over them, which would increase self-rule.

One of the issues was related to timber stumpage fund accounting. The 1910 law required that 8 percent of timber proceeds be set aside for management of the timber sales, but by the mid-1920s those funds were simply sent to the U.S. treasury with no accounting for how much of the money actually came back to the Klamath Reservation. In fact, Congress intended the Indian Service forestry division to use these moneys for any Indian reservation timber project in the country. Tribes with profitable forests like the Klamath subsidized federal employees not only on their own reservation, but on those of other tribes as well. Klamath tribal delegate Levi Walker told OIA officials that the tribes wanted "to whittle down as much as we can our tribal expenses." Some of the white employees did not seem to be working to benefit tribal members. And there seemed to be no way to account for where their money went.[17]

A 1930 Senate hearing reported that a Department of the Interior inspector found that although the Klamath incurred the eight percent charge for timber management, the actual logging and sale costs were less than 3.5 percent. At the same time, the Klamath did not receive the type of Indian Office support that other tribes did. Most of their children, for example, were educated in public schools without OIA support. In addition, expenditures were made based on an overcut of the Klamath forest that threatened to diminish it to the point that it would rapidly disappear.[18]

As early as 1922 tribal members began looking into the prospect of selling their reservation land to get out from under this paternalistic relationship. At the request of tribal members, a man named Frederic Baker prepared the first report recommending liquidation of their land base and assets in 1922–1923. He recommended selling all reservation land and assets to the United States to be held to protect the Klamath watershed and splitting the money evenly among tribal members.[19] Over the years tribal members would debate options including complete liquidation of assets, turning control of resources over to tribal management, or permitting some individual tribal members to sell their share of the tribal domain and give up their tribal membership. The intratribal debate over liquidation versus home rule or self-governance was thus intensified.

By the end of the 1920s two separate plans to prepare for the Klamath future emerged, with tribal members actually succeeding in having competing bills brought to Congress. One, written by Wade and Ida Crawford with the aid of the secretary of the Interior, called for incorporation of the tribes' forest under tribal management, with the federal government bowing out of that responsibility. The other, supported by Boyd Jackson together with Dice Crain and Jesse Kirk, called for the sale of the Klamath Forest and division of the funds received among tribal members. Neither of these plans envisioned federal oversight of Klamath matters. Though neither bill got past congressional committees, they did cement the factions that would fight each other for the next quarter century.[20] Throughout that time the Klamath factions would attempt one way or another to get control of their resources.

Continued federal theft of Klamath resources through the 8 percent administrative charge, and Klamath tribal members being shut out of decision-making, angered many in the tribes. They must have been especially irate when the Indian office forester J. P. Kinney set up a forestry training school on the reservation using Klamath funds and trained only white foresters. According to Secretary of the Interior Harold Ickes, "He wouldn't give a single Indian a chance at the training that they were paying for."[21] The Klamath forest was in the midst of a beetle infestation crisis, and Kinney had to oversee heavy cutting.

The 1910 law forced Kinney to pay for this with Indian funds.[22] But by freezing Klamath loggers out of the project and decision-making, Kinney deepened tribal anger at the federal government. Both Congress and the Indian bureau share the blame for the disaffection of the Klamath. As they had in the past, both groups ignored their fiduciary responsibilities as trustee.

Unfortunately, tribal members had no authority over the forestry budget, although they understood it better than the members of Congress who approved and appropriated it.[23] They were particularly incensed with the number of white supervisors assigned to the reservation.[24] Congress proved especially derelict in the 1920s and 1930s in fulfilling its trust obligations to the Klamath. Tribal leaders, therefore, tried various approaches to increase their control over their resources and moneys or, as Kirk desired, to sell it.

As one observer wrote, "The Klamath political struggles of the 1930's provided an impetus for the later termination act."[25] In 1933 newly appointed Commissioner of Indian Affairs John Collier appointed Wade Crawford as agency superintendent. As Secretary of the Interior Harold Ickes later recalled, "It was John Collier's policy, which had my full support, to give the Indians themselves the fullest possible representation in managing their own affairs."[26] In the Klamath case, this decision would intensify the tribal conflict that would last for two more decades.

Collier preached home rule but severely circumscribed the ways in which tribes could practice it. Crawford was the first Indian that Collier appointed as agency superintendent. Collier initially supported Crawford's efforts at forest incorporation, saying that the plan was "the most important new step in Indian affairs since the general allotment act."[27] But within a few years they came into conflict, which ended in Crawford's dismissal. This only served to intensify Crawford's anger at the Indian bureau.[28]

Long before the 1950s termination fight the Klamath became quite sophisticated in using the federal system. When they sent delegates to Washington (or Chicago and Washington during the second world war), they were well prepared to fight for Klamath interests.[29] In a fairly typical occurrence, in 1943 Boyd Jackson was sent with instructions from the business committee to lobby for sixteen different bills or issues involving the tribes. He met with the commissioner's staff, the secretary of the Interior's staff, the Oregon congressional delegation, and various committees on capitol hill.[30] Business committee instructions were approved by the tribes' General Council, which consisted of all adult members of the tribes.[31]

Nonetheless, or perhaps because of the Klamath's keen understanding of the disadvantages that paternalistic federal policy inflicted on them, conflict could not be avoided. It continued through the 1940s. The tribes' General Council approved a resolution written by Jesse Kirk at its December 27, 1940, meeting that was a step toward self-governance. In part the resolution read, "Any employment shall be exclusively of members of said enrolled Indians, namely: the Klamaths, Modocs, and the Yahooskin band of Snake Indians." The General Council then authorized Kirk to write a full resolution. In it he argued that Klamath tribal members should manage the reservation's economy. These were sent to John Collier, but since the second resolution had not been sent to the General Council for approval, Collier did not comment on it. However, he did state that the current Indian bureau program was "to re-establish and help him ['the Indian'] to become economically self-sufficient."[32]

Meanwhile Wade Crawford switched his perspective and emerged as leader of the minority faction push for "liquidation" bills that would eliminate communal control of Klamath resources. He did so when traveling to Chicago and Washington DC as a delegate on behalf of the tribes, but at the same time lobbying against the expressed wishes of both the Business Committee and the General Council.[33] In the years after the Second World War these "liquidation" bills came on a regular basis.

In 1946 Crawford, as an official tribal delegate, testified in favor of Senate Bill 1313, a Klamath liquidation bill. But he did so against the instructions of the Business Committee. He narrowly avoided having his report rejected by the General Council.[34] Crawford was concerned that the Klamath lacked individual property rights on reservation trust lands. He told the General Council, "The important thing that I discovered in the Indian Bureau, is that the Bureau does not intend to make the Indians unrestricted citizens of this country, rather it is the intention of the Bureau and their friends in Congress to consolidate the Indians' property into a Communistic system and administer the property under strict regimentation."[35]

Crawford was especially adamant about individual property rights. He and others wrote Oregon senator Wayne Morse after a contentious general council meeting. "We understand freedom of speech and the defense of property right to be the reason for this terrible war for which so many have lost their lives." They added, in exasperation, "Some of us believe that Hitler is not dead, that he is here, in complete charge of the Klamath Indian Reservation."[36]

Then in 1947 Crawford again ignored tribal instructions. He testified before Congress in favor of Senate Bill 1222, another Klamath liquidation bill, when the tribes officially condemned it. This bill was titled "To remove restrictions on the property and moneys belonging to the individual enrolled members of the Klamath Indian Reservation in Oregon, and to provide for the liquidation of tribal property and distribution of the proceeds thereof, to confer complete citizenship upon such Indians and for other purposes."[37] The title clearly stated the bill's purposes. William Zimmerman supported the measure on behalf of the Indian office, saying, "The bill that I suggest for the incorporation of the Klamath Tribe follows very closely . . . the bill supported by Mr. Crawford and introduced at his suggestion in 1932."[38]

Boyd Jackson and Crawford were sent to testify against it, and though they had once worked closely together for "Full Citizenship and Property Rights" of the Klamath, their testimony "was contrary one to the other."[39] Seldon Kirk then requested the General Council to remove Crawford from his position as delegate for "insubordination." Kirk added, "He is working for the liquidating of the reservation without the consent of the Klamath Indians." The council approved the removal in a vote of 88–4, with some abstentions.[40]

But the damage was done. Senator Arthur Watkins used Crawford's testimony to argue that the Klamath supported liquidation. In a statement he would mirror later with the Menominee, Watkins told Senator James Murray of Montana, "We have had a large number of witnesses testify here that they wanted that type of legislation, and the testimony of the Indian Service is that this tribe is far enough along in development that it could be put on its own."[41] Crawford would continue working with federal officials pushing Klamath termination, and members of Congress would continue to bring bills to accomplish just that.

In response to Crawford's antics, the General Council, in the summer of 1948, authorized creation of a special committee to devise a plan with three key features: "1) the defeat of any plan of liquidation of this reservation (2) the ending of further raids on our tribal funds, and (3) the assumption of self-government on our part."[42] Anthropologist Verne Ray published a report in 1948 on the liquidation proposals and found "that a substantial majority of the Klamath oppose it."[43]

By 1948 tribal members felt pressured by Congress to terminate the federal trust. At the same time, the internal split over individual withdrawal from the tribes versus remaining as a unified community continued. Oregon Senator Guy Cordon expressed his exasperation with the "anti-liquidationists" for what he viewed as negativity and instructed Boyd Jackson to bring Congress a positive resolution to the tribal schism over termination.[44] Tribal leaders, and the members at large, worked for a compromise.

Under this cloud, the tribes would push Congress to pass a law shifting supervision of all tribal activities from the federal bureaucracy to the tribes that would take full effect by 1965; they would push for a law permitting individual members who so desired to withdraw from the tribes; and at the same time they would oppose liquidation of the reservation. As tribal member Dorothy McAnulty said in response to Wade and Ida Crawford's efforts to push for liquidation, "We that do not want the liquidation we are trying to put a bill through where those that want to leave can do so."[45] Boyd Jackson spoke of the proposed voluntary withdrawal bills as a compromise: "The move . . . to liquidate created a problem, and for us to say we don't want to do it was insufficient to meet the thinking of our people as a whole."[46] These efforts continued into the future.[47] As one outside observer noted, the Klamath were enmeshed in "a cat and dog fight amongst tribal members who will never be able to unite in a program if they were to meet for the next 50 years."[48]

As a way around the intratribal impasse, Boyd Jackson, as official delegate from the tribes, lobbied congressional members and bureau officials throughout the 1948 congressional session for two bills. One offered voluntary individual emancipation from the tribes for those members who so desired. The other proposed "self-government by the Tribe after a period of years," providing the tribes could vote in advance on any bills brought before Congress.[49]

TERMINATION

Congress and the BIA continued to intensify their pressure on the tribes to accept termination. Unfortunately for the Klamath, their efforts to have Congress authorize a per capita payment to individuals out of tribal funds coincided with the peak of Congress's termination push that occurred over the next several years.[50] In fact, the termination debates in Congress and at Klamath subsumed events so that the per capita discussion is barely legible in the documentation. Just before the Klamath termination bill was introduced in Congress, an attorney new to the Indian Service told the tribes' General Council, "Its [*sic*] your program. We are only under a directive from Congress and the Secretary that you should have the right to manage your own affairs and withdraw from federal control. . . . But in the final analysis the decision must be yours not ours."[51]

However, Commissioner of Indian Affairs Glenn Emmons had already told the tribes that Congress had the final say, and even if the BIA and the tribes agreed on changes, Congress could do as it pleased.[52] Emmons was only affirming the long-standing policy granting Congress plenary power over tribal affairs.[53] The Klamath termination bill was introduced in Congress in January 1954, shortly after this meeting. The tribes, meeting in General Council, "provisionally accepted" the bill but established a special committee to work with the executive committee of the tribes to ensure that "some workable productive measures will be worked out to assure the safe-guarding of the interests and welfare of the membership of the Klamath Tribe."[54]

Boyd Jackson informed tribal members, "The bill did not originate with us." It was "instigated by the Bureau."[55] Tribal leaders protested that they had never been informed that the Bureau was going to include them on Zimmerman's infamous 1947 list of tribes ready for termination. They also believed there was no evidence that they had reached the point that they could "now take over the management and operations of the business of the Klamath Tribe."[56] At this point the tribes created a special committee of six to advise the executive council and selected Boyd Jackson and Jesse Kirk as delegates to go to Washington to monitor the bill.

Wade Crawford, a strong proponent of termination, was defeated in the election, but he went to DC anyway. He and his wife Ida had developed a strong friendship with Al Grorud, the Senate staffer for the Indian Affairs committee and subcommittee, over a period of decades.[57] Wade was a familiar and, in terms of termination legislation, friendly face in Congress. In June 1954 he "participated actively in negotiations leading to enactment of Public Law 587 [the termination bill], and was again compensated from tribal funds for salary and per diem on instructions from the Secretary of the Interior." In fact, he hired an attorney to help write amendments favoring those who wished to withdraw from the tribes and get their money.[58]

Secretary of the Interior Douglas McKay had written to Seldon Kirk that "under no circumstances" would the department pay salary or expenses for any unauthorized tribal member "who travels to Washington prior to receiving authority from this Department."[59] Nonetheless, McKay's office argued that it did have the prerogative to make that expenditure from tribal funds, even if the tribes opposed it. Interestingly, Indian bureau commissioner Dillon Myer had promised to crack down on delegates who arrived in DC without funding by helping them find work and referring them to missions for shelter but did not do so in Crawford's case.[60] Instead, the bureau paid Crawford with tribal money.

In fact, when Seldon Kirk, the president of the tribes' executive committee, protested to McKay, the secretary overrode his own policy. Kirk stated that McKay told him "that it was his policy he wished to get expression from minority as well as majority group so he would know what to do." McKay wrote to Kirk, "It was my belief that Mr. Crawford in his testimony at the hearing on the bills, performed a valuable service for a substantial number of the members of the Klamath Tribe and therefore justified being compensated at rates equivalent to those paid to tribal delegates." Kirk protested that the General Council's wishes should be deferred to by the Interior department and asked "that future elected delegates of the Tribe . . . be duly recognized as authentic." Myer simply said that he would defer to Secretary McKay.[61] In this case, the BIA failed to observe even a pretense of respecting tribal sovereignty.

William Zimmerman presented a counter view. After he left the Indian bureau he took on a role as field director of the Association on American Indian Affairs, the AAIA. He believed that "Crawford was recognized because he favored the policy generally advocated by the Department, rather than the policy advocated by the successful [delegate] candidate who defeated Crawford." The tribes' attorney, Glen Wilkinson, agreed. In other words, because Crawford supported termination, the secretary of the Interior's office paid his salary and expenses out of tribal funds to travel to Washington and advocate for termination.[62] Once again, the tribes' funds were used in support of federal goals and in opposition to tribal wishes.

Zimmerman's and Wilkinson's assessment were accurate. In the decade leading up to termination, Crawford was a favored witness among U.S. congressmen. Frederic Baker, who had a long career in public service, having worked for the Klamath in the 1920s and later working with California Indians, warned Senator William Langer of North Dakota, "Were I to be called upon to choose a witness to advise me what to do with the Indian Service he [Crawford] would be the last man I should call for this purpose."[63] His admonition was ignored.

Zimmerman put it succinctly: "The administration stands for consultation, after which it forces the Indians to accept what it says is good for them, whether they want it or not. The Klamath Indians were compelled to take a termination bill when all they wanted was a $500 per capita payment." (A payment of money from their own funds.)[64] A statement attributed to tribal leader Boyd Jackson but written by attorney Glen Wilkinson elaborates on this deal: "The Klamath Termination Act was enacted only because the Klamaths were trying to persuade Congress to distribute some tribal funds in the United States Treasury to members of the Tribe. Officials of the Bureau of Indian Affairs and members of the House Committee on Interior and Insular Affairs refused to approve such legislation unless the Klamaths agreed to 'termination' legislation."[65]

Assistant Secretary of the Interior Orme Lewis admitted that the Klamath bill was rushed to Congress without providing the tribes time to study it properly or to have the Bureau of the Budget provide an analysis. He declared that Congress had pushed HCR 108 for quick movement.[66] Oregon Representative Edith Green, in her efforts to slow the enactment of the termination until the law could be properly amended, blamed "this Administration's apparent policy of wholesale precipitate termination of government obligation to Indian Tribes" for rushing a poorly conceived bill into law. She argued "that the proposed plan was ill-advised and premature and might well result in disaster to the Tribe as well as serious injury to the local community of which it is part and to the State of Oregon."[67] But her voice was ignored.

Klamath tribal members and officials continued to protest passage of the bill up to the time it became law and even after that occurred.[68] But it was too late. In part, the tribes' political divisions aided the United States in its efforts to bring termination. As one observer said, "The Klamaths are divided into two strongly entrenched groups led by men who have been in personal conflict for more than 20 years."[69] Despite the fact that Crawford's support was relatively small as evidenced by his censure in general council, he had an outsized influence with Congress and the Indian bureau. The will of the majority of tribal members was thwarted by Congress in favor of Crawford's view, which paralleled their own.

Even just two weeks before the termination bill passed in the House, and shortly after it passed in the Senate, Jackson and Kirk reported to the General Council. They were frustrated in their hopes to have a per capita bill passed and to delay the termination bill. "Until recently we had not abandoned attempts to obtain passage of the Klamath per capita bill while deferring action on the withdrawal bill. We attempted this in order to obtain more time for careful consideration." The Senate committee considering the bill met in executive session "without additional consultation with the delegates," and so the delegates had no opportunity to advocate for themselves after the hearings were held.[70]

Anthropologist Patrick Haynal has clearly stated the outcome. "Congress was determined to terminate the Klamath and the joint sub-committee let it be known that Congress would not release funds to pay a $2.6 million dollar federal court judgment until the tribes endorsed the principle of their termination."[71]

Members of Congress and Orme Lewis of the Interior Department misled Senate president Richard Nixon and the joint subcommittees that held hearings on the bill concerning the economic preparedness of Klamath tribal members for termination and liquidation of their forest. They said that Klamath family income was about the same as the income of white families in the Klamath Valley. While this was technically true, they failed to point out that 75 percent of that income was received in per capita payments that were derived directly from the tribal resource—which the tribes would lose at termination. The Interior Department's analysis of the bill actually noted this fact, but public statements ignored

Fig. 5. Klamath Tribal Executive Council, 1955. © *The Oregonian*.

it. This reflects another abuse of tribal funds. In this case, these moneys were misrepresented as individually earned income, when even the Interior department's analysis described it as "unearned income" that came as payment of profits from forest operations. Oregon representative Sam Coon testified that "nearly all" of the Klamath families were "self-supporting."[72] Once the forest income would disappear, the average Klamath family would have just 25 percent of the annual income of its white neighbors.

Shortly after the bill became law tribal members asked Commissioner Emmons at a General Council meeting whether it could be repealed or amended. Rex Lee answered bluntly for the commissioner, denying the possibility, and saying, "Congress as well as other American people insist we do have some type of readjustment that would put some of the groups, the more advanced groups, on their own feet." In fact, much of the discussion by tribal members when the commissioner attended the meeting focused on either repealing or changing the law.[73] No change would occur.

Unlike the Menominee termination law, which incorporated the tribe's forest, the Klamath termination law liquidated the forest and provided "each adult member of the tribe," the "opportunity to . . . withdraw from the tribe and have his interest in tribal property converted into money and paid to him, or to remain in the tribe and participate in the tribal management plan to be prepared."[74]

Oregon senator Richard Neuberger suspected that the forest sale was slipped into the bill at the last minute through lobbying efforts of lumber interests.[75] The forest was appraised at more than $121 million in value.[76] Tribal members were left with the choice of relinquishing their tribal affiliation for cash or retaining their tribal membership and sharing the resources that remained after the rest of their compatriots had been bought out. In the end, 1,659 of the 2,133 members of the tribes—more than three fourths of tribal members—chose to leave the tribes and accept the money.[77] A significant number, apparently, believed that they could both accept the money and remain members of the tribes even after the law went into effect. An official preliminary planning report published in 1956 said, "Many believe they will be able to stay in the Tribe and at the same time obtain in cash their pro rata share of Tribal assets."[78]

In 1958 an article that appeared in the *American Indian*, a publication of the AAIA, lamented, "Their forest, which they were once allowed to retain because it had no value to the white man, has now become a coveted prize—to be preserved as a shrine to the white man's destruction of the natural resources, to be logged for the benefit and profit of the white man's civilization. But for the Klamath no place is provided in the white man's society." The article concluded, "The Klamath Indian has a historically well-founded fear that his children's estates will be subjected to legal looting."[79]

In 1958 Senator Neuberger shepherded a law through Congress to protect the forest from lumber interests by having Congress purchase it and add it to the National Forest system. Secretary of the Interior Fred Seaton wrote to Neuberger that he supported this sale of the Klamath timber, which was recognized as one of the finest ponderosa pine forests in the country. It would be a boon to the National Forest system. To achieve this the federal and Oregon state governments must do two things, he noted: protect Klamath property rights and provide for sustained yield management of the forest. "Public ownership would accomplish both of these objectives."[80]

Neuberger recognized that, though the forest was saved, the Klamath people were injured and wronged in the process. He said that the Klamath experience had taught a "valuable" and "expensive" lesson. "Secretary Seaton now insists that it would be 'absolutely unthinkable' for any Indian tribe to be 'forced' into a termination proceeding without its full understanding and consent. Mr. Seaton also has said that it would be 'incredible, even criminal, to send any Indian tribe out into the stream of American life until and unless the educational level of that tribe was one which was equal to the responsibilities it was shouldering.'"[81] But that is exactly what Klamath termination achieved. Neuberger's and Seaton's epiphanies occurred four years too late for the Klamath. With the loss of the forest and a one-time payout to a portion of tribal members—which brought them spending money but not wealth—Congress had essentially taken a financially independent group of people and impoverished them.

Neuberger observed, "Few of [Oregon's] influential citizens believe the Klamaths measure up to the standards prescribed by the Secretary for merging with 'the stream of American life.' Yet the egg cannot be put back into the shell." He concluded, "Nobody in our state talks very much these days about getting the United States government out of 'the Indian business.'"[82] He recognized the crisis that Congress had created. But he believed it was too late to fix it, despite the fact that Congress held plenary authority over Indian affairs.

The decades-old factional dispute between Crawford, on the one hand, and Jackson and Selkirk, on the other, continued after the termination bill became law.[83] But by then termination was a fait accompli. When termination went into effect in 1961, the 1,659 tribal members accepted a one-time payout of $43,000 and were bought out of their tribal rights, while a few more than 470 retained rights to their share of the forest in common in exchange for modest quarterly payments.[84]

Unlike the Menominee, when the Klamath gained restoration of their federal relationship in 1986, they had no land base on which to rebuild a tribal economy. Those who had left the tribes were permitted to return, however. The Klamath restoration act called for enrollment of all who were on the final tribal census roll in 1954 and any eligible descendants.[85]

The former Interior official infamous for his 1947 termination list, William Zimmerman Jr., now head of the Washington DC offices of the AAIA, tied the disastrous Menominee and Klamath experiences together. He saw their problems as part of the larger pattern of federal duplicity in managing Indian affairs. At the 1954 NCAI meeting in Omaha, in a speech to tribal leaders from across the United States, Zimmerman said, "The present [83rd] Congress have approved bills dictating what the [AAIA] board terms *The Extermination* of the Indians as such." He said that tribes were forced to accept these bills under pressure. He went on to say that "examples of duress, were, *When it was made clear to the Menominee Indians of Wisconsin and the Klamaths of Oregon that they would be permitted to withdraw thier [sic] own funds from the U. S. Treasury only if withdrawal was coupled with the Termination Bill.*"[86] In other words, they were bribed with their own money.

The Governors' Interstate Indian Council, an organization of states with Indian populations, had passed a resolution in its fall 1954 meeting urging Congress to defer passing termination bills "until the Claims of the specific tribes against the United States [were] adjudicated and settled."[87] The Menominee termination was tied directly to the settlement of their longstanding forest case against the U.S. government. Most Klamath claims, filed with the Indian Claims Commission, were not completely settled until the 1960s and 1970s, with more than $25 million awarded.[88]

Yet in both cases tribal funds paid to individuals in per capita payments were used to force termination on the tribes. With the Menominee it was judgment money. With the Klamath it included judgment money that the tribes wanted to pay out per capita—which had been a long-standing practice using funds derived from their forest. Oliver La Farge, director of AAIA, argued, "Reluctant consent of the Klamath and Menominee tribes of Indians to the termination or abandonment acts to which they have been subjected was strongly influenced by a flat refusal to allow them access to their own funds—large sums of money that are rightfully theirs—unless they would signify consent." He also observed, "As the termination process moved forward for these two tribes, both of them holders of extremely valuable timber lands, it looks as if one of its chief results would be the dissipation of their most important assets."

It was not only tribes with forest resources that Congress and the Indian bureau tried to bribe with their own money. Both the Three Affiliated Tribes at Fort Berthold in North Dakota and the Seneca Nation of Indians in New York received multimillion-dollar payments for taken lands when Congress decided to flood their reservations with the building of dams. Federal officials tried to withhold those funds until those tribal nations accepted termination. Though the cases occurred almost a decade removed from each other, both tribal nations found themselves in fierce battles for the welfare of their communities as they fought off termination efforts. The Three Affiliated Tribes came under siege at the beginning of the termination era, in the same years as the Menominee and the Klamath, and fought with the same congressmen and some of the same Indian bureau officials.

PART 3

Dams and Termination

CHAPTER 6

The Three Affiliated Tribes of Fort Berthold

> Whenever the Indian Office want to do something they generally do it regardless of what the Indians say.
>
> —Floyd Montclair (Three Affiliated Tribes), U.S. Congress, "Fort Berthold Hearings," 1946

When development occurs, whether agricultural, industrial, or through resource extraction, the work can cause devastating environmental changes to the land. These impacts usually fall most heavily on communities with little power and influence. In the United States these communities include communities of color, both urban and rural, and rural communities more broadly. The idea is that some people must relinquish a healthy landscape and home for the greater good. Those with power consciously decide who has to give up what in an effort to maximize the greater good. Those who are affected live in what have come to be called "sacrifice zones."

Sacrifice zones are a well-documented phenomenon. Analysis of them has become commonplace in environmental literature relating to both the developed and the developing world.[1] Craig Colten refers to the assignation of places as sacrifice zones as "the drive for industrialization and economic gain" taking "precedence over environmental stewardship."[2] It also takes precedence over the rights of human communities.

On Indigenous lands the environmental destruction has disrupted economic, social, and religious lifeways for decades.

Treating Indigenous lands as sacrifice zones is a long-standing feature of internal U.S. colonialism. This means that resources and goods flow out of Indian country but other goods and services do not flow back in. Sometimes the lost resources are tangible goods such as timber. Other times Indigenous lands are sacrificed for something less readily visible. Dams that flooded Indigenous lands to provide electric power or irrigation for their white neighbors are an example. And often environmental destruction is merely considered the price of progress, if it is taken into account at all.

In the book *Wastelanding*, Traci Brynn Voyles refers to such practices as "energy injustice" grounded in environmental racism. The American "treadmill of production," she argues, "requires 'wastelands' from which resources are increasingly extracted." And so Indigenous uses of and relationships to land and resources are discounted so that the lands can be defined as valueless except for their contributions to American growth and security and development.[3]

Vanesa Broto and Martín Calvet have observed that "Energy industries are an integral part of national imaginaries of modernization."[4] In the 1940s and 1950s, as the United States was both developing nuclear resources and weaponry and trying to become energy independent, federal bureaucrats viewed the Great Plains of the American west as a sacrifice zone for national security purposes. Indian reservations, which were economically and politically weak in relation to their white neighbors and state and federal officials, were disproportionately disadvantaged when it came to protection of their lands and resources.[5]

Great Plains industrial and agricultural development included oil and gas and other mineral sources and a massive series of projects damming up rivers for flood control, irrigation, navigation, and the production of electricity. The Department of the Interior actively supported stripping tribal resources from Indigenous peoples in the 1950s and 1960s, as it long had. As historian Laurence Hauptman put it in a discussion of dams, "Ironically, a department—Interior—that was supposedly committed to carrying out the government's trust responsibility to federally recognized

American Indian nations was instead increasingly working with the Army Corps of Engineers and private and public power interests and sacrificing tribal lands in a concerted effort to develop hydropower."[6] The Missouri River dams added electricity to the power grid and benefitted white agriculturalists with irrigation needs while disproportionately flooding Indian reservation lands.

When dams flooded Indigenous lands, Congress compensated tribal nations for the losses or the "takings." In the 1950s and even in the 1960s Members of Congress and federal bureaucrats attempted to tie dispersal of these compensatory funds to termination. When this happened to the Three Affiliated Tribes of Fort Berthold in North Dakota in the postwar years, the tribes suffered a gut-wrenching loss that caused their most calamitous experience of the twentieth century. Federal officials attempted to leverage the disaster they had wrought with elimination of the tribes as a legal entity by using funds for the taken lands in an effort to bribe the Three Affiliated Tribes to accept termination of their political relationship with the United States.

FLOODING THE RESERVATION

The Three Affiliated Tribes—the Mandan, the Hidatsa, and the Arikara—brought corn to the bottomlands of the Missouri River in what is now central North Dakota hundreds of years ago. The river served as a source of food, water, and rich soil for crops. Even today the tribes continue to grow the "four sisters": corn, squash, beans and sunflowers.[7] Prior to Lewis and Clark's trip through their homeland in 1804 their villages had become the major trading territory in the northern plains. Trade goods from the Northwest coast to the Atlantic and Gulf coasts and places in between passed through Mandan and Arikara villages, sometimes through middlemen. The villages themselves were treated as safe zones where people from a broad variety of backgrounds visited unmolested.[8]

The 1851 Fort Laramie treaty established an enclosed homeland for the Mandan, Hidatsa, and Arikara but the exterior limits of the reservation diminished considerably until 1910, when its current borders were finally determined by federal law. As the three tribes became geographically confined, they lost access to hunting and gathering and fishing grounds.

These had provided important supplements to their agricultural economy, especially in years of hardship such as drought.

Beginning in 1886, even before passage of the Dawes Act, reservation lands were allotted. They were surveyed and divided into parcels that were turned over to individuals with the idea that they would take up American-style farming. The plots of land were too dry to farm and too small to run enough cattle to be profitable. Before long the best use for the lands of many of those who held allotments was simply to lease them for meager payments.[9] Nonetheless, agriculture and ranching remained an important base of the reservation economy into the 1940s, when the United States made the decision to sacrifice much of the Fort Berthold reservation to flooding.

When plans for damming the Missouri River at Garrison, North Dakota, began to circulate the Three Affiliated Tribes immediately protested the proposal to flood their lands. As the Army Corps of Engineers and the Bureau of Reclamation argued over how to control the Missouri River, one of the plans in the early 1940s proposed the building of Garrison Dam. The Three Affiliated Tribes expressed their opposition to this plan even before the passage of the 1944 Flood Control Act initiated the process of seriously remaking the Missouri River. A 1943 tribal council resolution repudiated the proposed dam, stating that it would "destroy by permanent flood all the bottom land of the said reservation, causing untold material and economic damage to the Three Affiliated Tribes." The dam was, ironically, intended in part to prevent flooding downstream.[10]

As the plan developed, a tribal delegation telegraphed Commissioner of Indian Affairs William Brophy, "We Indians on the Fort Berthold Reservation oppose the construction of the Garrison Dam one hundred percent." Brophy then wrote the chair of the Senate Indian Affairs Committee, Joseph O'Mahoney, "saying, in effect, that it was too late to do anything but try to see that the Indians were amply compensated for their losses and granted lieu land if the residual reservation should prove inadequate." The tribes, through their attorney, hired an engineer. He showed that the river could be managed about as effectively by damming it in other places that would not flood the reservation. But this would harm the tribes' white neighbors and did not impact congressional intention to build the dam.[11]

The eminent legal scholar Felix Cohen got involved. He wrote that although Congress had the right to abrogate treaties, the flooding of reservation lands was contradictory to "the history of our Federal negotiations with these Indians" which included "not merely guaranties against private trespass, but were preeminently guaranties against any future taking of Indian land for governmental purposes."[12] Cohen also observed that although Congress had authorized eminent domain takings on allotted lands, it had never done so on tribal lands outside of New Mexico.[13]

Tribal representatives appeared before a Senate subcommittee in 1945 and stated that they had long lived in their homelands and they planned for their children and grandchildren "to occupy this land continuously forever." They argued that the flooding would violate the 1851 treaty, destroy their lands, flood their cemeteries, and push them from their historic homes. Senator William Langer told tribal chairman Martin Cross, at the hearings, "You and your mothers and fathers have been in that territory, hundreds and hundreds and hundreds of years." He also said of the Army corps, "They are going to take by far the best of the land. What is left will be tops of hills, it will not begin to compare with the fine rich loam soil of the valley."[14] The taking would, in addition to flooding the tribes' cultural heritage and patrimony, be economically destructive. This would be a textbook example of internal colonialism creating a sacrifice zone.

Chairman Cross argued at the hearing "that the treaty law between the United States Government and the Indians is binding and not subject to eminent domain." The proposed flooding, he added, would take "the best lands we have along the river, the best irrigable land," and destroy 436 or 437 of the reservation's 531 homes. When asked by Chairman O'Mahoney if the tribe would be willing to accept other lands for those lost to flooding, Cross simply replied, "No, sir." He described the lands chosen for relocation by the War Department as "good country for rattlesnakes and horned toads." When asked about the bottomland's value, Cross guessed it to be worth $150 per acre. But he told the committee, "I am not here to sell land. I am here to keep the land." He also said, "The Indians will not gain any benefit from this dam."[15]

Fig. 6. Martin Cross, chairman of Three Affiliated Tribes, Elbowoods ND, 1952. State Historical Society of North Dakota (B0673-0001).

Instead, the tribal council passed a resolution asking that the dam be built where the Missouri flowed into the reservation. "We have offered to the United States, as a gift, all the tribal and allotted lands needed to build a dam on the Missouri river in the northern end of our Reservation," chairman Cross said. "All we ask in return is that the proposed dam below our Reservation not be built."[16] If the dam were built where the tribes proposed, the flooding would occur upstream from the reservation.

A 1946 Department of the Interior press release said, "Acting Commissioner Zimmerman stated that the Indians' bottom lands, which lie within the reservoir site provide an almost ideal physical setting for the conduct of the livestock enterprise and for the location of their homes, with a large area of timbered lands and balance between upland range and valley haylands and shelter. The offered lands along the west bank on the Missouri River several miles below the Garrison Dam would not be comparable in quality, he said."[17] Shortly after he left his post as secretary of the Interior, Harold Ickes said that the three tribes should have been given priority rights to irrigation in the deal. He added, "It is just another of these heartless things that the whites have perpetrated in this country."[18]

Ickes's successor, William Brophy, however, did not support the tribes. In part he was stymied by Congress.[19] In July 1947 the tribes' attorney Ralph Case reported to the council that Congress had appropriated the funds for the dam and that contracts were being let. "Our fight to stop construction of Garrison Dam has been lost."[20] After Brophy wrote to Senator O'Mahoney that it was too late to reverse the decision, future negotiations would focus on monetary and land compensations for the land that would be destroyed, not on protecting the reservation resources.[21] As these negotiations dragged on, and the Three Affiliated Tribes faced utter devastation of their way of life, Congress and the BIA began to try to legislate the tribes out of existence altogether.

Over the next several years the tribes unsuccessfully fought with Congress to improve nonmonetary compensation for the lands that would be lost in the flooding. A national letter-writing campaign orchestrated by the new tribal chairman Carl Whitman Jr. and Ruth Bronson of NCAI brought voluminous correspondence supporting the tribes to the Senate.

Even so, the tribes failed to secure hunting, fishing, or irrigation rights in the deal. After all, Congress was increasingly viewing termination as the future for Indian nations.[22]

Just before the law was approved, Whitman stated the tribe's wrenching position in stark terms. "This will be a dismal Christmas for us . . . Indians. We will soon be evicted from our homes and will never see them again. They will be covered by the waters of the Garrison Reservoir. We are losing our valley lands, the remnant of a vast domain, and must eke out a living on the barren uplands."[23] Unfortunately, the Indian bureau proved itself the weakest of federal agencies time and again when dealing with damming of tribal lands during this era.[24]

The Senate Appropriations Committee offered just more than $5.1 million for the taken lands. Whitman said, "We did not willingly agree to it." But the tribes were forced to accept it.[25] Whitman told Secretary of the Interior Oscar Chapman: "We take this step sadly [since it] brings us closer to our exile." But the tribes voted to accept the law. "If we should reject the Act," they reasoned, "the next offer of the government would probably not be even as good as the one we were considering." Tribal members hoped that by accepting Congress's offer a more favorable amendment would be added in the future.[26]

O'Mahoney first got an amendment passed into law permitting the tribes to sue in the Court of Claims for additional losses, but eventually an additional $7.5 million in compensation was added to the award instead.[27] This still amounted to a significant undervaluation of the lands and the losses that emanated from the flooding. At the time of taking, the Three Affiliated Tribes believed they would incur nearly $22 million in losses of the value of lands and resources. This amounted to almost 90 percent of the reservation's monetary value.[28] Congress agreed in 1949 to provide $12.5 million for the land-taking and relocation costs.[29] More than forty years later Martin Cross's son Raymond Cross would successfully work through Congress for a $149.2 million compensation bill for the taken lands, providing a stark record of how much the tribes had been cheated in 1949.[30]

Eighty percent of all reservation roads were flooded, as were all the schools on the reservation. More than a quarter of the reservation was

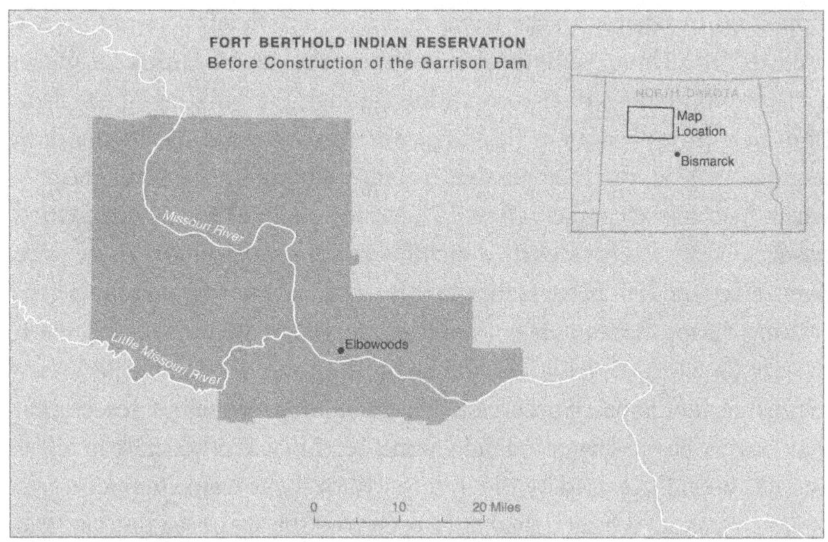

Map 5. Fort Berthold Reservation, North Dakota, before the flood. Courtesy Aileen Clarke.

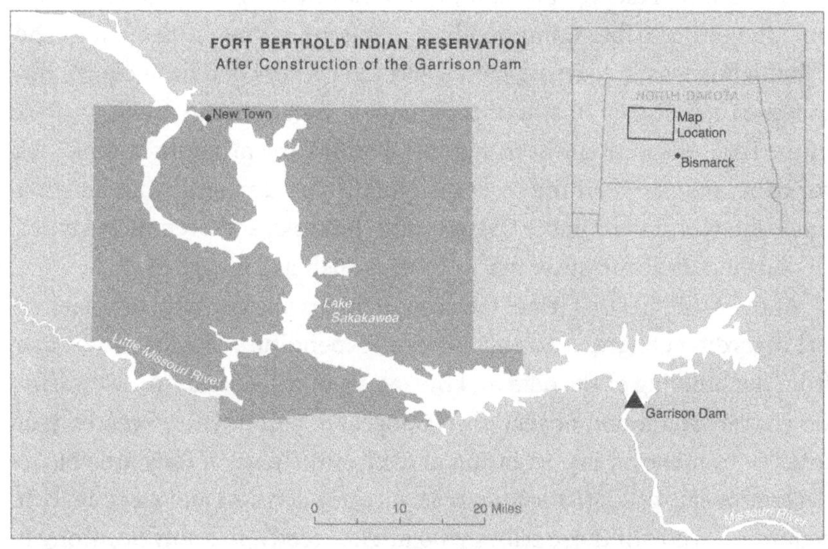

Map 6. Fort Berthold Reservation, North Dakota, after the flood. Courtesy Aileen Clarke.

lopped off in what both the tribes and federal officials referred to as a "taking." The Three Affiliated Tribes suffered a loss of 94 percent of the agricultural land on their reservation through the building of Garrison Dam and the subsequent flooding. The authorizing law for the dam required that "land . . . comparable in quality and sufficient in area" be provided the tribes as compensation.[31] The tribes, and the Indian bureau, tried unsuccessfully to provide tribal members with similar lands. There were none, since the rich bottomlands that they had worked for countless generations disappeared to the bottom of the newly created Lake Sakakawea.

In 1950, when the tribal council finally approved the taking, Secretary of the Interior Chapman observed, "The remaining area within reservation boundaries, consisting of upland grazing territory, is practically roadless and has been little used by the Indians. With the extreme temperatures of North Dakota winters, they have preferred the sheltered bottom land adjacent to the Missouri River."[32] They had learned, with centuries of living on the land, what locales were habitable and productive.

A meeting with Aberdeen Area Office personnel in April 1951 hinted at even bigger problems to come. By then it was abundantly clear that the remaining reservation land did not have enough resources to support the entire tribe. Compounding this issue, some 60 percent of the tribal lands was in heirship status and the owners had little choice but to lease them for small amounts of money to non-Indian ranchers. Part of the federal solution was to support a relocation program finding jobs for tribal members off the reservation.[33] This began with an office that made job placements in the Dakotas and Nebraska and eventually spread to placements in far-away urban centers such as Chicago.[34]

At the April meeting tribal members held discussions with BIA personnel regarding congressional support for expenditure of tribal funds due from the building of the dam and the taking of tribal lands. Area director G. Warren Spaulding observed, "[Congress] requires the Secretary of Interior to make an investigation of each tribe to see if they are able to determine cut-off date for Indian Service supervision and assistance. It requires a study of those tribes who are not ready, to know how long it will be." He added, "I think that anything we can do here to come up with agreements as to ideas would be helpful to all of us and to Congress."[35]

Spaulding asked several times during this meeting whether the tribal council "want to get out from under the wing of the government." He wondered if they "still want[ed] government service," or if that was "a good time to cut the strings." Council members pointed out that some 85 percent of tribal members wanted the Indian Service or Congress to fulfill its obligations to the tribes. One council member said, "The Indians should take the severance step themselves, individually." Ben Young Bird strongly opposed this idea, telling the group, "I think we need more supervision rather than being taken out of supervision at the present time." He argued that this would not be an issue if the army had not flooded their lands.[36]

THE TERMINATION PLAN

In 1952 several tribal members called for withdrawal of federal supervision over the Three Affiliated Tribes. The tribes rejected the plan which would have authorized this by a vote of 476 to 92.[37] Of those voting, 84 percent opposed termination. In June the agency superintendent told tribal members, "Whenever the Tribes want to put an end to some part of the trusteeship . . . the Indian Bureau will be glad to put staff members on the job working out the needed legislation to do this." The tribe's attorney, James Curry, instead proposed that the Indian bureau could simply permit a change to the tribes' constitution that would provide them "entire control" of their "tribal funds."[38] The tribes preferred home rule—local control—under federal protection.

This vignette provides insight into the disagreement between federal officials and tribal officials who agreed with their attorney. Both sides believed the tribes should have greater control of their resources. But the bureau believed the best way to bring that about was through congressional legislation relinquishing federal authority, while the tribes believed that it should occur under federal trust protection.

In the 1952 tribal elections the candidates who eventually won clarified the tribes' wishes in relation to federal involvement in their affairs. They said, "We are opposed to the withdrawal by the government of any *help* that they give us. We only oppose their *interference* with our management of our own property and money." They also referenced

Curry's message to Martin Cross, which said that no "legal basis" existed "for the claim that granting of home rule would result in withdrawal of the federal aid."[39] In other words, the tribes wanted the United States to continue to fulfill its trust responsibilities but to provide the tribes with the opportunity for more robust self-rule.

Nonetheless, by the fall of 1952, the Aberdeen Area Office was hard at work planning for full or partial withdrawal of federal services to Indians throughout the region, which would impact the Three Affiliated Tribes. Spaulding, now the Director of Programs in the Central Offices in DC, made it clear that the Bureau's orders from Congress were to prepare to withdraw federal services from tribes. New commissioner of Indian Affairs, Dillon Myer, had stated that that was his job. Spaulding told bureau employees from the agencies under the Aberdeen jurisdiction that when tribes opposed termination they would stand in opposition to the bureau. He declared, "We can go to Congress and tell our story to Congress. We would go to Congress with a bill. We would present that bill to Congress and the Indians would have every opportunity to present their side. Congress will pass or not pass the bill."[40] In this atmosphere it is no surprise that the Three Affiliated Tribes felt increasing federal pressure to agree to termination.

In October 1952 the tribes requested, and six months later received, a $200 per capita payment from the land-taking fund. Then in March 1954 the tribes made another request for a $200 per capita payout to individual tribal members. The BIA disapproved this request, intending to use the money to coerce the tribes into accepting termination.[41] When the tribes insisted on the per capita payment, the commissioner's office presented them with a termination plan. "The Commissioner had a suggestion for making a per capita payment from the dam money," agency superintendent Ralph Shane told tribal members. "He calls it a comprehensive plan for Fort Berthold." This comprehensive plan called for immediate incorporation, giving the tribes five years to create their own termination plan, which might not be implemented for another five to fifteen years after that.[42]

Homer Jenkins, a BIA program officer based in Washington DC, visited the reservation on July 16 and 17, 1954, to explain the plan to tribal members. He began the meeting by saying, "Personally I am no traveling salesman and I am not here to try to sell you this plan but presenting it to you for your consideration." But he added, "It is something that will be of benefit to you in the long run."[43] Jenkins did not believe it was proper for the federal government to seek consent from Indian tribes to terminate their trust relationship with the United States.[44]

He noted that the Klamath had recently presented a termination plan to the bureau and recommended that "every tribe in the United States study this situation carefully." He implied that this was a national program that would be fully implemented. Tribal chairman Martin Cross responded the next day: "I will not consider or recommend my people to consider this draft and I am sorry to see it."[45]

Cross's response reflected tribal anger and the bewilderment expressed by tribal members at the two-day meeting. Ben Young Bird asked the tribe's attorney Quentin Schulte his opinion of the bill. "I don't think it is fair that the termination bill is tied onto the per capita," Schulte said. "The Indian Bureau is setting up the per capita as a plum to get you to take the termination bill." Philip Adkins said, through an interpreter, "I thought these discussions were to be about per capita, but it seems the main discussion is about termination." Martin Fox, also through an interpreter, added, "The people will disagree with this bill. Our land should remain tax exempt forever." Otherwise, he said, they will lose the land. Tom Spotted Wolf, also speaking through an interpreter, said, "Yesterday I said I didn't want this bill and I advised Mr. Jenkins to pack up his things and go back to Washington and not bring any more bills. Who asked for this bill to be prepared? We asked for a per capita and not a [termination] bill."[46] Jenkins disliked the opposition to his proposal and was apparently upset with his treatment at the council meeting.[47]

At this point, on July 17, Martin Cross took over the meeting. The tribal council immediately passed two resolutions—one calling for the new commissioner of Indian Affairs, Glenn Emmons, to release the $200 per capita without strings, the other rejecting the so-called comprehensive plan.[48] The council called the bill "detrimental," "unfair and ungracious," and contrary "to settlement of the Garrison Dam Controversy."[49]

Helen Peterson, executive director of the National Congress of American Indians, advocated for the tribes from her base in Washington DC. NCAI was a ten-year-old membership-based coalition of tribes whose staff in the nation's capital regularly worked on behalf of member tribal nations and Indian country issues before Congress and with the BIA.[50] Three Affiliated Tribes Business Council member Peter Star was also a member of the NCAI executive council. Soon after Peterson became executive director, Star and Martin Cross had hosted her on a visit to North Dakota, not only bringing her to meetings with the Fort Berthold tribal council but to visit the Turtle Mountain Chippewa tribe and Fort Totten as well. They seem to have built a strong relationship, as Star and Cross helped recruit tribes to join NCAI.[51]

Peterson and Ruth Bronson met with Jenkins in his Washington DC offices in early August 1954. Peterson reported to Mandan, Hidatsa, and Arikara council members that Jenkins was upset that the tribal council rejected the termination plan without any consideration. "However, Ruth and I kept insisting that the money on deposit was your money," she wrote.[52]

Peterson and Bronson added, "We further pointed out, in the strongest language that we know how to use, that it was insulting to tell people that this was not a termination bill when, in our opinion, it is in fact a termination bill. The very word 'termination' or 'withdrawal' frightens an Indian tribe, as it certainly frightens me." Jenkins responded that when the tribes received their money from the dam they would have no more assets anyway. When Bronson and Peterson told him that the tribes should be able to get hold of their own money without agreeing to termination, he told them that Aberdeen area director William Roberts would take the next step.[53]

Bureau officials in the Aberdeen Area Office revised the plan, purportedly based on tribal input. The new draft would split the tribes by blood quantum, granting fee patent ownership of lands to all tribal members of "half-blood" or less in three years' time. Those tribal members of more than "half-blood"—and their heirs, so long as they remained at "half-blood" quantum or higher—would have the option of retaining their land in trust status or claiming it in fee patent.[54] This proposal fell in line with Arizona senator Barry Goldwater's failed bill to do the same, an on-again, off-again racialized federal policy dating back more than a hundred years to diminish the size of tribal nations by removing "mixed-blood" citizens and redefining how tribes identified their citizenry or membership.[55]

This bill, too, lacked tribal support. As Robert Rietz, former Fort Berthold relocation officer, wrote in November 1954, most tribal members desired "an opportunity to administer their own affairs." However, they would only accept a bill making the per capita payment contingent on termination "under such conditions of sorrow and anger as no one would want to countenance."[56] Rietz's observation was borne out in a nearly three-hour-long General Council meeting held in New Town on the afternoon of January 14, 1955. Most tribal members who spoke opposed the bill, either outright or in the draft form in which it was presented.

Some viewed the bill as a form of trickery on the part of the federal government. Bill Deane spoke up, saying, "Homer Jenkins was a salesman trying to get the Indians to sell out for per capita." Both Guy Fox and Percy Rush agreed. Fox said, "The Secretary of the Interior has the authority to disburse the per capita money. This bill is being used as bait for a trap." Rush added, "When you go fishing, the bigger bait, the bigger the fish. . . . The Indian Bureau is using big bait to catch us like fish, but I think we should leave the pole in the water longer and not grab at this bait." Both Guy Fox and Jim Hall said they believed the bill was being "forced" on the tribes.[57]

Several people believed the bill was simply an effort to snatch valuable resources from the Indians. Arthur Mandan observed that oil companies had their eye on the tribe's oil reserves and were interested in leases. Nathan Little Soldier and Ben Young Bird also stated they were concerned about the tribe's oil resources. Young Bird also expressed his fear for the loss of ranch lands. "I object mainly to the possibility of white speculators having an opportunity under the wording of this present bill to obtain key tracts of land with waterholes for range areas."[58]

In addition to concerns about resources, the land itself was an important issue to several of those who spoke up. Kenneth Fredericks, a member of the tribal Stockmen's Association, declared that the bill did not sufficiently take into account complicated heirship cases, and he expressed concern over the future tribal status of such lands.[59]

Some attending the meeting believed that termination of some sort was a fait accompli and hoped to blunt the impact to the extent possible. Maggie Grinnell supported this idea, saying she would like to be offered termination on a personal basis so that she could get her land in fee patent status. She argued that those who had accepted fee patents in 1921 still lived among the tribes. Jim Hall countered that most who had accepted those fee patents had lost their lands to taxes or mortgages but had not lost their rights as Indians. "By this bill we would lose our Indian rights," he said. Reflecting the concerns of Arthur Mandan, Young Bird, and Little Soldier, Hall added, "The white man is after our land now because of the discovery of oil and uranium, etc. They realized the value of our lands and are trying to work out some legal method by which they can get them away from us."[60]

Numerous people stated that both those of under "half-blood" and those of over "half-blood" should be involved in decision-making. Nathan Little Soldier told the council, "We should all get together, forget our personal differences, and work as a team to preserve the reservation lands for the Indians." Sam Mathews, Rufus Stevenson, and Percy Rush all agreed with him. In addition, Mathews and Arthur Mandan said that it was important for young people to express their opinions since their future was at stake.[61]

In early March 1955 the tribal council met again to discuss plans for termination, including how to deal with health care coverage and land issues.[62] They were not in favor of going ahead with termination at the time but had begun planning how to deal with these issues if it occurred. A couple of weeks later the tribal council traveled to Washington DC for a series of meetings with Bureau officials and congressional representatives. On March 21 they met with Emmons, several other Bureau members including Homer Jenkins, and their own attorney Quentin Schulte, to discuss their per capita payment. Cross clarified at the beginning of the meeting that the tribe intended to receive the per capita payment without considering termination as part of the deal. Emmons and others agreed. When Guy Fox insisted that they discuss the per capita first and then termination, "Cross halted Fox in order to remind him that there was no termination in connection."[63]

Jenkins groused, "We have produced one good program. . . . They turn[ed it] down and I don't know the reason."[64] Jenkins expected tribes to happily create their own termination laws.[65] Cross himself was startled at the turn of events. "I'm surprised to know, Mr. Emmons, when you said termination will not be discussed now," he said.[66] Two days later at a meeting with North Dakota senator Milton Young and North Dakota congressman Otto Krueger, Young inquired whether termination was planned as part of the per capita payment. Cross said, "It was stated clearly by the Indian Bureau personnel present that there was no termination legislation considered in connection with this payment and the subsequent payments."[67]

This was a stunning turning point for the Three Affiliated Tribes. All at once the cloud of termination was lifted. At the same time, their per capita payment was approved. It was little wonder that Cross was surprised. NCAI immediately issued a press release that opened triumphantly: "One group of Indians talked back to the Bureau of Indian Affairs here this week—and won the argument, the first in a long time to make such a stand, let alone to win." The press release pointed out that "requests for Secretarial approval of per capita distribution from the tribes' own funds had been refused unless the Indians would accept the termination agreement" originally proposed by "top officials in the Bureau."[68] But the tribes successfully quashed that effort.

This decision came in the wake of five termination bills that had already been forced on dozens of tribes from Oregon, Texas, Wisconsin, and Utah. This did not put an end to termination. Seven more termination bills, also affecting dozens of tribal communities, would be passed throughout the rest of the 1950s, and one would come as late as 1962.[69] However, it was a signal that the pushback to detrimental federal policies, from local tribes and on the national level, could be successful. Significantly the tribes had the support and backing of North Dakota's governor and two senators, and from their two representatives in Congress as well.[70]

At one point Martin Cross wrote to Helen Peterson about his response to Jenkins regarding his straightforward opposition to the termination rider that was proposed for the per capita payment bill. "I have been criti[ci]zed for the way we treated the visiting dignitaries as to abruptly turn it down."[71] Jenkins did not like the way he was treated. And tribal political diplomacy often included politely listening to American proposals, even when tribal leaders disagreed. But this direct confrontation was an American style of politics, and in this difficult time in tribal history it helped limit the damage.

The people of Fort Berthold already suffered much sorrow, not to mention economic and cultural decimation that stemmed from the flooding of their historic homelands and their forced relocation to higher ground. They successfully opposed termination by steadfastly refusing to connect it to the acceptance of their settlement money. Martin Cross recognized the BIA effort for what it was and charged that the bureau was "using" the per capita money "as a way of bribing us to accept termination." The bureau gave up on the idea of termination, and Congress eventually provided the per capita payment that tribal leaders requested.[72]

The Three Affiliated Tribes had lost their battle to thwart the damming of their lands. But tribal leaders gained significant experience negotiating with federal officials. They had spent more than a decade in intense battles with the BIA and Congress by the time the BIA tried to leverage the money the tribes received for the taken lands to force termination upon them. Tribal leaders stood their ground, sought allies in the national Indian community and with statewide officials, and beat back the termination threat.

But this was just one of a number of efforts by federal administrative and congressional officials to use access to tribal funds as a weapon to force termination. And damming of rivers was not confined to the western United States. In fact, nearly a decade later—after even Congress recognized the failure of termination and the damage that the policy had caused—a similar attempt was made against the Seneca Nation of Indians in New York. This would draw significant national attention.

CHAPTER 7

The Seneca Nation of Indians and Kinzua Dam

> Sometimes it has seemed to the Indians as though the site of a dam had been selected deliberately to flood their lands in preference to those of white owners with perhaps more political weight.
>
> —Roy W. Meyer, "Fort Berthold"

> In the final analysis, the whole structure of our existing society will be undermined.
>
> —DeForrest Billy, Seneca Nation of Indians Negotiating Committee to Wayne Aspinall, March 13, 1963

More than a decade after the Three Affiliated Tribes succeeded in halting federal termination plans, the Seneca Nation of Indians in New York found themselves in a remarkably similar situation. The Army Corps of Engineers proposed to flood a significant portion of their Allegany reservation. The Senecas adamantly opposed it. Eventually, they hired an engineer who showed that other sites for the dam would actually be more effective at flood control. The Kinzua Dam was built anyway, and its waters inundated a significant portion of the reservation. The Seneca Nation and the United States fought over the issue of compensation. Eventually, Congress attempted to tie that compensation for the taking of land to termination. The Senecas were forced to fight against this ugly turn of events even as the flooding caused great economic and cultural suffering among them. And eventually they defeated the termination plan. Like the Three Affiliated Tribes, the Senecas were able to gain support from both the public and congressional allies. While suffering their greatest loss of the twentieth century, they avoided an even more horrific fate.

The Seneca Nation of Indians consists of people of two territories in New York state, the Allegany Reservation and the Cattaraugus Reservation. They established their modern political system in 1848, creating a written constitution long before most tribal nations. Laurence Hauptman has observed that the Seneca Nation "political system has always been shaped by fears that outsiders want Seneca lands and resources."[1] Hauptman also notes that, "to [Seneca Nation] tribal members, the Kinzua Dam crisis is considered the third worst event in [the] nation's history, the first two being the American Revolution and its immediate aftermath and the Buffalo Creek Treaty of removal of 1838."[2] In all three of these catastrophic events outsiders threatened Seneca sovereignty and reduced Seneca land and resources.

The Senecas signed numerous treaties with the United States, but they view the 1794 Treaty with the Six Nations, more commonly called the Pickering Treaty, as having established an unbreakable alliance with the United States. In the treaty they were guaranteed permanent control over their remaining land and resources. The treaty, according to its preamble, was made for the purpose of "establishing a firm and permanent friendship with them." This agreement was sanctioned by President George Washington, and the Seneca have honored their side of the friendship since its signing.[3]

The treaty went on to guarantee the Seneca permanent control over their land and resources. After describing the limits of Seneca lands, the Pickering Treaty reads, "Now, the United States acknowledge all the land within the aforementioned boundaries, to be the property of the Seneka nation; and the United States will never claim the same, nor disturb the Seneka nation . . . in the free use and enjoyment thereof; But it shall remain theirs, until they choose to sell the same to the people of the United States, who have the right to purchase."[4]

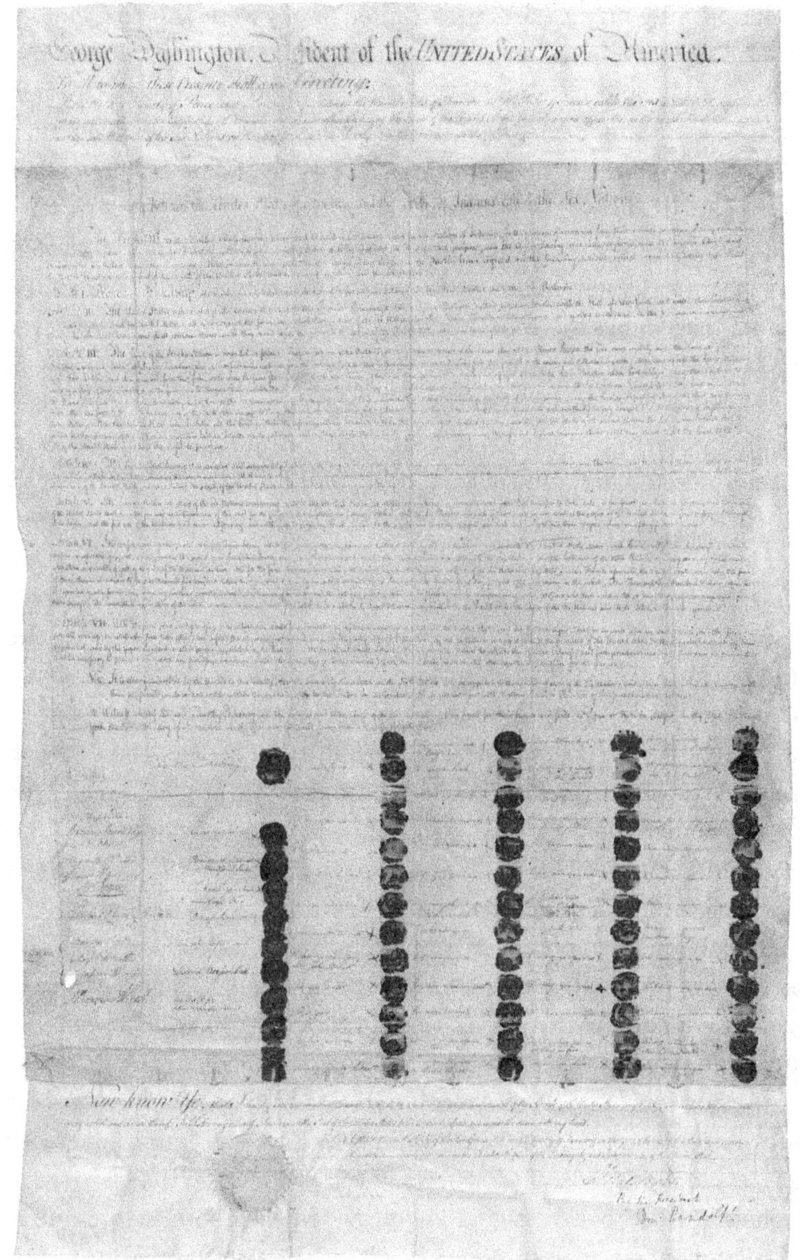

Fig. 7. Treaty with the Six Nations or Pickering Treaty, 1794. National Archives and Records Administration digital copy.

This promise on the part of the United States would not last long. In 1797 the Senecas signed an agreement known as the Treaty of Big Tree limiting their land base and establishing boundaries under U.S. law. Just five years later came the first of a series of treaties shrinking their land base even more.[5] The United States broke its promise of protection, ignoring its trust responsibilities time and again.

The Senecas were swindled out of their land in New York in an 1838 treaty but fortunately reacquired some of their lost territory in 1842. (During these times the Tonawanda Senecas separated from the Seneca Nation and created a separate polity.) Unlike the Senecas at Cattaraugus, those at Allegany became heavily surrounded by non-Indians in their own land, due to the growth of Salamanca, a railroad city located on the reservation. This influx of a white population increased significantly in the late nineteenth century and into the twentieth century. Congress gave ninety-nine-year leases on Seneca land in the town of Salamanca to non-Indians in 1890 in a case that made national headlines when the leases expired, for example.[6] Over the years non-Indians were able to build houses on land that they leased for as little as one dollar a year and often refused to pay even these meager amounts. This was a gross abdication of the federal trust responsibility to protect the Senecas' land and resources. This action denied Senecas the access to their land and also denied them the income from the land's use by outsiders. This prompted John Mohawk to observe that the Senecas could earn more from their land if it were cornfields than if it remained a town site.[7]

Like other contemporary tribal nations, the Seneca Nation was also targeted for termination beginning in the late 1940s. They were listed together with all the Iroquois Nations in New York in William Zimmerman's infamous 1947 list of tribes ready for immediate termination.[8] At the same time, largely as a result of the Seneca Nation gaining some control over land leases in Salamanca, New York legislators convinced Congress to move federal jurisdiction over New York's tribal nations to the state. A 1948 congressional law provided New York with criminal jurisdiction, and a 1950 law added civil jurisdiction to the state's legal control over tribal nations.[9] Then U.S. House Concurrent Resolution 108, the 1953 termination enabling bill, listed New York Indians as among the tribal groups that "should be freed from Federal supervision and control" "at the earliest possible time."[10] It was under this cloud that the Allegany Reservation was threatened by the building of the dam that would submerge much of their land under Allegheny River water.

THE DAM

In September 1966 the United States began operation of the Kinzua Dam in Pennsylvania.[11] It flooded one third of the Seneca Nation of Indians' Allegany Reservation upriver in New York, displacing hundreds of Seneca individuals. They lost their farms, their homes, and their historical and cultural connection to the taken land. They were forced to move thousands of graves. Their schools were inundated. Sacred and ceremonial sites disappeared under the waters of the reservoir.[12] The result was heartbreaking, mirroring the devastation felt by the Three Affiliated Tribes in North Dakota.

The Army Corps of Engineers said the purpose of the dam was flood control. But according to historian Paul Rosier, the key proponents of the dam championed it as a method to create industrial economic development. It was critical, they argued, for Pittsburgh's future.[13] Pennsylvania politicians viewed it as providing a path to energy independence. One observer has argued that although "the conflict centered upon matters of national policy and the interpretation of treaties . . . in a real sense it was fought upon the drawing boards of civil engineers."[14] The dam was also a product of backroom deals between federal officials in the executive and legislative branches and powerful corporate interests.

The dam was first proposed in the 1930s as part of a larger flood control and power production plan. By 1946 the Army and New York state officials were circulating plans, one of which included taking the entire Allegany Reservation from the Seneca Nation and moving its residents elsewhere.[15]

The Quakers, through their "Society of Friends Kinzua Project of the Indian" committee, described the damming as the result of "30 years of deliberate effort to divide and overwhelm the Seneca People" which had "disturbed Seneca community life and demoralized many families."[16] Prior to final official approval of the dam site over an alternative, tribal

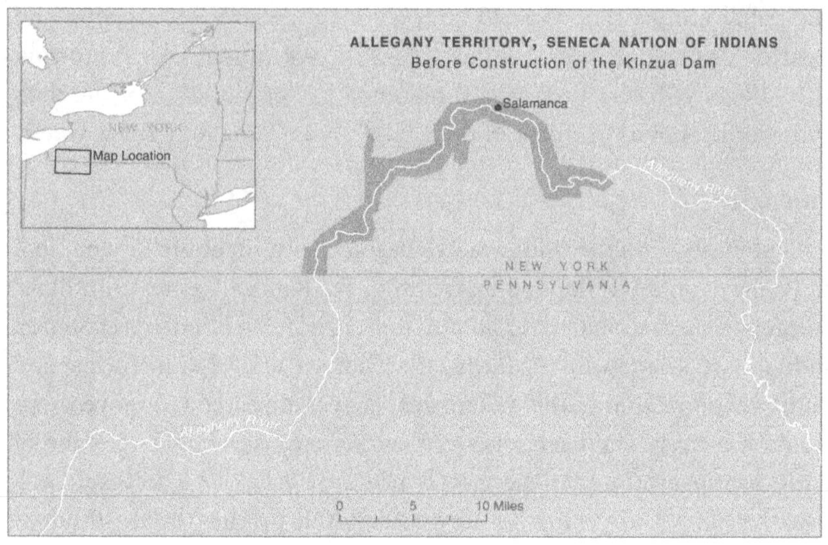

Map 7. Allegany Reservation, New York, before the flood. Courtesy Aileen Clarke.

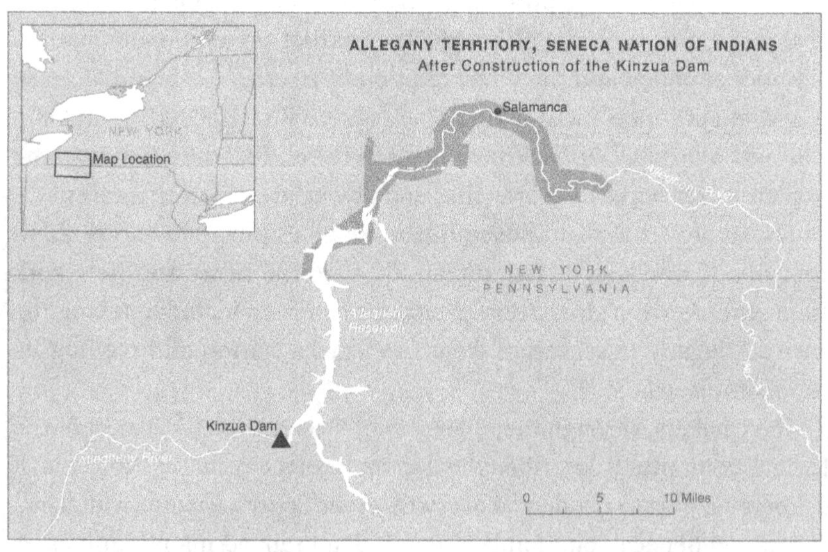

Map 8. Allegany Reservation, New York, after the flood. Courtesy Aileen Clarke.

leaders spoke and gathered opposition to the flooding of their lands. They also brought in an engineer to study alternative sites for the dam. Tribal President Cornelius V. Seneca reminded congressional leaders that the 1794 Pickering Treaty defined Seneca-U.S. relations, and asked, "Has this Government changed so much in the last century and a half that the assurances given to my people by George Washington, the Father of this country, are no longer to be honored?"[17]

President Seneca told 1957 House Public Works subcommittee members, "My people have steadily maintained the position that if the construction of this proposed Kinzua Dam was the only economic and engineering solution for the prevention of floods to downstream Allegheny, we would not oppose the taking of our lands. But when it can be shown by competent engineers that the construction of this dam and the deprivation of our homelands is not sound engineering, then my people can see no justification in having their lands taken from them in direct violation of the treaty rights guaranteed by the Congress of these United States 163 years ago."[18]

Unfortunately, the engineer the Senecas hired to suggest other options had long-standing conflicts with the Army Corps of Engineers, which got in the way of serious consideration of his proposed alternative. Just as important, "Charles Congdon, a city father and attorney in Salamanca, New York, perceptively observed in 1964: 'Flooding the [alternative site] would provide more water for Pittsburgh, but it would flood out white folks! They vote [unlike many Iroquois].'"[19]

James Haley, a Florida congressman who chaired the Indian Affairs subcommittee, made a similar observation. He said, "The alternative, of course, would probably have dislocated some additional Pennsylvanians and New Yorkers who might have gone to the courts to make the proponents of the Dam show public necessity. It was much easier, at least some of your political leaders thought so, to flood out the Seneca Tribe by breaking a treaty signed in 1794 by our first President and running over a small group of people to whose ancestors we are deeply indebted."[20] Unsurprisingly, white needs overshadowed treaty rights and the impacts of the decision on Indigenous communities.

Haley also observed that when the Eisenhower White House sought an independent evaluation of the two proposals, the company the president's office hired could not have been expected to be objective. "I call attention to the fact that this 'independent' firm gets more business from the Army Engineers than from any other sources, and also that some of its principal partners were former Army Engineers," he said.[21] Under these circumstances, Haley believed, this firm would clearly side with the corps over the Seneca Nation's engineer.

George Heron, then Seneca tribal treasurer, expressed his opposition to the dam in relation to his own patriotism to the United States. He served in the navy and fought in both the Pacific and the "African-European Theater" in the second world war. "Along with my fellow Indians, I fought to preserve and maintain this government in the full belief that this government would preserve and maintain my homelands."[22]

In a 1957 hearing, the tribe admitted that Congress had the right to abrogate the treaty, to which Missouri congressman Clarence Cannon responded, "But, it would have to be a solemn act of Congress . . . passed by both houses and signed by the President."[23] President Eisenhower would not support the tribe, although his son, John, argued that he was sympathetic to the Senecas. He stated that the president "believed that the construction of the 'dam would be wrong if the Indians do not desire it, unless it is essential rather than merely desirable' and that it 'is particularly essential that our word be kept with the Indians.'" But it was not to be.

When Eisenhower suggested he wanted Secretary of the Interior Fred Seaton's advice, an intermediary who had a strong desire to see the dam built told him that the attorney general had already said that from a legal perspective, the dam could be built. That intermediary was Eisenhower's longtime friend and head of the White House Office of Public Works, General John Bragdon.[24] This allowed the president to ignore any federal trust responsibility to the Seneca Nation.

Since they lacked support from the legislative and executive branches, the Seneca Nation sued in federal district court to stop construction of the dam. They contended that the act authorizing the building of the dam did not include congressional authorization for taking their lands. Both the district and appellate courts ruled against them in 1958.[25] The appellate court declared that Congress recognized, in a 1941 law, that "the Chief of Engineers plainly showed that the project he recommended would flood the [Seneca] lands . . . in violation of the treaty of 1794." That seventeen-year-old law, together with a 1958 budget line item that would kick off the project, was enough for the judges to rule that Congress had consciously exerted its plenary power and had authorized the taking of Seneca lands.

The decision reads in part, "It is undisputed (1) that the proposed flooding will infringe Indian rights acquired by treaty in 1794, . . . and (2) that Congress can authorize a taking by eminent domain despite the treaty." The court also noted that "Congress knew (1) that the Seneca lands would be flooded, (2) that the Seneca Nation was unwilling to relinquish any of its rights in the lands, and (3) that the lands could be taken by eminent domain."[26]

The Supreme Court refused to take the case. The Association on American Indian Affairs observed that by 1959 the tide was turning against termination policies but that the Kinzua Dam got caught in the "undertow" when Congress approved the release of funding for the dam.[27]

So in 1960, when Representative James Haley, chair of the Indian Affairs subcommittee, voiced opposition, it was already too late. He observed that the House had not initially included funding to start the project in a public-works bill, but "in conference, the House conferees gave in, and the prohibition was removed." Nonetheless, he urged, "The Congress of the United States should withhold any more money for construction of Kinzua Dam, and should initiate, on its own motion, a complete, impartial investigation of the alternative plan submitted by the Seneca Nation."[28]

The secretary of the Interior's office, which had been bypassed by General Bragdon when Eisenhower had asked to hear Secretary Seaton's opinion, attempted to throw the problem squarely onto the shoulders of Congress. "We concur in the recital of the resolution that the United States should avoid the taking of this Indian land unless there is no reasonable alternative. If a feasible alternative can be found which is acceptable to Congress and would not involve a taking of the Seneca lands, it would certainly have our wholehearted endorsement and support."[29] This was a weak statement in support of the federal trust responsibility, basically recognizing congressional plenary authority over tribal affairs.

Not surprisingly, a last-ditch appeal from the Seneca Nation to President John F. Kennedy went unheeded. As Hauptman observed, "The Senecas were fighting a losing battle from the start." The decision to build the dam was basically a done deal before Kennedy's election. "During the Eisenhower years," Hauptman adds, "Indian lands became sacrifice areas in massive flood-control and hydroelectric projects deemed essential in America's Cold War climate."[30] The policy initiatives that had dammed the west now moved to the eastern United States, with many of the same justifications.

In February 1961, on George Washington's birthday, tribal president Basil Williams wrote Kennedy to remind him of his campaign promises to uphold American Indian rights. "The construction of the Kinzua Dam notwithstanding our protests thus will violate Article III of the 1794 Pickering Treaty with the Seneca Nation and, of course, also is contrary to your own personal and Party commitments to all Indian tribes."[31] By May, unbeknownst to the Senecas, the Federal Power Commission had granted a preliminary permit to a private company to develop hydropower at the dam.[32]

In June Congressman Haley again voiced his opposition to the dam and exhorted Kennedy to honor the treaty. He told the president, "Not only am I concerned deeply about the effect this will have upon the Seneca tribe, but also I am concerned about the criticism our government will receive from other nations of the world because of this treaty-breaking." He scolded the president for ignoring a campaign promise to protect Indian rights. Haley reminded Kennedy of a letter that he had written to former American Association on Indian Affairs president Oliver La Farge while on the campaign trail. In it Kennedy said he supported the Democratic party platform that stated, "There would be no change of treaty or contractual relationships without consent of the tribes concerned." Haley added, "So, the United States insists upon its legal rights, and ignores the moral issue."[33]

In August Kennedy told the Senecas that he had "this matter looked into carefully" and that "construction of Kinzua must proceed." In reality, he owed a debt to Pennsylvania's governor for his help in the 1960 presidential campaign. Kennedy then promised to assist the Senecas in their efforts to relocate.[34] New York congressman Thaddeus J. Dulski, who had "been very much opposed to the construction of the Kinzua Dam," entered an editorial from a Buffalo newspaper into the *Congressional Record*. The editorial suggested, "The President . . . said, in effect that, treaty or no treaty, the material interests of the country of which the Indians are in a sense impressed citizens transcend in importance its moral obligation to live up to a treaty made 167 years ago." The newspaper opined that the United States should have studied alternate plans before Congress approved the action and that the Seneca Nation should seek a substantial material award as compensation for their lost lands.[35]

A *Washington Post* article also took a hard line. "George Washington's word was accepted as good; now it is being coldly and ruthlessly broken," the article said.[36] Haley later said in a speech to Seneca Nation members, "Let us not forget, however, the promise made by the Father of our country, General and later President George Washington, to the Seneca Indians that they would be secure in their lands and homes as long as they desired. This promise has been violated."[37] Walter Taylor, the Quaker coordinator of the Friends of Kinzua Project added, "History will forever include, though men may forget, the unilateral, unnegotiated violation of a solemn treaty between the United States and the Seneca Nation of Indians."[38]

Strong opposition to the building of the dam came also from the AAIA, the Quakers through the Friends' Indian Committee, the NAACP, and non-Indian citizens from across the nation, and continued into the Lyndon Johnson administration. Even Eleanor Roosevelt referred to the circumstance as "shameful." Hugh Downs reported on the broken promise on the *Today Show*. Newspapers across the United States reported on the fight and its aftermath.[39] Walter Taylor reported, "In my office there are over 2,000 unsolicited letters of concern over the moral issues and the engineering arrogance of the Kinzua Dam controversy. The letters come from nearly every state."[40] An Australian newspaper published an article with the headline "'Washington's Word Worthless." The opening sentence read "The word of George Washington, America's first President, who 'could not tell a lie,' is in doubt—at least among the angry Seneca tribe."[41]

The evening of the famous August 1963 civil rights March on Washington, New York senator Jacob Javits hosted a party for the event's leaders.

At the party Clyde Warrior (Ponca), then a student at the University of Oklahoma, confronted a New York representative about the dam project, while "nearby, his friend, Marlon Brando" discussed racial discrimination.[42] A significant portion of the American public was incensed by Congress and the presidents' breaking of this treaty. Unfortunately for the Seneca Nation, "Long before anti–Kinzua Dam lobbying efforts had been organized and implemented" the Eisenhower administration had moved the project past the point of no return. As for Javits, despite his support for civil rights, he "never testified against the Kinzua project before its construction."[43]

In early 1964 the House of Representatives passed a compensation bill for the flooding that included more than $16 million in rehabilitation costs. This would help pay for industrial and economic development. George Heron, now president of the Seneca Nation, wrote the chair of the House Interior and Insular Affairs Committee, Wayne Aspinall, thanking him and the committee for ushering the bill to passage in the house. "It is our fondest hopes that we will be accorded the same fair treatment by your counter-parts in the Senate," he said.[44] Unfortunately, that was not to happen.

As Seneca Nation leaders and the house subcommittee worked to gain equitable compensation and provide a plan for removal of those families whose land would be flooded, the Senate moved in another direction.[45] The bill was amended in the Senate Subcommittee on Indian Affairs at the urging of Democrat Frank Church of Idaho and Republican Peter Dominick of Colorado. They succeeded in cutting nearly $10 million from the Seneca rehabilitation compensation. At the last minute, adding insult to injury, as the subcommittee approved the bill on March 18, 1964, Dominick inserted a termination rider. This addition to the bill would give the Seneca Nation two years to draw up a termination plan to present to the secretary of the Interior.[46] The Senecas immediately expressed shock at this addition through their attorney, pointing out that termination was "not even mentioned during the thirteen days of hearings" in the house, nor in the one-day senate hearing.[47] It was sprung on them without any advance notice, let alone consent or even consultation.

THE TERMINATION THREAT

Though early efforts to terminate the Seneca Nation's political relationship with the United States fizzled, the threat never clearly or cleanly died.[48] And so once again the Senecas had to fight the battle to keep the destructive policy at bay.

Through its planning newsletter, which was established to disseminate information to the Seneca Nation and update its citizens on council meetings, the Senecas blasted the termination rider. Merrill Bowen, the editor of the newsletter, wrote to Seneca Nation members in March 1964 that the termination rider "is completely unrelated to our rehabilitation bill and is cleverly disguised." He argued that the sole purpose of the rider was to take land away from the Senecas.[49]

Bowen's description of the termination amendment to the bill angered its author. Senator Dominick responded with a scathing letter which Bowen printed in the newsletter's next issue, in May 1964. In it Dominick objected to the way Bowen portrayed the senator, saying it was "contemptibly inflammatory." He then complained about Bowen's "failure to consult with me or any member of the committee" prior to publication.[50]

The irony of Dominick's complaint was not lost on Bowen. He apologized for language in one of the sentences in the article which he deemed as "unfortunate" and brought on by "the momentary loss of emotional control" due to the knowledge "that Seneca Indians regard the Termination Amendment as a most serious threat to our survival as a people." He then chided Dominick for his comment on consultation, writing "We are sure you will understand our reaction about the introduction of a termination amendment to H.R. 1794 without any notice whatever to the Seneca Nation and without consideration in any public hearings."[51]

In his letter defending Seneca termination Dominick also declared, "If termination is completed, the Tribe will be free to develop its reservation property in the manner it desires without regulation by the Bureau of Indian Affairs or anybody else."[52] Of course he failed to say that the property would be subject to New York state taxes. Bowen responded that Dominick misunderstood the relationship between the Seneca Nation and the United States. Since Congress had already passed legislation beginning in 1948 that turned criminal and civil jurisdiction of Seneca Nation lands over to the state of New York, the amendment "serves no purpose other than to alienate our lands."[53] Except for the purpose of working out details on the Kinzua Dam the BIA was not even located in Seneca territories. In fact, federal officials exerted virtually no "'supervision over the property and affairs' of the Seneca Nation and its members," Bowen told Dominick. Unlike the Three Affiliated Tribes, the Seneca Nation argued that it had little interference from the BIA since the 1948 and 1950 laws had withdrawn much of federal supervision over New York tribes.[54]

"The idea of 'emancipation' of Indians through termination is entirely false," Bowen continued. "Termination could only free us from a heritage which we hold very dear and separate us from what is left of our land, the very source of our continuing identity." Like Indigenous people across the hemisphere the Senecas had developed a millennia-long relationship with the place where they lived, which encompassed the social, economic, political, and religious foundation of their nation. "We are loyal Americans," Bowen added, "but we do not believe that we should be compelled by the Kinzua Dam to stop being also Seneca Indians."[55]

In April 1964 Walter Taylor of the Friends of Kinzua Project observed, "The amendment to terminate the Seneca Nation has added confusion and fear as well as amazement to the anxiety which already prevails among Seneca families because of their anticipated eviction within the next six months." He added, "Termination seems to Seneca Indians and their friends an added injury rather than any kind of reparations for damages resulting from the Kinzua Dam."[56]

The nation through its well-known Indian rights attorney Arthur Lazarus Jr. strenuously objected to the termination rider. Lazarus wrote to Senator Jacob Javits that "the Seneca Nation is unalterably opposed to the termination section in the legislation." He argued that if Congress were serious about termination it should be taken up in a stand-alone bill. He observed that the current bill was intended "to compensate at least partially for the Government's great wrong in breaking the Treaty of November 11, 1794, and in destroying the Allegany Reservation."

Instead the termination rider gave the bill the opposite effect. "To convert this worthy bill by a termination rider into a vehicle for doing

Fig. 8. George Heron and Walt Taylor in a 1961 meeting. Theodore Brinton Hetzel Papers and Graphics, box 20, Haverford College.

away with the remaining obligations of the United States to the Senecas is literally to add insult to injury." After commenting that termination would lead to land and resource loss, the end of tribal hunting and fishing rights, the loss of tax-exempt status, and abrogation of the 1794 treaty, Lazarus told Javits, "Needless to say, the Seneca Nation vigorously opposes the loss of any of these rights for which it bargained and to which the United States agreed years ago."[57]

As the bill was debated in Congress the Senecas expressed opposition to the termination rider through Lazarus. He wrote to Representative Haley that when the rider received pushback, its supporters argued that it was merely meant to keep the BIA from establishing a permanent office in New York state. If that were the case the bill could easily say so. With the blessing of Seneca Nation president George Heron, Lazarus proposed language that would clearly state Congress's opposition to a New York

BIA office.[58] Instead, the requirement for development of a termination plan was clearly spelled out in the bill.

Senator Paul Douglas, an Illinois Democrat, strongly opposed the insertion of the termination amendment to the bill. "The effect of this amendment is to make the treaty with the Seneca Nation null and void because it puts their land back into tax status," he wrote, although their land had never been taxable. "It is my hope," he continued, "that the committee will . . . make the necessary recision."[59]

The *New York Times* took notice. In commenting on the Senate's efforts to significantly diminish the compensation to the Seneca Nation, the paper's editorial staff observed, "The well-being of about 130 families and nearly 700 persons depends on the generosity—and sense of decency—of the Congress." If the Senate version of the bill were to pass, "the Federal Government [would] be committing a double perfidy."[60] In reality, termination, on top of the land takings and undercompensation, would have amounted to a triple perfidy.

As the compensation and termination bill languished in the Senate, *Times* columnist Brooks Atkinson penned an acerbic criticism. After excoriating federal officials for breaking the 1794 treaty he turned his attention to termination. "The Senate would like to get rid of the Seneca Nation," he asserted. By the senate's action, he argued, the "[termination] amendment . . . completes the annihilation of the Seneca Nation." To "thousands of Americans" Atkinson wrote, "The consistent harassment of the Seneca Nation constitutes an intolerable stain on the honor of the United States." He concluded, "The Senate couldn't care less."[61]

Other non-Indian citizens took notice as well. The Philadelphia Religious Society of Friends immediately cabled Colorado congressman Wayne Aspinall, urging the House to "Delete the unnecessary and undesirable termination amendment." Within days the Indian Rights Association telegraphed, "Delete the termination amendment."[62]

Despite vociferous public opposition Congress passed the law on August 31, 1964. It provided some $15 million in compensation for the damming to the Allegany Seneca Nation of Indians. Approximately $2.2 million paid for damages and losses of homes, schools, fishing sites, sacred sites and more. Some $12.1 million was earmarked for economic development. That law, in its final sentences, called for termination and adjusted the timeline from two to three years, providing merely that the secretary of the Interior would consult with the Seneca Nation about it.[63]

After passage of the bill, Heron wrote Haley to express his thanks for getting the bill pushed through. However, he finished the letter by stating, "One cloud, of course, remains on the horizon. The Seneca Nation still strongly opposes the termination of our special relationship with the Federal Government." If it were to occur, "such action would further violate our treaty rights and expose our lands to involuntary alienation under State Law." He urged Haley to continue to support the Senecas as they fought against termination.[64]

Shortly after the compensation and termination law was passed Commissioner of Indian Affairs Philleo Nash visited Salamanca and spoke about termination. He compared the Seneca Nation to "Squanto and Sacajewea, [who] extended the hand of fellowship and hospitality to settlers and explorers." He added, "History now repeats itself as the Senecas yield up their lands for the benefit of their neighbors downstream."[65]

Nash went on to praise both Congress and the Seneca Nation for supporting "the onward march of civilization." He lauded Congress because, "in recognition of the extraordinary sacrifice being made by the Seneca people, the Congress of the United States [went] far beyond payment of the direct and indirect damages required in the taking of private lands."[66]

In this tone-deaf speech Nash also told Seneca citizens, "The Congress as it authorized this program of rehabilitation, concluded that it offered so much hope of economic self sufficiency and self determination that we all ought to look forward, actively and affirmatively, to an end of the special Federal-tribal relationship." He told them that the bureau, in consultation with the Seneca Nation, was to bring a termination plan within three years.[67]

In this case Congress believed it was throwing so much money at the Senecas that they would rapidly develop their economy to a point where the federal government would no longer need to uphold its treaty and trust responsibilities. At the first community meeting after the nation lost the fight to stop the dam, in 1961, one of the first questions that had arisen was whether treaty rights would be extended to replacement lands.[68] The thought of diminishing those rights was never one that the Senecas considered.

The Senecas acted to protect themselves from termination as the date for it approached. In the summer of 1966 the Seneca Nation wrote President Lyndon Johnson to be sure they would be consulted on any termination legislation. That fall Harry Watt contacted Representative Haley, reminding him that the termination "rider would be contrary to the conditions and terms of our 1794 treaty relationship."[69]

By 1967 Seneca opposition to termination was strong. In fact, off-reservation newspapers reported that it was unanimous. Seneca citizens were aware of the travails of the Menominee tribe; they had screened a half-hour film called *The Last Menominee*. Seneca president Calvin John wanted the viewers to understand the "hardships" that Menominees faced after termination. Daniel Jemison and Robert Hoag attended the termination hearings of Washington's Colville tribes to report back to the council. And the Seneca Nation made an hour-and-a-half-long television program themselves to let the local Seneca and white population know of their disapproval of the idea of ending their relationship with the United States.[70]

On March 27 and 28, 1967, the council held meetings in both the Allegany and Cattaraugus communities, and afterwards the council reported "It was ascertained that the majority of the Seneca people were opposed to any form of termination." This led the council to adopt a resolution in May that read, in part, "The Seneca Nation is opposed to altering the relationship which now exists between the Federal Government and the Seneca Nation and specifically is opposed to any form of termination."[71]

In the summer of 1967, Seneca leaders Harry Watt, Ernest Mohawk, and Abner Jimerson met with President John on behalf of the Seneca Indian Longhouse. The people of the Longhouse faith, who were followers of Handsome Lake's Code, addressed a letter signed by the Faith Keepers to Secretary Udall. Watt, Mohawk, and Jimerson asked John to seek tribal council approval of the letter. The letter said, "After a period of discussion the feeling expressed was unanimous against termination." It argued that the Seneca Nation should not be forced into termination. "The disruption caused by the U.S. Government's violation of the Treaty with the Six Nations of 1794," with the flooding and taking of their lands, "has created a disturbance from which our people have not recovered." The resulting threat to their "way of life" and "tradition" was ongoing.[72]

Leaders of the Longhouse emphasized that Handsome Lake's Code, which dated to the years following the American Revolution, provided a "warning to those who would sell or part with our lands." This could "only lead to great hardship." They argued that termination would "definitely lead to the loss of our lands to the State through the inability of many of our people to keep up with the taxes that is expected to be imposed. These lands are our heritage—earth is mother to us."[73] As the Seneca Nation had when opposing the dam, they urged the United States to honor the 1794 treaty and its own trust responsibilities. "Grant us the peace that is so badly needed in these troubled days and permit us to occupy our lands without further molestation or disturbance."[74]

In this case, a proposal of termination was tied directly to the payment for the takings of land. But by 1967, when the proposal was due, Congress was becoming increasingly reticent to terminate tribal nations. Both the abject failures of previous terminations to improve Indigenous quality of life and the burgeoning civil rights movement dulled congressional appetite for such legislation. In fact, all fourteen of the termination bills that eliminated the political relationship of more than one hundred tribal nations to the United States were passed by 1962. The BIA, too, began to falter in its enthusiasm for the policy.

Just one month before the termination bill was due to be sent to Congress, Commissioner of Indian Affairs Robert Bennett met with Seneca Nation community members. "We would not be presenting a plan if we were not instructed by Congress to do so," he said. However reluctant Bennett was, the BIA was required by law to bring a termination bill to Congress. Bennett also warned the Senecas, "Complete termination means [that they] will no longer own their reservations, but will pay land taxes as any other New York State property owner." He told those listening that termination could not be put into effect by federal officials unless a majority of Senecas voted for it and also informed them that three tribes had voted to reject termination—the Florida Seminoles, the Osage, and the "Flatheads of Montana" (the Confederated Salish and

Kootenai Tribes). He said this just days before the Faith Keepers wrote their letter.[75]

President Calvin John reported in July, "Perhaps the most important topic at the present time, in the minds of the majority of people of the nation residing on the two reservations, is the word 'termination'." He reported that the nation's attorney, Arthur Lazarus Jr., was optimistic, having said, "I for one don't believe the American people will stand for a final breaking of the Treaty."[76] Nonetheless, this battle must have been especially galling since it came when the nation was in the trying process of rebuilding its communities and economy in the wake of the coming flood. The Senecas had to divert their energy from that work to fight off a termination that had simply been inserted into their flood compensation bill.

When Secretary of the Interior Stewart Udall sent the bill to Congress, a BIA press release reported that he did so "in keeping with a Congressional directive." It said, "The Seneca Tribal Council recently passed a resolution which says that while the tribe recognizes the necessity of the legislation, a majority of its members are 'opposed to altering the relationship which now exists between the Federal Government and the Seneca Nation and specifically (the tribe) is opposed to any form of termination.'"[77] When Washington senator Henry Jackson brought the Seneca termination bill before the Senate in 1967 it went to committee and died there. The bill apparently never even made it to the House committee.[78] Ironically, Jackson would sponsor a Senate resolution condemning termination just four years later.[79]

Even after the Senate and President Nixon repudiated termination, the fear of it still permeated the Seneca Nation. In 1972 the Indian Claims Commission found that the Senecas had been cheated in the 1797, 1826, and 1838 treaties and were owed approximately $4.5 million.[80] When meetings at Seneca were held to discuss a vote to accept the judgment and payment, opposition arose—in part based on a fear of termination.[81]

The fear—certainly justified from Seneca and broader Indigenous experiences over the past couple of decades—was based on false information spread by an activist from Sisseton, South Dakota, Meredith Quinn. He was able to convince some Seneca citizens that the 1964 compensation act's termination rider had actually gone into effect in 1967. Incendiary fliers titled "SENECA NATION TERMINATED—LANDS TO BE TAKEN" were circulated throughout the community, and contentious meetings were held in early September 1973. These were followed up with a meeting at the Newtown Longhouse on September 11.[82]

All of this chaos caused "The Nosey Reporter," a regular contributor to the Seneca community newsletter, to write, "We have been hearing a lot of rumors to the effect that we are not citizens or we are citizens. We are terminated or we are not terminated. You don't know what to believe. So we asked a reliable source. The reply was 'We Are Citizens' since 1924 and *we are not* terminated."[83]

The misinformation also caused both Longhouse leaders and Seneca Nation political leaders to publicly respond. The Longhouse leaders simply said that such meetings should be held at other sites and not in religious spaces.[84] The political leaders refuted Quinn's assertions by reprinting a "Termination Report" written by Calvin John and published a year earlier, as well as the 1967 letter opposing termination from the Faith Keepers to Secretary Udall. That letter had been endorsed by the tribal council. The council also banned Quinn from the reservation.[85] After twice having had brushes with termination, in the 1950s and again in the 1960s, the fear of it held power over Seneca Nation citizens.

After more than a quarter century of opposition to the flooding of their lands, the Seneca Nation had received its compensation that came with an effort to terminate them. The painful destruction of their homelands by flooding was brought about by a betrayal by the U.S. Congress of a sacred promise made to the Seneca when George Washington was president. In 1986 Laurence Hauptman reported, "Even today, more than twenty years after the flooding of their homeland began, Seneca elders have difficulty speaking of this modern time of troubles. . . . To them, the relocation and removal of Seneca families from the 'take area' was their second 'Trail of Tears,' comparable only to these same Indians' loss and removal from the Buffalo Creek Reservation in the first half of the nineteenth century."[86] Then Congress tried to diminish the Seneca Nation even further by destroying not just the economic and cultural foundation of the community that the flooding brought but the very political foundation of their nationhood. Tying termination to not only an infusion of money but to loss of a significant portion of their homelands represents a particularly insidious effort to use bribery to end the relationship between an Indigenous nation and the United States.

The threats of termination to the Mandan, Hidatsa and Arikara, and the Seneca Nation in two different parts of the country, occurred a decade apart from each other during very different political climates. Both were tied to compensation when lands were taken and their reservations were flooded. The Three Affiliated Tribes' threat came in the heart of the termination era; the Seneca Nation's on the cusp of a policy shift toward Indigenous self-determination. Yet they both carry eerie similarities. For both nations, the idea of termination was sprung on them without prior consultation. Congress decided to tie it to economic development or compensation for the losses they would incur for the taken lands flooded by major dams that would benefit surrounding white communities, one largely agricultural, the other largely urban. At the same time it would have destroyed these nations' political standing and put an end to their sovereignty.

Since the first treaty of cession, Indigenous lands have been treated as internal colonies that would become sacrifice zones for United States and local or regional economic development. But Indians have also long contested that. The Seneca Nation leader George Heron later framed U.S. actions in breaking the 1794 treaty in terms of contemporary foreign policy issues. He referenced Secretary of State John Foster Dulles's excoriation of the Soviet Union for breaking agreements in East Germany and President Dwight Eisenhower's affirmation of the necessity for the United States to hold to its agreements in order to maintain moral standing in the world.[87]

Yet both Congress and the executive branch of the federal government viewed the breaking of such agreements as necessary to advance the national interest. And these were not isolated cases. With a kind of circular logic, federal officials argued that an infusion of cash prepared Indian people to stand on their own and that Indigenous communities that were prepared to stand on their own could use that cash to find and secure their place in modern America. For their part, tribal nations and individuals generally viewed these machinations as underhanded and shameful methods to both acquire Indigenous land and resources and to destroy the possibility of separate sovereign American Indian polities in the country's future. To them, the security they desired regarding their place in modern America was largely contingent on the United States maintaining—not abandoning—its responsibilities to tribal nations.

PART 4

Land and Termination

CHAPTER 8

The "Mixed-Blood" Utes

> We do not want to sell a foot of our land—that is the opinion of all.
>
> —Ouray in 1872, quoted in O'Neil and McKay, "A History of the Uintah-Ouray Ute Lands"

> My clients would still be willing to get all of the land back, rather than a cash consideration, were that possible. There can therefore be no complaint on the part of the government that the amount involved is large, for the government is itself responsible for the taking.
>
> —Ernest Wilkinson, *Daily Sentinel*, Grand Junction, Colorado, August 13, 1947

Arguably, losses of land brought the most devastating impacts to Indigenous communities in the pre-reservation years. Plant and animal foods, materials for clothing and building, medicines, religious sites, graveyards, and more all disappeared as former homelands were taken by white invaders. Tribal economies lay in ruins. Political power vanished. Cultural practices were disrupted. Indigenous nations were vastly underpaid for the value of lost land and resources. Almost as soon as it happened, tribal leaders attempted to gain fair compensation for the losses or to have the lands returned. Those fights continued into the twentieth century and beyond.

When in 1950 the Ute people of the Uintah and Ouray reservation in northern Utah succeeded in a series of decades-long claims cases to gain a positive judgement, Congress and the BIA almost immediately used that money in an attempt to bribe them to accept termination of their federal relationship. The federal effort was partially successful as the tribe agreed to termination of the rights of the portion of its membership that had a high degree of out-marriage—people who both the Utes and federal officials referred to as "mixed-bloods."

Historian R. Warren Metcalf tells us that "the story of what happened to the mixed-blood Utes defies classification into the usual categories and patterns of American Indian history."[1] Indeed, the story of their termination is both ugly and complex. They had the misfortune of being represented in the Senate by Arthur Watkins of Utah, who wanted to use the Indians of his state as the model for the termination policy he touted, much as Douglas McKay had wanted to use Oregon's Indians for the same purpose.

Like the Klamaths, the Utes also became embroiled in an intratribal fight. Theirs was over membership rules and was intensified by the Utes' success in a lawsuit brought in the U.S. Court of Claims in 1938 over lost lands in Colorado. Those combined cases generated a $31.9 million judgment in 1950 just as Congress became serious about its termination program. The tribe benefitted from being charged minimal offsets, since Ernest Wilkinson, the Utes' attorney, was able to have the Indian Claims Commission rules on offsets applied to this case, even though it was decided in the Court of Claims.[2] And so the money awarded was not diminished the way other judgments had been in the past.

These two factors—the membership fight and the claims victory—would have a dramatic impact on the Utes. It would permanently break the tribe apart as some tribal members were able to avoid termination while the "mixed-blood" members were banished in a fight similar to modern disenrollments in casino-wealthy tribes.[3] Unlike the Klamath case, there was never a reconciliation. This was all done as disbursement of the judgment funds was held up in order for Watkins to coerce Ute termination. While partial termination was a unique response to federal failure to uphold its trust responsibilities, it was devastating for those affected by it. Although all three cases ended in terminations, the story of the "mixed-blood" Utes would end differently than the Menominee and the Klamath termination stories.

CLAIMS CASES AND MEMBERSHIP BATTLES

"Historically, the Ute people lived in several family groups, or bands, and inhabited 225,000 square miles covering most of Utah, western Colorado, southern Wyoming, and northern Arizona and New Mexico." These bands thought of themselves collectively as "the people." They hunted and gathered across the landscape, shared religious views and practices, and "ethical beliefs," and they were related to each other through marriage.[4] Some of that marriage was to neighbors of other tribal backgrounds.

The United States acquired the right to negotiate for most of Ute lands from Mexico in the 1848 Treaty of Guadalupe Hidalgo. During the latter half of the nineteenth century the Utes lost most of these lands through cession, theft, and federal collusion with local white settlers and businessmen. As a result of these losses independent Ute bands would be divided geographically, with the Southern Utes, located near what is now the Colorado, New Mexico, and Utah borders, and the Northern Utes on the Uintah and Ouray Reservation in Utah.[5]

In 1861, by executive order, President Abraham Lincoln established the Uintah reservation in Utah. Then an 1868 treaty established a fifteen-million-acre reservation of Ute lands in western Colorado.[6] This was adjacent to the reserved Ute lands in Utah. In 1880, according to ethnohistorian Sondra Jones, virulently anti-Indian white Coloradans joined forces with the U.S. military and U.S. president Rutherford Hayes to force the White River Utes to move onto the Uintah Reservation and the Uncompahgres to move onto the adjacent Ouray reservation in Utah Territory shortly after Colorado earned statehood. The two reservations were later combined. In essence, in the 1880s White River and Uncompahgre tribal members were banished to join the Uintahs, where their infertile land was allotted for farmsteads.[7] These three bands would become the Ute Indian Tribe of the Uintah and Ouray Reservation.

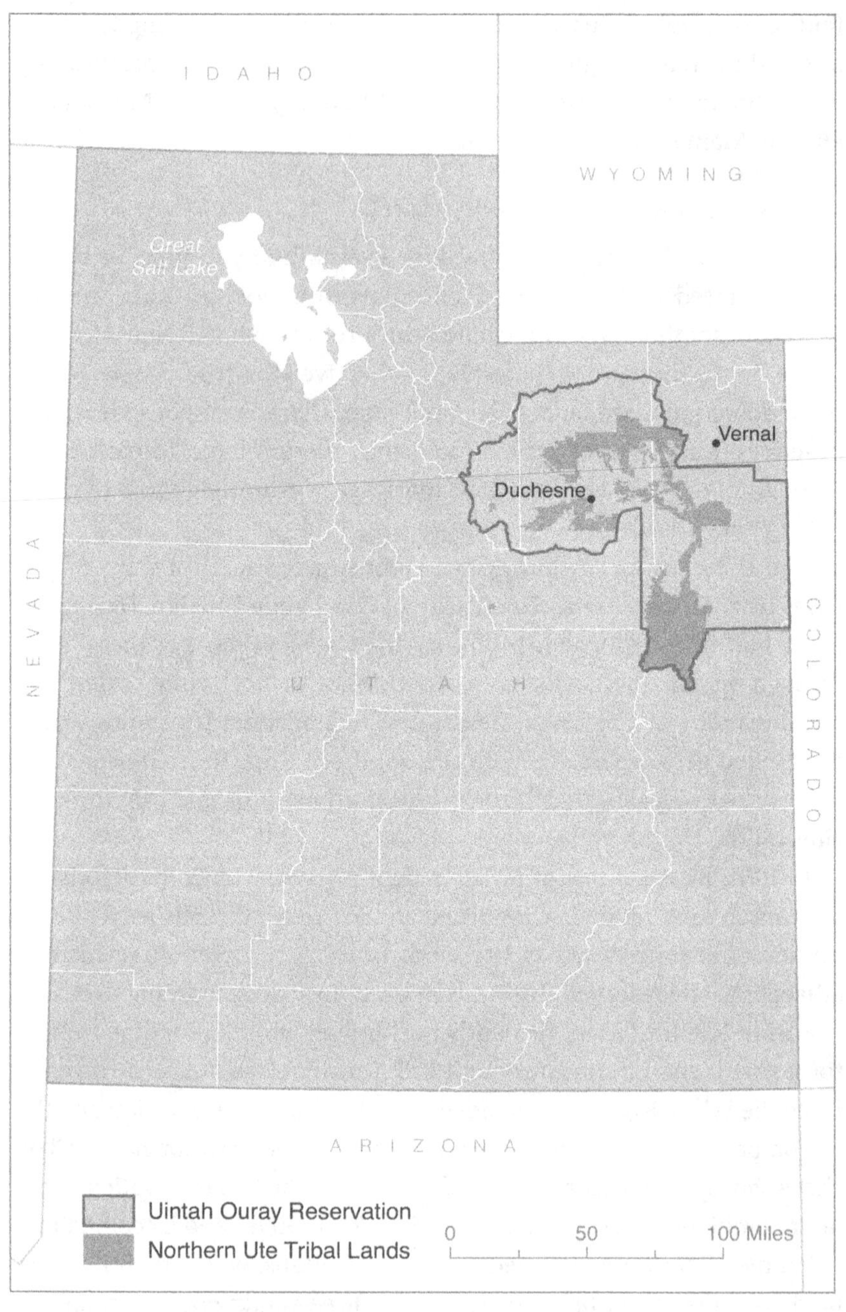

Map 9. Uintah and Ouray Reservation, Utah. Courtesy Aileen Clarke.

Floyd O'Neil and Kathryn McKay tell us that many Utes refused to sign the 1880 agreement; so in order to reach the three-fourths threshold of adult male signees required to authorize it, one of the commissioners spent $2,800 bribing Ute men with two-dollar payments.[8] In the agreement the White River and Uncompahgre Utes lost almost 11.8 million acres of their land in Colorado.[9] One of the stipulations of the agreement provided that the federal government would sell that land at $1.25 an acre. The income would first pay federal expenses for the negotiation and implementation of the agreement, but "the remainder" of the funds, "if any," would be "deposited in the Treasury as now provided by law for the benefit of the said Indians."[10]

This agreement was the subject of a suit in the Court of Claims that was decided in 1910 in which the Utes were awarded partial value for some of the lands taken. In this claim they also unsuccessfully sought interest payment for the lands not sold.[11] Then, in 1938, Congress simply took the unsold lands without compensating the Utes. They were able to do this under the so-called Adams Amendment. The amendment, named for Colorado Senator Alva Adams, whose stock-raising constituents opposed removal of the lands from the public domain, was attached to a law that permitted the Utes to sue the United States for land and resource losses. The amendment reads, "that the Ute lands 'to the extent that they have not been disposed of by the United States are hereby declared to be the absolute property of the United States.'"[12]

This language was written by the tribe's own attorney, Ernest Wilkinson, who said that he drafted this language for the bill as a compromise. Adams had wanted to disallow the land to be restored to the tribe and also to prevent the Utes from receiving any compensation for the loss.[13] Under the Adams Amendment the Utes lost more than four million acres of land whose surface and subsurface values would eventually be determined to be more than $24 million.[14]

In addition, Wilkinson later said, "We discovered that the United States had disposed of some 1,361,993.22 acres of Ute lands as free homesteads for which no accounting or payment had ever been made to the Utes." That land was supposed to have been sold at a minimum of $1.25 an acre, with the proceeds benefitting the Utes. Tribal member Oran Curry in

1926 wrote, "It is understood that the Gov't had an option on this land to pay us (Indians) up to 1925, it's one year past Due now." The land was later valued at $1.93 per acre at the time of its taking.[15]

The United States also took almost four million acres of the lands lost in the 1880 agreement for National Forest lands. Though the Utes were partially compensated for this in their 1910 claims case, they had still been shortchanged.[16] All of this was enough to convince Ernest Wilkinson to take the Utes' case before the Court of Claims on a contingency basis.

These claims were initially taken up by Raymond Bonnin, a Yankton Sioux who worked for the Indian bureau on the Ute Reservation at Uintah and Ouray beginning in 1902.[17] He reportedly "felt that the Utes had grievances against the United States, and after he returned from World War I as an infantry captain he was engaged by the Indians to prosecute their claims." In 1935 he referred the Utes to the law firm of Hughes, Schurman and Dwight where Wilkinson worked as an attorney. Two years later Wilkinson took over the case. Bonnin did a lot of the legwork in the Ute communities to pave the way for Wilkinson and continued to do so up until his death in 1942. At that time Wilkinson estimated the value of the claim in the $1–2 million judgment range.[18] Years of research by the attorneys proved the valuation significantly higher.

The lawsuit was complicated, including both northern and southern Utes in a four-part claim for lands lost as well as surface rights, oil, and various minerals agreements. Thirteen other suits were eventually included as part of the judgment. These included efforts to gain just compensation for previous land sales, compensation for resources on those lands, and accounting errors.[19]

The work to bring the case to judgment was monumental. In order to prove that the tribe had been unpaid and underpaid for lands and resources Wilkinson, as lead attorney, worked with a team of seventy lawyers who spent sixty-two thousand hours on the claims cases over nineteen years. They worked on several fronts: ushering bills through Congress supporting the claims work, recreating the historical and financial history of Ute lands and resources, and litigating the cases.[20]

Since federal officials had kept poor records of transactions, and in some cases no records at all, the attorneys had to search documents in the War Department, the Department of the Interior (including the Indian bureau, the Bureau of Land Management, the Geological Survey, and the Bureau of Mines), the Department of the Treasury, the House, the Senate ("some of which were located in unclassified boxes in the attic of the Senate Office Building"), and the National Archives.[21] They used all of these to piece together their cases.

In the meantime the tribe's attorneys were able to get more than 600,000 acres of land returned to the tribe. In 1945, after ten years of negotiations, the secretary of the Interior returned 217,000 acres under the Indian Reorganization Act. According to the Court of Claims, "The Utes preferred the restoration of this land to a suit for its value." Then in 1948 the 80th Congress returned 427,015 acres.[22] At the same time, the claims cases for the rest of the taken lands continued.

As the cases wended their way through the court system, tribal members became increasingly antsy over the distribution of funds, attorney fees and costs, and even whether any actual money would ever be paid out.[23] By the late 1940s the frustration that tribal members felt spilled over into tribal business committee meetings.

At a meeting in October 1949, with Wilkinson present, several tribal members vented their frustration. Most tribal members were extremely poor, and constantly in need of loans or support to supplement their grazing or their hunting activities, and even their daily needs. "Connor Chapoose stated that in the back of the Indians [*sic*] minds was the question of when some of these cases would be settled, or were the funds going to be exhausted on attorneys fees on processing these claims. They would like something to come in for their benefit. He said it seemed to the Indians that things were in the same shape they were twelve or thirteen years ago." Tribal leader Della Curry added, "We should derive something from the money that we put up. We have waited thirteen or fourteen years now, and we haven't seen anything." Elder James Atwine echoed their concerns.[24]

At this same time Congress, with the help of Indian bureau officials in Washington DC, attempted to find ways to end the U.S. legal and political relationship with the tribe. The first real hint of trouble to come for the tribe occurred in 1948 when Utah senator Arthur Watkins visited the Uintah and Ouray Reservation. Despite the fact that he lived near the Ute reservation and his parents owned an allotment there, Watkins knew very little about the Utes and their long history of dispossession. But even in 1948, early in his first term in the Senate, Watkins believed termination was the answer to the "Indian problem."[25] Tribal member Lawrence Appah later recalled, "Senator Watkins in Duchesne said 'Turn the Indians loose.' A certain whiteman at Duchesne said 'The Senator probably does not know the condition of the Indian people.'"[26]

At a special meeting of the Business Committee Watkins told tribal members that he had secured funding for a new high school where the Indian children would be sent to attend with white high schoolers. James Atwine, a non-English speaker, opposed the idea, believing that the Indian children would suffer discrimination. Watkins responded, "The United States Government wants to put the Indians on their feet so they won't have to be taken care of and the only way for the Indian children to learn is to mingle with the White children, especially the Indian children between the age of 14 and 20, they should go to white schools to learn the White people's ways so they can take their place as citizens the same as any one else." He concluded the meeting by telling tribal members, "I want to see you Indians . . . stand on your own feet."[27] He believed assimilation into white society was the way to accomplish that.

Agency superintendent Forrest Stone reported his deep concern regarding Watkins's intentions to the BIA central office. He wrote that the senator "made himself very clear to practically everyone with whom he talked" that his goal was to put the Indian Service out of business.[28] Stone, however, naively believed that Indian leaders would play a key role in determining the future of the Indian service.[29] Unfortunately for the Utes, Stone's view clashed not only with Senator Watkins but with Indian bureau officials in the central offices in Washington DC and with Congress.

The confederated tribe consisted of three bands, the Uncompahgre, the White River, and the Uintah. Where money was involved members of the three groups increasingly bickered with each other. When oil money came as per capita from the Uintah territory in 1948, for example, the business committee debated whether it should be split among all members or solely among Uintah members. Julius Murray, who was

Fig. 9. Chief Ouray with his wife, Chipeta, 1880. Library of Congress #LC-DIG-cwpbh-04477.

Uintah, argued, "All the people on this Reservation are incorporated into one Tribe and are recognized as one Tribe, we should all share and share alike." Otherwise, tensions would only increase.[30] The tensions, however, dated to the establishment of the reservation and would not readily disappear. Ethnohistorian Sondra Jones describes it this way: "From the first, the Uintahs resented having to share their reservation with the White Rivers while already struggling to survive themselves; when they were later compelled to share it further with the Uncompahgres, their resentment grew. For their part, the Uncompahgres resented the White Rivers for precipitating their expulsion from Colorado, while the White Rivers still resented the Uncompahgres who had been led by the Washington-appointed Ouray to the 'detriment' of the other bands. The [federal] government perpetuated these factions as they continued to deal with each band independently and partially."[31]

These longstanding tensions spilled over into membership fights. There was a feeling among the poorer and the "full-blood" members of the tribe that the cause of the problem was the tribe's Indian Reorganization Act government. Many believed that it favored those with more wealth and people of "mixed-blood," or those who married outside of the tribe, whether they married white or other Indian people.[32] Even membership within the tribe could be contentious.

One of the tribe's attorneys, John Boyden, warned, "There is the question of intermarriage how are you going to decide whether people are Uncompahgres, Whiterivers or Uintahs. There must be a decision one way or another, a problem never gets better until brought out in the open."[33] The problem extended to marriage outside of the tribe as well. John Nick, an Uncompahgre, bluntly told the council, "I think something should be done about inter-marriages, especially Indians marrying whites, if an Indian girl marries a white man he should take care of his family, get them off the rolls."[34]

Reginald "Rex" Curry, whose father Oran had originally asked Raymond Bonnin to investigate Ute claims, urged unity at least until the lawsuits were settled. "I believe that Conner [Chapoose] was right when he says that we have to stick together on this thing. We are fighting the Government, and if we are going to be split up among ourselves we will lose. We have to have unity. It can be ironed out later, after the case is won against the Gov't."[35] However, these split opinions would only increase over the next decade. This conflict made it easier for federal officials in DC to drive a wedge between factions in the tribal community.

The process of splitting the tribe began in earnest in May 1950. The Business Committee proposed to constitutionally change enrollment rules so that Indian blood would be counted toward tribal membership only if it was Ute Indian blood. A proposal was made at that time to increase the blood quantum standard from one-fourth Indian blood to one-half Ute Indian blood for those born in the future.[36] Blood quantum requirements had incrementally crept up, from one-eighth Indian blood in 1937 to one-fourth in 1939.[37] The new proposal brought immediate protest from a group of "mixed-blood" people, who argued that the new law would separate some tribal members from their land and resource rights and would prevent children from inheriting their parents' land.[38] In July 1950, however, the tribe decided to continue to recognize all Indian blood as Ute blood, potentially keeping the membership rolls broad.[39]

That same month the Utes won what was then the largest judgment against the United States. On July 13, 1950, the U.S. Court of Claims awarded the tribes $31,938,954.23.[40] Some $18 million of this would go to the Uintah and Ouray Utes. This would provide Watkins and the Indian bureau the opening they sought to push termination, and it would fuel the "full-blood"–"mixed-blood" conflict over the division of judgment money and tribal membership.

THE UTE PARTITION ACT

As the judgment became reality, Senator Watkins and Commissioner of Indian Affairs Dillon Myer insisted that the tribe develop a termination plan. In November 1950 when the tribe requested emergency per capita funding, "Myer and the 'higher authorities' demanded a 'permanent constructive plan' in exchange" for action, according to R. Warren Metcalf. The "higher authorities" were Watkins and the Senate Indian Affairs subcommittee. "In Myer's vernacular, 'permanent constructive plan' meant a long-range termination plan."[41]

In August 1951 Congress authorized the tribal business committee to expend judgment funds "for such purposes, including per capita payments," as it saw fit. The legislation immediately authorized a $1,000 per capita payment but then required the tribe to get congressional approval for future payments.[42] Myer told Watkins with satisfaction that the tribe had created a three-year plan and would use some of the award money "to submit a permanent long range program."[43] Of course Watkins already knew this. Both of them viewed the infusion of funds as paving the way toward termination of federal trust responsibilities. With the tribe's ability to use its funds controlled by the whims of Congress, Watkins held a stout stick that he hoped to use to beat the Ute people into submission.

In 1952 the BIA's Phoenix Area Office reported with enthusiasm, "The manner in which the Ute Tribe of the Uintah and Ouray Reservation has handled its financial affairs and rehabilitation program has brought wide public commendation to the tribal officials, members of the tribe, and to the Indian Service." To prove this, an editorial from the *Deseret News* was included in the office's annual report. The editorial waxed positively on the responsible ways in which tribal members had spent their recent per capita payment. "This sensible beginning of rehabilitation of the Utes is an event that all Utahns, Congress, the nations of the world . . . might note and applaud," the newspaper opined.[44]

This attitude permeated the area office by the next year. In its 1953 report the area office declared that though tribes had initially opposed the federal withdrawal plans, once bureau officials explained the benefits to tribal members, there was "lessened resistance."[45] This commentary ignored the intratribal conflict developing on the Ute reservation.

After the business committee had recognized all Indian blood as Ute blood, council member Della Curry pushed hard that only Ute blood be counted. She argued, "It is not fair to our people to enroll all these others, soon there will be no Utes."[46] This would be devastating to the "mixed-blood" Ute population. While some Ute women had married white men, much of the "mixed-blood" population included Navajo, Paiute, and Shoshone intermarriage, some of which had predated establishment of the reservation.[47]

In May 1953 a tribal ordinance moving blood quantum to one half for new-born members was enacted. The General Council approved the measure in a vote of 107–1. The business committee then passed a resolution stating, "Hereafter, no person born subsequent to the adoption of this Ordinance shall be enrolled in the Ute Indian Tribe of the Uintah and Ouray Reservation unless the degree of Ute Indian Blood of such person shall be one-half or more."[48] Ute Indian blood was defined as being from the Ute Indian Tribe of the Uintah and Ouray Reservation.[49] In the end this would be interpreted as more than one half, not one half and more. Everyone at precisely one-half blood quantum and below would be excluded.

The conflict dated to the 1880s when the White River and Uncompahgre Utes were moved to the Utah reservation. The intermix of blood from various Indian nations both predated that and was continuing. And the conflict was further complicated by the way the tribe had been organized under the Indian Reorganization Act. Tribal member William Reed first petitioned and then wrote senators urging an investigation that would return control of tribal affairs to the tribe. He believed that the IRA government, which had put all three bands into one governing unit, was the basis of unescapable conflict. But he emphasized, "Nothing herein is to be construed as a request or suggestion, that all governmental restrictions over the Uintahs be removed, as many of my people are unprepared for such a development."[50]

Nonetheless, Watkins wrote a letter in May 1953 pressing the council to develop its termination plan.[51] In September 1953 the tribal attorney, John S. Boyden, informed the council "that although he didn't wish to be pessimistic . . . it looked very much like the U.S. Government [was] planning to withdraw their services from Indian Tribes and perhaps faster than the Tribes [were] ready."[52] This was clearly the case. The tribe did want to receive per capita payments to individuals from the judgment funds, but they were not interested in terminating their relationship with the United States.[53] Watkins increased the pressure in early 1954 in terms that historian R. Warren Metcalf has referred to as "economic blackmail."[54] In February 1954 Watkins wrote that until the tribe created its termination program, "further legislation for aid or assistance" would be in jeopardy.[55]

The tribe faced pressure on its resources and land on many fronts. A non-Indian organization, for example, the Uintah Water Basin Association, wanted to take control of management of the local irrigation project since its members were not at all protected. The association's president told the tribal council, "We are not trying to take any rights of any nature, it is the waste of money and supervision we want to get away from." Council members were not so sure. Vice Chairman Russell Cuch cautioned, "All this must be thought out carefully. We must watch our step."[56]

Rex Curry added, "We understand that the policy of the Government is to get out; we want to work it so it won't be a detriment to the Indians." The tribe had invested more than one-and-three-quarter-million dollars in the irrigation project. If changes in control were to be made, the tribe would want that money back. Curry was not confident that Congress would agree to that. This was an issue that the General Council would have to decide, Curry said.[57] He apparently worried that the federal desire for withdrawal of services would play into the hands of the non-Indian water association to the detriment of the tribe. Lack of tribal control over its own water resource and money were issues here that were compounded by federal termination plans. The water association's efforts to take water from the Utes paralleled the efforts of non-Indians in North Dakota to get hold of the Three Affiliated Tribes' oil and gas resources. In both cases, tribal members clearly recognized the threats.

Robert Bennett, director of program for the bureau, along with Rex Curry and Francis McKinley, two of only four college-educated Utes on the reservation, concocted a plan to preserve a majority of the tribe. Bennett brought with him a letter from Watkins to Curry and the Business Committee saying, "Congress will expect you to keep very fully and completely your promises made to the Committee when this legislation [the three-year program] was approved." He meant that he expected them to develop termination legislation.[58]

The decision to award the tribe judgment funds had exacerbated the "mixed-blood"–"full-blood" division within the tribe. Together Bennett, Curry, and McKinley devised a proposal that would split the funds between "mixed-bloods" and "full-bloods." Bennett "argued . . . that the partitioning process would result in the immediate termination of the mixed blood Utes." This would serve to relieve pressure on the "full-bloods," since the portion of the tribe to be terminated would be the members most likely to succeed without receiving trust benefits from the federal government.[59]

Watkins was satisfied that the bill he proposed would serve two purposes: it would create a termination in Utah that could be used as a model for future terminations across Indian country, and it would eventually lead to termination for the remaining Utes. A "compromise" reached as the bill was being written strengthened the former possibility because it redefined "mixed-blood" in a way that did not conform with tribal law. Instead of "mixed-blood" being defined as being less than half Ute, it was defined in the law as half or less Ute. That meant that anyone of exactly "half-blood" was written out of the tribe. The tribal ordinance

Fig. 10. President Harry S. Truman and (*l to r*): Reginald Curry of the Uncompahgre Ute Tribe, Lawrence Appah of the White River Ute Tribe, and Julius Murray of the Uintah Ute Tribe, all of Fort Duchesne UT, 1946. Image 68–1893, Harry S. Truman Library.

had defined "half-blood" individuals as tribal members; this law excluded them. According to the final tribal rolls as published in the federal register in 1956, more than 90 of the 450 individuals listed as "mixed-blood"—fully 20 percent—were categorized as precisely one half. However, in the end this did not lead to termination of the entire tribe. Metcalf tells us, "Once the mixed bloods had been cut off . . . the tribe no longer felt the pressure to develop a termination program."[60]

Despite the fact that tribal consent was theoretically a basis for termination, the "mixed-bloods" in this community did not consent to the fate that befell them. In fact, though Watkins reported to the Senate that the tribe had consented to termination, the BIA consistently argued that only consultation was necessary. In the hearings on the Utes' termination bill, Commissioner of Indian Affairs Glenn Emmons told Congress, "I might say, however, that consultation does not mean that Indian consent must necessarily be obtained before terminating a particular Federal trusteeship. As trustee, the Federal Government must make the final decision and assume the final responsibility."[61] The difference between consultation and consent has long been problematic for tribes.

Very few "mixed-bloods" attended the most significant meeting that pushed their termination forward, on March 31, 1954.[62] Despite Emmons's perspective, Watkins conflated the practice of consent with consultation.[63] As with the Menominee, Watkins led his Senate colleagues to believe that the Utes had asked for termination or freedom, as he defined the policy. Even the eminent Indian rights attorney Arthur Lazarus Jr. assumed the tribe had requested termination.[64]

Even the "full-bloods" seemed surprised, or at the least confused, by the passage of the law, signing petitions asking the president to veto the bill. They gathered their signatures too late to submit them before the bill became law.[65] In a petition calling for accountability, the Uncompahgre band later said that a "delegation of Utes allegedly representing the Ute Indians resulted in the enactment of Public Law 671," the Ute Partition Act. They went on to say, "the United States Government and Members of Congress claim that Public Law 671 was enacted because of request and petition made by the Ute Indians and not through any specific recommendations, influence, and pressure from the United States Government and Members of Congress." This, they argued, was not true, since their own chosen delegates were refused participation by the Ute Tribal Business Committee.[66]

Just before the partition act became law, the secretary of the Interior's office, through Orme Lewis, told the House Committee on Interior and Insular Affairs that "the bill was drafted by the tribe and introduced at the request of the tribe." He added, "It is an excellent example of initiative and planning on the part of the Indians, and their efforts deserve commendation." As a result, the committee recommended passage of the Ute Partition bill, which it said was "the result of proposals by the Ute Tribe of Indians in Utah." Committee members clearly believed that the tribe supported termination, writing, "The mixedbloods propose a termination program; the fullbloods propose to develop within 3 months after the enactment of this bill a program to prepare them for that termination at a later date."[67]

The division within the tribe presented the opportunity for a portion of the leadership to kick the "mixed-blood" Utes out of the tribe. They did so in collusion with Congress and the BIA. This action was obfuscated with language both stating and implying that the "mixed-bloods" were part of the process in the development of the plan that forced them out of the tribe.

The National Congress of American Indians too was seemingly taken by surprise when the bill became law, splitting the tribe and terminating the "mixed-bloods." Helen Peterson, who had a strong working relationship with the tribal chair Rex Curry, visited Fort Duchesne on August 26, 1954, the day before the president signed the bill. She described the experience as "interesting and confusing. It seems . . . the tribe would be divided in two." She added, "Rex had to go with the mix bloods. They will call themselves Affiliated Ute Citizens." She also observed, "The mix-bloods will have to join NCAI separately as the 'Affiliated Ute Citizens' if they want to be members."[68] At this point NCAI was willing to recognize the "mixed-bloods" as Indian, even despite their termination. It would do them little good.

A small group of White Rivers and Uintahs, the "Special Committee of Independent Ute Indians," organized to oppose the implementation of the law after its passage but before termination went into effect. They became known as the "True Utes."[69] In December 1960, according to the *New York Times*, they endorsed a proclamation denouncing their American citizenship and seceding from the United States. Their primary concern in this case was the tribe's lack of control over its resources. Echoing the frustration of tribal leaders across the United States, "The True Utes have said the money is not being spent correctly and want control of it themselves rather than have it in the hands of the Bureau of Indian Affairs."[70] Their fight had begun with the tribal council itself, where under the leadership of Julius Twohy they conducted a sit-in to try to take over the tribal offices earlier in the year.[71]

The "full-blood" faction had little sympathy for the "mixed-blood" tribal members after years of wrangling. They argued that termination "came as a voluntary request by the mixed blood members." Immediately after termination went into effect in 1961 the Ute tribal newspaper reported that "mixed-blood" members' reactions were mixed—from resignation, to "elation," to being "bitter at being classed as an ordinary white man." The story added, "A few were hoping that the termination could be overruled and the Indian rights restored in view of the announced policy of Secretary Udall that termination as a policy for Indians will no longer be pursued."[72] This change in policy, of course, came too late for the "mixed-blood" Utes, as the "full-bloods" had kicked them out of the tribe and the Ute Partition Act had already become law.

The "mixed-blood" protests continued to the end of 1961 when a General Council meeting devolved into disunity over efforts of the Affiliated Ute Citizens who had been cut out of the tribe to have Francis McKinley removed from the Business Council. Tribal leaders again evinced little sympathy for those who had been terminated. "Harvey Natches, Chairman of the Tribal Council, said that . . . the meeting probably was inspired by malcontents from the Affiliated Utes who were now going through the throes of living as private citizens."[73] But the "mixed-blood" noncitizens of the tribe were by then powerless in tribal affairs.

Most of the "mixed-blood" Utes were devastated financially both before and immediately after their formal termination in August 1961 despite receiving a share of the judgment money and the forest. This occurred through the contrivance of their own attorney and bureau officials. As R. Warren Metcalf put it, "It seemed that Senator Watkins's objective had been realized at last: these Utah Indians vanished into the mainstream of American life, many of them to become welfare recipients or to take menial jobs in the unfamiliar urban centers of the West." In fact, most were cheated out of both their rangeland and cattle and their annual income from oil and gas revenues. They were even cheated out of judgment money that was finally awarded in 1963 in another successful Indian Claims Commission lawsuit. They had sold shares in the latter to stave off poverty. Non-Indian purchasers benefitted.[74] Ironically, the termination of the "mixed-blood" Utes was pushed through when the tribe received $18 million dollars in judgment funds and then they were frozen out of the next infusion of cash, at the same time as they lost their ability to be self-sufficient.

At the same time, Watkins and others in Congress targeted the "full-blood" Utes for termination, albeit more slowly. When the partition bill was sent to the full Senate, committee members made it clear that they supported the Interior department's plan to include termination in the ten-year development plan for those remaining in the tribe.[75] The law itself said that the development plan was to be written "with a view of eventually terminating all Federal supervision of the tribe and its members."[76] However, neither the Department of the Interior nor Congress pursued this termination as they shifted away from supporting that policy in the 1960s.

Shortly after passage of the 1954 termination bills, Montana representative Lee Metcalf expressed anger and frustration at being misled into believing that tribal nations had supported termination when in fact they had not.[77] As with the Menominee and the Klamath, the Utes' desires were misrepresented by the secretary of the Interior's office to the congressional committees recommending approval of the termination acts. Tribal leaders did *not* propose termination, they proposed getting control of their assets. At the behest of Watkins and allies of his within the BIA, tribal leaders were willing to resolve a long-standing intratribal conflict by forcing "mixed-blood" members out of the tribe. For the Utes this meant an $18 million judgment, and the price was a forced, partial termination. Congress initially intended a full termination of all tribal members' relationships with the United States but in the end settled for the partial termination that shut "mixed-blood" members out of the tribal realm. Unlike the Menominee and the Klamath tribal nations, the "mixed-blood" Utes never regained tribal membership or federal recognition.

The Utes were not the only tribe whose land losses would lead to a termination fight. The Colville tribes in Washington state would face a similar conflict when they tried to get lands that had been illegally taken from them returned.

CHAPTER 9

The Confederated Tribes of the Colville Reservation

> The Act [Public Law 772] was negotiated after 7 years of extreme duress and pressure. The Colville Tribe was apprehensive that they would not ever get their lands back.
>
> —Affiliated Tribes of Northwest Indians Resolution #9 draft, October 1971

> Factionalism can be bad for communities, but I refuse to give that word power over the Colvilles when outsiders—be they scholars or members of other tribes—use it as a theoretical critique of our identity.
>
> —Laurie Arnold, *Bartering with the Bones of Their Dead*

The story of the Colville termination efforts is unique and has been well told by Sinixt Band of Colville Confederated Tribes historian Laurie Arnold in her book *Bartering with the Bones of Their Dead.*[1] Deep divisions among members of the tribes living on and off the Colville reservation in Washington state caused great turmoil from the 1950s into the 1970s as the Colvilles debated whether to accept or reject termination. Many of the supporters and the opponents of termination desired greater control of their funds and resources, though they differed sharply on the extent to which that control should be through the tribal entity under the protection of federal trust versus in the hands of individuals. This conflict provided a wedge that U.S. officials would try to exploit and would lead to a congressional bill requiring the Colvilles to develop a termination plan.

The Colville tribal division dated to the early reservation years. Eight separate bands were initially assigned to the Colville reservation when it was established in 1872, and four more were added over the years.[2] These communities thought and acted autonomously and responded to the loss of land resources in different ways. It was not until 1938 that the Colvilles established a confederated tribal government. They did so after rejecting the Indian Reorganization Act. Tribal members clearly desired home rule. They wanted the Office of Indian Affairs to get out of the tribes' business.[3] By establishing a government that was not under the auspices of the IRA, they hoped to join together to accomplish that end but still retain U.S. trust protections. But their unity remained fractured, and a unified tribal vision of the future did not coalesce. This gave Congress the opportunity to further divide the Colville tribes as it would refuse to return taken lands without consideration of termination.

TAKEN LANDS

In large part both the confederated tribes' and federal efforts to push for termination hinged on the Colville tribes' demand for the return of lost reservation lands. Unfortunately for the confederated Colville tribes, the federal government had blackmailed them long before, and that was the origin of the postwar termination debate. Their reservation, established in eastern Washington by executive order in 1872, originally stretched from the Canadian border in the north to the Columbia River in the south and east, with the Okanogan River establishing its western boundary. In 1892 Congress passed a law taking more than 1.5 million acres of the land—over one half of the total reservation holdings, referred to as "the northern half." This land was placed in the public domain and opened to non-Indian homesteading and settlement.[4]

The tribes were to be compensated for this land from the money paid by white settlers who claimed it. The amount due the tribes from the sales totaled $1.5 million. In 1905 James McLaughlin (known for having ordered the arrest of Sitting Bull that led to his death in 1890), then an

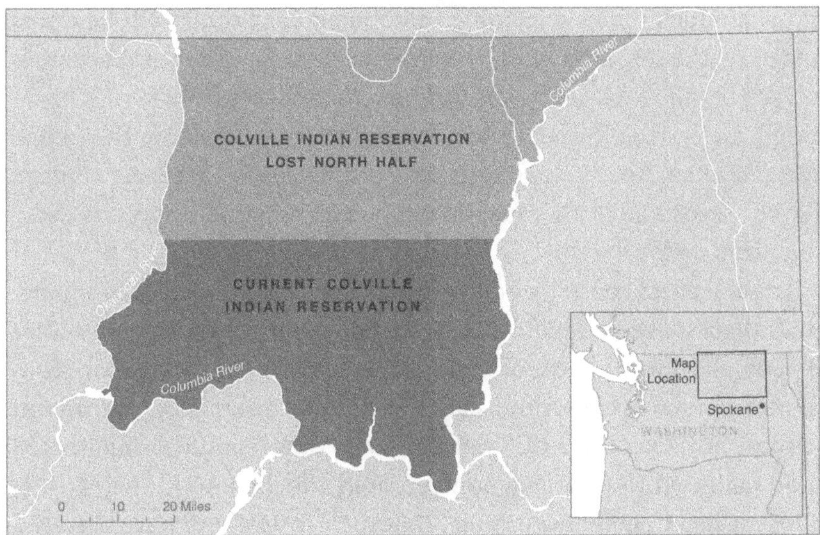

Map 10. Colville Reservation, Washington, showing the north half. Courtesy Aileen Clarke.

Indian Inspector in the Department of the Interior, told tribal members they would receive their money only if they agreed to allot the southern portion of the reservation—that is, divide it into individual plots for tribal members. They would also have to open the leftover unallotted lands to non-Indian settlement. A significant portion of tribal adults signed this agreement with McLaughlin.[5] Congress never paid the tribes for the northern portion of the reservation, which thus was stolen by the United States.[6] In essence, they were not bribed with their own money in this case; they were bribed with the *promise* of obtaining their own money, which never came to them. This loss of the North Half of the reservation served as a catalyst for future battles between the tribes and the federal government over return of lost lands. It would also bring the tribes to the brink of termination.

The McLaughlin agreement allotted almost three hundred thousand acres of land to individual tribal members in the southern portion of the "diminished reservation" as it came to be called. In addition, nearly a quarter million acres were lost there to outside non-Indian settlers. The status of much of the remaining 818,000 acres of south-half land was frozen by the Department of the Interior in the mid-1930s. The tribes worked in the 1930s and 1940s for the return of these lands, which was complicated since the tribes had refused to organize under the Indian Reorganization Act.[7] As we saw in the Menominee case, the Indian bureau did not accord non-IRA tribal governments the same respect as those organized under the IRA.

Tribal leaders correctly believed that they were tricked into signing away their southern land rights in exchange for the money they were already owed for the loss of their northern lands. In 1949 tribal council members articulated this claim in a report asking for restoration of those 818,000 acres of southern lands that remained unpatented and unallotted to trust and confederated tribal control. They wrote, "Present-day Colville leaders feel that their forefathers were betrayed by the government probably through erroneous interpretation when Mr. James McLaughlin negotiated the agreement of December 1, 1905, when it was stipulated that payment for the north half was contingent on the Indians signing away additional portions of their diminished land base."[8] This foreshadows the method used in case after case a half century later when federal officials used moneys already owed to tribes in an effort to push termination on them. Tribal leaders seeking to regain control of and payment for their lands referred to them as "the Colvilles most priceless possession."[9] Laurie Arnold called the losses "the single most distressing event in Colville history."[10]

Washington representative Don Magnuson would later succinctly describe the basis of the conflict that would consume the tribes for decades: "By departmental executive orders of 1934–35, the unsettled and unallotted land in the southern half of the reservation was withdrawn from public entry, and has remained in this uncertain status to the present day. This is the approximately 818,000 acres which [a proposed restoration bill] would restore to tribal ownership."[11]

In their 1949 report Colville leaders also argued that a sound economic future based in ranching and timber practices could only occur if the taken lands within the reservation boundaries were returned to tribal control. Significant chunks of land were necessary for both ranching and timber if either was to be a path to economic independence. Individual allotments had been too small to be successful. “It seems rather obvious that since 160 and 320-acre tracts did not prove to be successful operating units amongst the [non-Indigenous] homesteaders, that Indian allotments of 80 and 160 acres would prove to be less so,” they pointed out.[12]

The leadership concluded, “The restoration of these lands to tribal ownership will insure permanence to the prosperous communities built up around the timber resources, the range resources, the agricultural resources, the recreational resources and the potential mining possibilities.” They added, “It is the Colvilles most priceless possession, their heritage, their hope. May it be restored to give the present generation and generations to come the needed opportunity for progressive self-development.”[13]

Long before the phrase “land back” was popularized, Indigenous leaders across the United States sought in a variety of ways to regain lost lands and resources. This included aboriginal territories lost outside of reservation borders and land within reservations. Throughout much of the twentieth century the confederated Colville tribes expended an inordinate amount of political energy in an effort to regain control of the majority of their lands within the reservation boundaries. The federal government simply held these lands in limbo. The glaring failures of the federal trust responsibility created poverty, insecurity, and anger among community members who merely wanted the opportunity to develop a sustainable economic, social, and cultural system with the abundant resources that had been unjustly taken from them.

The Colville frustrations with lack of control over the resources they still controlled can be seen in a 1946 conflict they had with non-Indian fishermen over the use of their lakes. The Colville tribes lost much of their fish resource with the building of the Grand Coulee Dam. Prior to that they had been able to catch enough Columbia River salmon to last the year, according to a member of the tribes’ game committee. In an effort to procure revenue, the Indian bureau convinced them to let white sport fishermen use Lakes Buffalo and McGinnis for two-dollar tribal permits. But the white fishermen did not want to pay and regularly trespassed on tribal waters.[14]

Fig. 11. Colville men fishing from wooden platforms built over the rocks at Kettle Falls WA, before the Grand Coulee Dam flooded and destroyed the fishing site. Northwest Museum of Arts and Culture, neg. no. L93–75.31.

"We Indians on the game committee look at it this way our fish and game on this reservation is our food not sport," the committee member wrote. Fish had long been a staple food source for the Colvilles. The tribe attempted to get funding to create their own fish farm, but instead the state took over responsibility for stocking the fish in the reservation lakes.[15] The

Fig. 12. Colville women at Kettle Falls WA in 1939, smoking salmon over fire at the "Ceremony of Tears," which was held in commemoration of the salmon and salmon habitat to be lost when the area was flooded by the building of the Grand Coulee Dam. Northwest Museum of Arts and Culture, neg. no. L95–80.1.

non-Indian sporting community in Spokane Washington was incensed by the tribes' efforts to control tribal waters. A local attorney offered free legal services to any white man arrested by the tribal police for illegal fishing. The state officials clearly sided with the non-Indians. The Spokane *Spokesman Review* reported that "Game officials recently, in Spokane, made the statement that if the 'Indians persist in this action, the state game department will not plant another fish in the reservation lakes.'"[16]

Indian bureau officials stated that they would do what they could to protect the tribes' rights.[17] This must not have been much of a comfort to the tribes, however. "What the white man wants He always gets," a tribal game committee member glumly concluded.[18] The bureau more often obscured tribal rights than upheld them, violating its trust responsibility. Shortly after this the Indian bureau again attempted to exert control over the Colvilles.

Commissioner of Indian Affairs Dillon Myer tried to wrest authority over attorney contracts from tribal nations across the country, beginning in November 1950. One of his primary targets in this effort was James Curry, who represented the Colville tribes in a claims case. The Colville protested this action in a January 1951 press release.[19] Myer had disapproved the Colville attorney contract because the tribe paid fees to Curry, and Myer insisted that attorneys in claims cases could only be paid by contingency in the event that they won the cases. Former Interior secretary, Harold Ickes, protested this ruling to current secretary of the Interior Oscar Chapman, who overruled Myer and let Curry continue as the attorney for the Colville claim.[20]

At the same time, Colville members were strongly divided on whether the council should purchase lands for the tribe or, as a minority hoped, dissolve the tribal body and pay the tribal funds to individuals. The Business Council, following recommendations of the General Council, vehemently opposed per capita payments to individual tribal members. A 1952 statement reads, "The Colville Business Council has expressed strong opposition to this enforced liquidation of tribal assets for the reason that this liquidation would have a very adverse affect [*sic*] on the tribe in general by weakening the economic structure of the tribal program on the reservation." At the same time, both the General Council and the Business Council strongly opposed all so-called "'emancipation' bills" before Congress.[21]

On the other side, a nonelected group calling themselves the Colville Indian Commercial Club directly lobbied Congress for per capita payments and dissolution of the Indian bureau. They opposed existing legislation. They wrote that it gave "the so-called '*governing body*' of our Reservation and the National Congress of American Indians and the Indian Bureau [the opportunity] to continue to spend and dissipate our money for matters that will only disrupt our progress as American Citizens." They were especially upset that the tribe was buying back land and putting it into the tribal estate. "We are Individualists—and don't want any Communistic ownership of land on our Reservation," they told Congress. "We want to be American Citizens under the United States Constitution and not under the Wheeler-Howard Act of 1934."[22] They failed to recognize that the tribes had rejected the Wheeler Howard Act, which was also known as the Indian Reorganization Act. At any rate, this division foreshadowed the political split that would divide the tribes over the next two decades.

This dispute spilled over into a fierce debate over opening the southern half of the reservation to mineral development in the early 1950s. The Commercial Club met with local non-Indian groups and convinced them that the tribes supported this mining venture. Local non-Indian interests worked with these "independent Indians" rather than with the tribal government. The Business Council opposed opening the southern portion of the reservation to mining—not because they opposed mineral development but because they did not want it to occur until their "frozen" southern lands were returned to their control. At that point development could be managed legally by the tribe on those lands.[23]

Laurie Arnold determined that from 1953 to 1972 tribal members organized between four and six pro- and anti-termination committees that "operated at any given time."[24] By 1954 one, the Colville Indian Association (CIA) was established by dissident members of the tribes. The association was organized as a protermination entity to protect individual interests in the tribal estate and would hold together for more than a decade.[25] They described themselves this way: "We shall not willingly submit to the narrow bondage of tribalism." They likened this "to a living death for the pleasure of fossil hunters and museum builders," and "to being embalmed with a dead culture [and] to be entombed in a dead era."[26]

This is how they described their focus: "We are not in opposition with the Colville Business Council if, they will handle our business efficiently. The purpose of this organization is to keep the business council in line in managing the business of the Colville Indian Tribe and to eliminate the unnecessary dissipation of tribal funds, which has resulted in the past with no benefit to the tribe."[27] The commissioner of Indian affairs's office described them as "a political faction within the Confederated Tribes of the Colville Reservation," which "is vociferous in its opposition against the Colville Business Council, which is the official tribal governing body."[28]

The bureau was careful to deal with the official governing body of the tribes, while the CIA tried to gain traction for termination by appealing to their U.S. senator. The proterminationists also went to the new secretary of the Interior, and they said "Mr. [Fred] Seaton assured us that he would give consideration to the Colville Indian Association as representative of the people of this tribe."[29] In the following years more pro- and anti-termination groups organized themselves, and a complicated and heated debate broke out among tribal members both on and off the reservation.[30]

The CIA referred to official tribal leadership as "the Bureau supervised Council." CIA president Thomas Edwards argued, "The Bureau of Indian Affairs through many years of ruling has been able to present an image of a supposed Tribe while at the same time completely obscuring the fact that the true situation is that of having an Indian Estate being held in trust for its heirs." One of the key problems, the CIA believed, was the way the bureau handled their estate: "The Bureau of Indian Affairs has erred in its handling of our estate. It has brought about an unjust situation." They thought that this locked them out of access to benefits from their resources.[31] The Colville Business Council pushed for restoration of southern lands that could be used for economic development; the CIA members wanted them liquidated.

Underlying the conflict was an effort by the confederated tribes to have the lost lands on the diminished reservation returned. The effort came to be called restoration.[32] A land restoration bill was stymied in the Senate even after passing the House on more than one occasion. Montana Representative Lee Metcalf observed, "when the bill to restore lands was before Congress, the Indian Bureau put in a contingency. The Bureau refused to consent to the restoration until the Colville Indians had submitted an agreement for termination."[33] The Senate Committee on Interior and Insular Affairs under the leadership of Hugh Butler of Nebraska also insisted that termination be tied to the bill. The restoration bill, Public Law 772, would pass in 1956 but include termination. Unfortunately, this was still at the height of the termination era.

RESTORATION AND THE BATTLE OVER TERMINATION

In February 1954 an attorney for the confederated Colville tribes wrote to Senator Henry Jackson, seeking support for the south-half Colville restoration bill. "The bill has passed the House twice but we have never had very much luck with Senator Butler and, perhaps more importantly, his cohort, Albert Grorud, on the Senate Committee staff," he said. Grorud, in what was clearly a conflict of interest, served as an attorney for the protermination Colville Indian Association. Since the bill was not getting through the Senate, the Colvilles offered to provide financial support to Ferry and Okanogan counties, in which they lived.[34] They hoped this would cause county officials to support the restoration effort. The offer of aid to the counties would cause conflict with other tribes.[35] Jackson responded that he would do what he could to "jar it [the bill] loose from the Committee."[36] He was unsuccessful.

In June 1954 Washington congressman Walt Horan met with the general membership of the confederated tribes and told them "that he doubted that Congress would pass a bill that did not include some kind of termination provision tied to restoration."[37] By August it was clear that the restoration bill was being held hostage. Late in the month the Business Council held a "Special Session" to discuss the restoration and termination. Several council members recognized at that meeting that Congress would not approve restoration of the lands without including termination as part of the bargain. Council member Steve Cleveland conceded that if a majority of tribal members supported adding termination to the restoration bill but that Colville would still "retain their hunting and fishing rights, water rights, and other rights and privileges," he would support legislation to bring that about. But Cleveland personally opposed dissolution of those rights because he felt they "should be retained in perpetuity."[38]

Cleveland's view of what termination should look like differed significantly from federal perspectives and those of tribal members who simply wanted to end the tribal relationship altogether. To him the Colvilles' rights as Indians remained paramount. This reflected a view across Indian country that the federal trust responsibility remained foundational to tribal rights in the modern world and must continue, even if Congress forced termination.

Cleveland was right. The Supreme Court would later rule in one of the most high profile termination cases—that of the Menominee Indian Tribe of Wisconsin—that tribal members had retained their treaty rights even as they had lost much of their political relationship with the United

States.[39] It may have been difficult for federal officials in the 1950s and 1960s to envision continuation of separate Indigenous rights after termination, but tribal leaders could and did envision the continuation of Indigenous trust rights and federal responsibilities.

As historian Laurie Arnold has suggested, Colville members increasingly viewed termination as inevitable. They viewed restoration as the far more significant part of pending legislation than the termination that was attached to it.[40] Though the Colville people wanted more control over their resources, and some pushed hard for full elimination of the trust relationship, others were reticent. Agency superintendent Floyd Phillips, at an April 1, 1955, meeting in the BIA's Portland Area Office, "stated that there had been fear instilled in the hearts of the people in that they had to take termination with restoration."[41]

At another meeting council member George Friedlander suggested that the tribe could be split; that those who wanted to be bought out could get their share of funds and leave the tribe, and that those who wanted to retain tribal rights under the trust relationship could remain. James White, the tribal chairman, observed that Friedlander was talking about liquidation of a portion of the tribal resource, but that this could not be done since that part of the reservation had not been surveyed.[42]

At the April 1955 meeting in Portland, tribal leaders told Area Director Don Foster that the tribes' official position was "that no termination legislation be tied to or connected with the Restoration Bill." Tribal Business Council leaders said, "They do not want to accept termination in order to have restored the controversial lands." The Colville would also agree to begin negotiating with the BIA "looking forward to eventual release of all Bureau of Indian Affairs controls."[43]

This would take the decision away from Congress and put the tribes in a position where they were at least at the bargaining table. "Release" of "controls" could be interpreted in a broad variety of ways, but leaders agreed to discuss ways to bring legislation "for eventual release from Bureau of Indian Affairs controls." But they did not want to be bribed into doing it.[44]

Business Council vice chairman Glen Whitelaw stated the tribes' position clearly at the Portland meeting. "I would like to see restoration introduced without termination attached." Many Colville tribal members wanted to avoid the type of experience the Menominee Indian Tribe of Wisconsin faced with their disastrous termination legislation. Area Director Foster himself feared a repeat of the Klamath termination fiasco—the Klamath also were under his jurisdiction.[45] He was caught between unbridled support for termination from Congress and the BIA central office in DC and his knowledge of actual impacts based on his experiences and observations. Both the Menominee and the Klamath had been terminated in the first wave of termination legislation. Now, within a year, the glaring deficiencies in the legislation had become apparent, even before those terminations went into effect. Even tribes that were comparatively well-off, financially, were vastly unprepared to be released from federal trust, and both the Business Council and Foster recognized this.

The situation was complicated by congressional intransigence. Tribal leaders believed that if it were up to him, Congressman Horan would bring a stand-alone restoration bill. But he was under pressure from the House Interior committee to include termination.

In this case, the local BIA was not on the same page as Congress, or even the BIA central office in DC. Foster suggested that the Colville try to gain restoration before they considered termination. He supported the idea of termination—but separate from restoration and at a later date. He suggested these issues be addressed in two separate bills. But he pulled back on the plan to separate termination from restoration when he was told that Horan did not think a restoration bill would pass Congress if it did not include provisions for termination.[46]

At an April 18, 1955, meeting the tribal Business Council passed Resolution 1955–33, in which it agreed to develop a termination plan.[47] This paved the way for federal legislation that the Colville people hoped would restore their lost reservation lands. This legislation now had three components: a modicum of land restoration on the existing reservation, an annual payment from the confederated tribes to the two counties on which their reservation sat, and termination.

In May Representative Horan introduced a new restoration bill in the House. It included a section calling for the Colville tribes to develop a termination plan within five years. Representative Magnuson introduced a competing restoration bill that summer which did not include the termination section. These bills were referred to the Committee on Interior and Insular Affairs, which sought an opinion from the BIA central office. Assistant Secretary of the Interior Orme Lewis penned and forwarded the bureau's views to committee chair Clair Engle of California.[48]

In his response Lewis, a strong advocate of terminations, wrote that the confederated tribes had been deemed "one of the more advanced Indian groups in the country" by Zimmerman in his 1947 report. He added that the bureau had held termination discussions for several years with the Colville tribes and called for a tribal vote "to agree to the commitment" to termination "before the restoration of the ceded lands [became] effective."[49]

The committee met in March 1956 to consider the legislation. The two House bills represented "two different philosophies" in the words of one committee member. Another, Lee Metcalf of Montana, told the full committee that the subcommittee recommended putting Magnuson's bill forward without the termination clause. The idea behind this was twofold. First, the main purpose of the bill was to "restore lands that we all agree in equity and good conscience belong to the Colville Indians, and should be restored to them." Second, the tribe could develop plans for termination or not at a later date. He added, "My objection to this sort of legislation is that it is making a condition of restoring this land an obligation to plan for termination."[50]

By 1956 Metcalf recognized that he and other congressmen had been duped into believing that tribes had supported termination bills when that was not true. After this he argued regularly for federal support of tribal needs rather than for termination.[51]

Congressman Wayne Aspinall of Colorado observed that the Horan bill merely requested the confederated tribes to develop a termination plan. He added, "If they do not, there is no penalty attached." Others disagreed with both Metcalf and Aspinall. Washington Representative Jack Westland argued that the Colville tribes wanted termination to be part of the bill. The argument, then, turned to whether to amend the bill to include a section calling for a tribal vote to accept termination before it became law. Metcalf argued here that including all three parts of the bill—the restoration of land, the termination plan, and the payments to the two counties—would make the intentions of tribal members unclear regarding termination, since they might cast their votes primarily based on restoration. In the end, the committee accepted Horan's bill virtually unchanged, without the amendment calling for a tribal vote on termination, and sent it to the floor for approval.[52]

Four months after the hearings, in July 1956, Congress passed Public Law 772, which provided for restoration of the 818,000 acres of reservation lands "to tribal ownership to be held in trust by the United States to the same extent as all other tribal lands on the existing reservation." The bill also required (though not "requested" as Aspinall had suggested) the tribes to draft a termination plan within five years. Respected tribal member Paschal Sherman observed that it did not require the tribes to terminate.[53] It did, however, require the Colville tribes to send a bill to Congress; that is, to develop termination legislation. Section five of the law reads, "The Business Council of the Confederated Tribes of the Colville Reservation shall, in accordance with resolution numbered 1955–33, dated April 8, 1955, of the Colville Business Council, submit to the Secretary of the Interior within five years from the date of enactment of this Act proposed legislation providing for the termination of Federal supervision over the property and affairs of the Confederated Tribes and their members within a reasonable time after the submission of such proposed legislation."[54]

By the mid-1960s members of Congress and Interior department officials were increasingly reticent to support termination legislation. But the Colville fight continued. As was the case for other tribes contemplating termination, the Menominee experience served as a cautionary tale. But different people took different lessons from it. At the same time as the 89th Congress considered a Colville termination bill, Congress had a bill to provide significant aid to Menominee County, since Menominee tribal members had been impoverished and their welfare was no longer a BIA responsibility. The newly created Menominee County was the poorest in Wisconsin. Where federal aid to the Menominee had ranged from $20,000 to $70,000 annually prior to termination, it ballooned to nearly $2 million a year in state and federal aid during the first decade after termination.[55]

Congress recognized some of the mistakes it had made with the Menominee. Senate staffer James Gamble, for example, opposed a per capita payment the Colvilles had requested in 1963 since they would need the money to pay for a mineral survey in preparation for termination. "Congress learned in the Menominee situation . . . that it is very unwise to make per capita payments in advance of a final agreed-upon terminal plan," Gamble told Senator Jackson.[56] The per capita payments, however, were a major motivating factor for many of those tribal members who supported termination.

The next year, in 1964, the Colville Indian Association urged the U.S. Senate to provide a $350 per capita payment from timber funds. Marcel Arcasa of the CIA argued that over a ten-year period individual Indians had received "not even as much as a dime." He said, "We have never had an accounting of the proceeds from those large sales to this day." He also urged rapid termination "before the Indian Bureau dissipates the total [tribal] assets."[57] Thomas Edwards, president of the CIA, reminded James Haley, chair of the House subcommittee on Indian Affairs, that Public Law 772 called "for termination of Feederal [*sic*] supervision over the property and affairs of the Colville Indians."[58] On the other hand, a BIA study showed an annual payroll of $4 million to Indian loggers working in the forest, with the potential for that to increase significantly.[59]

In June 1965 Secretary of the Interior Stewart Udall wrote to the House committee considering Colville termination and warned the congressmen that Colville problems were similar to those the Menominee faced. The Senate had passed a Colville termination bill in 1964, but it had not made it through the House. Udall wrote, "If this bill is enacted into law and the referendum is affirmative, the annual income will be replaced by the distribution of a substantial sum in cash. The cash hunger of poor people is great, and the cash for many of them will not last long. At that point the welfare costs to Okanogan and Ferry Counties will begin to mount. Just as they have for Menominee County there will be a demand for State and Federal welfare aids."[60] Termination, it turned out, was more costly to the U.S. treasury than simply fulfilling its trust responsibilities.

In a House Indian Affairs subcommittee meeting in January 1966, when discussion of a Colville termination bill resumed, Representative

John Saylor of Pennsylvania instead turned the discussion to the problems that the Menominee faced in their termination and suggested that the committee begin to deal with those issues.[61] Congress was tiring of paying for and fixing problems caused by terminations. Just as the Seneca Nation termination bill died in Congress in 1967, so did efforts to terminate the Colville tribes in the 1960s.

None of the Colville termination bills brought to Congress passed. The Colville factions wrangled over whether to terminate for almost two decades, until an anti-termination tribal council was elected. That council finally put the issue to rest, and the tribes moved on, retaining their political relationship with the federal government.[62]

Laurie Arnold writes that "fervent disagreement" among tribal members "and refusal to compromise on the withdrawal process are ultimately what saved the Colvilles from termination." She adds, "What began as a simple hope, [land] restoration . . . , created unprecedented tribal turmoil from which the tribe still has not fully recovered."[63]

It is tempting to say that because the tribes initiated the effort to tie restoration of their lost land to termination, federal officials cannot be accused of bribing the Colvilles. But on the other hand, as with other tribes, many Colvilles believed that termination was inevitable. Their representative in Congress, Walt Horan, reinforced this when he told them those outcomes needed to be coupled. This led many to believe that the only path to restoration of the lost lands was, at the minimum, to plan for termination. In this belief they were probably right. In fact, the restoration law required that the tribes initiate and Congress consider a termination bill. But it did not require that Congress pass that bill into law.

As in 1905 the Colville tribes were asked to give up a significant portion of their rights in order to regain something that they never should have lost—in this case *the very same thing* that they had previously lost and never been paid for. And even after the bill became law the Colvilles had to continue to fight for decades to be compensated for their lost lands.[64] They were bribed with their own money *twice* and, even after feeling compelled to begrudgingly accept the bribes, both times gave up rights without receiving the promised compensation.

As with the Three Affiliated Tribes in North Dakota and the Seneca Nation of Indians, the Colvilles witnessed their resources and land used as bait to trap them into accepting termination. And as with those tribal nations, they avoided termination. But the merciless onslaught from Congress, with the aid of the BIA and the Department of the Interior, caused deep turmoil in already difficult circumstances. All three of these Indigenous groups faced their greatest disaster and challenge of the twentieth century. By avoiding termination they were spared what would have been significantly more destructive future challenges. Other tribal nations, including the Menominee, the Klamath, and a portion of the Utes, were not so fortunate. All had to battle against seemingly insurmountable odds to chart a viable future even while they were refused the opportunity to determine it for themselves. Instead, they saw their fates tied to accepting federal initiatives in order for Congress to release their own resources or money to them.

Conclusion

The Lasting Specter of Termination

> The United States of America, alleged champion of self-determination and democracy.
>
> —Jonathan Kamakawiwoʻole Osorio, introduction of Cornel West, Piʻo Summit 2022 Wai Sovereignty & Justice, Honolulu, December 15, 2022

> Every so often in the history of Indian affairs, two constant elements combine to form what the atomic scientists call a critical mass, resulting in an explosion. These elements are the ever-watchful group that desires to plunder what remains of the Indian estate, and the ignorant but well-intentioned, would-be friends of the Indians.
>
> —Oliver La Farge to Board of Directors and Executive Director, AAIA, August 7, 1953

> Throughout the history of the Indian trust relationship, we have recognized that the organization and management of the trust is a sovereign function subject to the plenary authority of Congress.
>
> —Justice Samuel Alito, *United States v. Jicarilla Apache Nation*, 2011

The long history of federal abuse of the funds belonging to Indigenous nations is deeply rooted in official misinterpretation of the federal trust responsibility as a license to control the lives of Indigenous people and the resources and destiny of Indigenous nations. A large part of the misinterpretation is due to the belief of members of Congress, bureaucrats, and the judiciary that Indian interests and resources must be sacrificed for U.S. policy goals, regardless of what Indigenous people have desired or what has been in the best interest of their communities' futures.

"The [federal] Government has often structured the trust relationship to pursue its own policy goals," Justice Samuel Alito observed in a 2011 Supreme Court decision. He adds that, "while trust administration 'relat[es] to the welfare of the Indians, the maintenance of the limitations which Congress has prescribed as a part of its plan of distribution is distinctly an interest of the United States.'"[1] In fact, Alito does not go far enough in this statement. The interest of the United States has often been the overriding feature of its application of trust responsibilities.

Both Congress and the Indian bureau share the responsibility for the misinterpretation of the trust responsibility and the abuse of tribal funds. The role of Congress is paramount in Indian affairs, but the Department of the Interior was charged with carrying out congressional dictates in the 1940s through 1960s. They worked hand in hand at times, separately at other times, to get out of the Indian business.

Congress passed the laws, and Senate staffer James Gamble reminded senators on the Interior and Insular Affairs committee to keep in mind that "the source of Indian policy is the United States Congress and *not* the Bureau of Indian Affairs. . . . The Bureau is to carry out Congressional policy."[2] This friction was embedded in a larger struggle in which Congress has tried "to protect its own centrality and prevent the bureaucracy from dominating, even marginalizing, the role of the legislative branch."[3]

The BIA pushed the policy ahead following the lead of its commissioners. At times the commissioners took orders from the secretary of the Interior. In the end both members of Congress and Interior department bureaucrats shaped and enacted Indian policy. Oftentimes they worked together. They generally kept each other informed of their actions. And both were responsible for the bribery and attempted bribery to coerce termination. In this way they followed in a long line of individuals who resorted to underhanded means to gain access to the Indians' estate.

At the same time, very few members of Congress exhibited interest in Indian affairs. And so the primacy of power embedded in the Interior and Indian affairs committees and subcommittees was especially potent in that era. American Indian leaders learned this, much to their dismay. When Seneca Nation officials lobbied Senate Interior and Insular Affairs committee members over proposed Indian Affairs subcommittee changes to the compensation bill for the Kinzua Dam in 1964, they were told outright, to their consternation, that the committee rarely made decisions overturning subcommittee recommendations.[4]

Thus a small group of congressional members, together with a handful of Indian bureau officials brought in to radically change Indian policy, were able to begin an all-out assault on dozens of Indigenous nations in the 1940s and 1950s to little national fanfare. And early on they were able to use what Walter Lippman referred to as "manufacture of consent," in essence unchallenged propaganda, to convince congressional colleagues and the press that the politics of termination represented freedom or emancipation for Indian people.[5]

The policy called for a liquidation of not only tribal governments and their relations with the United States but also the Indian estate, since there would be no tribal political entity to manage it and no federal trust protections for it. In addition, the policy aimed for rapid assimilation of American Indians into both local white communities that were hostile to Indians and a nationalist American identity that did not include their tribal heritage. This policy reflected a modern version of Richard Henry Pratt's dictum to "kill the Indian and save the man." In order to understand the role of bribery in the termination years, it is valuable to remind ourselves of the breadth of the postwar Indian policy initiatives. Not all the tribes that were terminated were bribed with their own money, and not all diminishment of federal policy was carried out with direct terminations. Bribery to bring about termination was one—but not the only—tactic used by federal officials.

The relinquishment of federal responsibility came quickly in a number of venues in the 1950s. Public Law 280 transferred jurisdiction from federal to state authorities in five states and Alaska. The BIA closed hospitals in tribal communities, farming out the Indian patients to local hospitals.[6] Indian Health Services was moved from the BIA to the U.S. Public Health Service in 1955. A similar effort was made for the bureau to get out of the work of educating Indian children and turning them over to local public schools.[7] Some members of Congress proposed eliminating the Indian Claims Commission in 1956, while many tribes were still preparing their claims, though the Department of the Interior opposed this initiative.[8]

To a significant degree, termination was meant to alienate American Indian tribes from their land and resources. This ran in direct contradiction to what constitutional law professor Charles L. Black Jr. called "the paired life-bases of property and autonomy."[9] An example of how readily the loss of lands could occur is apparent in regulations governing sale of four thousand acres in twenty-one parcels at the Pine Ridge Reservation in South Dakota. In the summer of 1955 "invitations to bid on Indian Trust Land" were advertised on the reservation. The rules, in the words of one observer, were "so perfectly legal, democratic, and equal, and so absolutely in favor of the outsider." They read, in part, "No preference or right will be granted to the Oglala Sioux Tribe or any member thereof to meet the high bid. It will be necessary for any Indian who desires to acquire the tract to submit a bid at the time the land is advertised to the general public, and that in order to acquire the tract it will be necessary that his bid be the highest."[10] In the first two years that the termination law went into effect, 1953 and 1954, more than five thousand parcels of Indian trust land across the United States, amounting to some half million acres, went from trust to fee-patent status, taking federal protections away from Indigenous landholders.[11] Federal officials viewed this as a positive step toward termination.

Policy leaders in both the legislative and executive branch of the federal government believed that the best way to empower American Indians was by destroying communal forms of governance and enacting policy measures that ultimately diminished already crippled tribal economies. The purpose was to thrust Indigenous people into American society on an individualized basis. Some tribes slated for termination were spectacularly unprepared for the loss of their relationship with the federal government. The Confederated Tribes of Coos, Lower Umpqua, and Siuslaw Indians, included in the swath of western Oregon tribes that were terminated by a 1954 law, had $47.48 in their U.S. Treasury account.[12] They were certainly not bribed with their own money but nonetheless fell victim to an unwanted termination. The Seminole tribe of Florida, who were threatened with termination, were identified by bureau officials as 90 percent "full bloods," a euphemism for being ill prepared to participate in modern society. The AAIA described them as in no way ready for termination.[13] Mercifully they avoided it.

Once the terminations began, federal officials quickly learned what many tribal members already knew—that the process of the federal government divesting itself of its responsibilities to Indians was very complex. It was more complicated than federal officials had anticipated. This would have disastrous results for the tribes on the receiving end of the legislation.

Even the case of the termination of four small bands of Pauites in Utah, totaling just 177 individuals, proved beyond the bureau's capabilities to effectively manage. The Paiutes were subject to one of the six termination bills passed in 1954, and their termination went into effect in 1956. In the fall of 1957, Commissioner of Indian Affairs Glenn Emmons wrote a lengthy memo reflecting on lessons learned in this case. Both the Central Office and the BIA Area Office in Phoenix were derelict in following deadlines. Some blamed it on the lack of personnel assigned to tasks related to specific tribal terminations.[14]

With a flood of termination bills pouring through the bureau, officials were forced to respond to tribal concerns throughout the country. In the Paiute case, as in others, the Indians being terminated had even less information available to them than did bureau personnel. The commissioner's office lamented that, among the lessons learned was "the need for more detailed planning prior to the submission of any future termination bills as to the needs and desires of the Indians concerned and the actions . . . required."[15] This would prove to be too late for the tribes already undergoing termination and would not stop termination bills from coming before Congress.

When Oliver La Farge of the AAIA wrote to President Eisenhower in the fall of 1955 that he believed a "sense of disappointment, even dread" was sweeping Indian country, Secretary of the Interior Douglas McKay responded that reports from staff in the field "reflect a widespread and warm appreciation [among Indians] of the forward-looking programs that have been initiated and the positive results that have been achieved . . . during the past two years."[16] It would still be a long time before bureaucrats would admit publicly that the unfolding policy actions constituted an intensification of crisis rather than a solution to the ills affecting Indian country.

McKay also told La Farge, "I find it particularly difficult to understand what is meant by your statement that present policies have tended to worsen the situation in regard to Indian economy and 'the wellsprings of Indian initiative.' I know of no factual evidence whatever that would support this assertion."[17] Study after study would bear out La Farge's allegations, but the studies had not yet been made in 1955.

Despite the years of planning and analysis that were to determine the order in which tribes would be terminated, in the end the fate of many boiled down to a matter of luck. This was even the case for tribes subjected to bribery. The tribes in Utah, including the "mixed-blood" Utes, came early simply because their senator Arthur Watkins wanted to use his state as an example of the policy he was pushing so hard. The tribes in Oregon, including the Klamath, came early and ended up accounting for more than half of all tribes terminated under the policy because their former governor, Douglas McKay, ran the Department of the Interior and wanted *his* state to serve as an example of the policy's efficacy.[18]

In 1955 Commissioner of Indian Affairs Glenn Emmons tried to convince tribal leaders that they were involved in bureau decision-making. "Consultation is one of the fine policies of this administration. By talking things over here, whether there is agreement or not—but its [sic] not a healthy thing for the government to go along and do something and tell the Indians about it later."[19] But by then, Indigenous leaders knew better.

The "consultation" that the Menominee received from both Senator Watkins and the bureau was farcical and disingenuous. The senator nor the bureaucrats were interested in Menominee goals, or even their thoughts about the future. They simply wanted a rubber stamp of pre-determined policy initiatives. Not only did Watkins fail to consult with the Menominee, by refusing to have the critical decision-making meeting translated into the Menominee language, he did not even let tribal members know what they were agreeing to. And although state leaders in Wisconsin did not approach the idea of termination with the fervor of Watkins and McKay, neither did they oppose termination or support the Menominee. In several ways they actively worked against them. This stands in contrast to other cases.

Indigenous leaders dealt with the termination threat in various ways. The Three Affiliated Tribes at Fort Berthold and the Seneca Nation of Indians in New York, unlike the tribal nations in Utah, Oregon, and Wisconsin, gained support from statewide politicians in their opposition to the policy. They also decided to challenge federal officials differently. Martin Cross at Fort Berthold directly confronted bureau officials in refusing to tie termination to the per capita payment due for land takings in the building of Garrison Dam. The Menominee, while developing significant non-Indian allies, treated bureau officials with a traditional form of Indigenous nonconfrontational respect. This method of politics led, in part, to their termination.

In some cases where tribes were divided, a significant number of tribal members did support termination. The Colville, the Three Affiliated Tribes, the Klamath, and the Ute all suggested splitting their tribal entities, with some members remaining in the tribe and others being bought out. Neither the Colville nor the Three Affiliated Tribes divided their membership. The Klamath members who supported termination accepted cash to buy themselves out of the tribe, even though they were able to regain status later. The Utes who were terminated, on the other hand, were permanently pushed out of their tribe against their wishes by those who remained in it, in a way similar to modern disenrollment fights.

The six tribes targeted in these case studies all fell victim to bribery or attempted bribery because of rich natural resources that they either held or had lost. The Menominee and the Klamath had fought bitterly for control over their forests since the nineteenth century. The successful Menominee lawsuit, and the disgust at federal mismanagement within the Klamath community that caused a significant number of individuals to ask that they be paid cash for their forest, both paved the way for successful bribe attempts.

For the Three Affiliated Tribes and the Seneca Nation at Allegany, the loss of their best reservation lands to flooding was the catalyst for significant compensation packages for the taken lands. Though the bribe attempts that accompanied the appropriations legislation to pay for the takings failed, both groups were forced to spend an inordinate amount of time and energy fighting them off.

Taken lands that the United States never paid for were the basis of bribery attempts for the Utes and the Colvilles. The Utes met the crisis by dividing the tribe and forcing some members out of it. The Colvilles were too divided for any legislation to pass before Congress tired of terminating tribes, but they continue to deal with the loss of their North Half. In all these cases, though, federal officials clearly believed that bribery was a practical way to gain tribal support for termination legislation.

Bribery was clearly an official policy initiative that put immense pressure on those Indigenous nations to whom it was applied. In all the cases portrayed here, tribal leaders desperately attempted to gain political and economic control of their resources. With the Menominee, the Klamath, the Colville, and the Ute, this battle had been fought over several decades. The Seneca Nation of Indians and the Three Affiliated Tribes of Fort Berthold were hit with the bribery effort just as they were dealing with the most disastrous events they faced in the twentieth century. In all six of these cases the pressure was intense to make quick decisions that would have long-lasting impacts on their communities and future generations.

Many Indian individuals who supported termination echoed the language of home rule even if definitions of it varied. Frank Parker of the Shoshone Bannock tribe from Fort Hall, Idaho, for example, argued that it was time for "withdrawal" of federal meddling in Indian affairs. When federal officials used that term, they meant withdrawal of the federal trust responsibility. When Indians used that term, for the most part they meant withdrawal of paternalistic oversight that quashed tribal self-determination. Some, like Parker, also viewed termination as inevitable and believed that tribes must prepare for it as well as possible. "We are looking forward to the time when federal controls can be lifted," Parker said in 1954. He added, "Although the general feeling of the NCAI is that they do not want federal supervision withdrawn, many forward looking Indians realize it must come about."[20]

The meaning of terms like *withdrawal* and *relinquishment of federal control* was interpreted in vastly different ways by federal officials and Indigenous people. The Indian Office preferred using the term *withdrawal*, and Congress preferred the term *freedom*. Indians for the most part, however, viewed the federal definitions of *withdrawal* and *freedom* as synonymous with liquidation of land and resources and termination of federal responsibilities.[21] This is a prime example of Ngũgĩ Thiong'o's observation of the colonizer using language to control the colonized.[22] Unfortunately, although the Native definition would turn out to be more accurate, the federal definitions won out in the 1950s.

In 1955 National Congress of American Indians executive committee members hotly debated whether or not to support termination in cases where tribes themselves called for it. The organization opposed termination wholeheartedly, but some board members wondered whether that put NCAI at odds with its support of tribal self-determination.[23] The belief among some tribal leaders that termination was inevitable clouded the issue for Indian rights organizations. Early on, NCAI went on record in favor of termination where they believed that tribes themselves supported or proposed it. In a document outlining the successes and failures of the 83rd Congress, NCAI had listed all the termination bills—those that passed and those defeated—as successes.[24]

Even as the Indian bureau continued to carry out congressional directives and push the policy, congressional opposition to its own termination policy began to develop shortly after it passed the first wave of termination bills. In 1959 Montana senator James Murray proposed a law that would have stopped the termination process altogether. In the words of the National Congress of American Indians, Murray proposed "that no termination of federal trusteeship or services to Indians shall take place unless the tribes affected have full understanding of the proposed termination and until Indians are on a parity in health and education with other Americans."[25] Support for termination, though, was slow to die. Still, although Murray's bill was unsuccessful, Congress passed just one termination bill after 1959 and rejected others.

Though many terminated tribes have successfully fought to have their government-to-government relationship with the United States restored, HCR 108 has not been overturned. Termination is a threat that tribal communities have continued to face on a regular basis for the past half century. The mere thought of it strikes terror across Indian country and revives trauma intergenerationally within tribal communities.

In 1983 the 32-million-member American Farm Bureau Federation, with organizations in 2,800 counties in 48 states, lobbied for "abolition of special treaty rights" in a bill that would "end special treaty rights and bring everyone under the full equality of the law." According to a tribal newspaper published in Sault Ste. Marie, Michigan, "The bill would end collective ownership of tribal land, prevent legal relief in the Court of Claims for land and water rights, . . . and close down the BIA itself." The article's headline read, "Termination is genocide."[26]

Though there was not much support for this at the federal level, for the past four decades, well-organized antitreaty and antitribal groups have pushed to end the federal trust responsibility toward Indigenous nations under the banner of equality for all. They argue that treaty rights are special rights that should not be accorded to Indian nations. Some of these organizations were behind the violent protests against tribal fishing rights in the 1980s and 1990s, and they continue their efforts today.[27]

Occasionally politicians and policymakers take up this battle, couching their language in terms eerily similar to that of the 1950s—freedom, equality, and emancipation. Recently the idea of termination was floated in the Donald Trump administration as a means to advance Indigenous economic development. In 2017 Secretary of the Interior Ryan Zinke created an uproar in Indian country when he asked, "Is there an off-ramp? If tribes would have a choice of leaving Indian trust lands and becoming a corporation, tribes would take it." To many Indigenous people this signaled a potential return to the termination era.[28] This fear was compounded in 2019 when William Perry Pendley was appointed as acting director of the Bureau of Land Management. Pendley had long been an advocate for selling off federal lands and worked as an attorney opposing treaty rights and tribal sovereignty for the Mountain States Legal Foundation. These efforts fizzled, but tribal leaders across the United States continue to be watchful for termination's resurrection.

Tribal governments have been trying to take control of their own destiny for centuries now. Until the federal government finds a way to rectify past policies that abused tribal funds and finds a way for tribes to operate safely under the protection of the trust relationship, the specter of termination will continue to haunt American Indian communities. Coos elder chief Edgar Bowen was fond of paraphrasing an old saying. He would often tell younger Indigenous leaders, "The price of maintaining our sovereignty is eternal vigilance."[29] That is nowhere more true than in the necessity to protect and retain the federal trust responsibility, which one set or another of politicians or bureaucrats or non-Indian Americans is always scheming to take away.

APPENDIX

Table 5. Termination laws (alphabetical), by tribe or region

Tribe or Region	Law (date)	In Effect
Alabama and Coushatta TX	68 Stat. 768 (1954); PL 83–627, August 23	1955
California Rancheria Act (37–38) (41 listed in bill; 7 added in 1964 amendment, 37–38 terminated)	72 Stat. 619 (1958); PL 85–671; August 18, amended 78 Stat. 390	Various 1961–67
Catawba SC	73 Stat. 592 (1959); PL 86–322, September 21	1960
Coyote Valley Rancheria CA	71 Stat. 283 (1957); PL85–91, July 10	1957
Klamath OR	68 Stat. 718 (1954); PL 83–587, August 13	1961
Lower Lake Rancheria CA	70 Stat. 58 (1956); PL 84–443, March 29	1956
Menominee WI	68 Stat. 250 (1954); PL 83–399, June 17	1961
"Mixed-Blood" Utes UT	68 Stat. 868 (1954); PL 83–671; August 27	1956
Ottawa OK	70 Stat. 963 (1956); PL 84–943; August 3	1959

Peoria OK	70 Stat. 937 (1956); PL 84–921, August 2	1959
Ponca NE	76 Stat. 429 (1962); PL 87–629, September 5	1966
Southern Paiute UT	68 Stat. 1099 (1954); PL 83–792, September 1	1956; proclaimed 1957 by Department of the Interior
Western Oregon (61 tribes & bands)	68 Stat. 724 (1954); PL 83–588, August 13	1956
Wyandotte OK	70 Stat. 893 (1956); PL 84–887; August 1	1959

Table 6. Termination laws, by date

Law (date)	Tribe or Region
68 Stat. 250 (1954); PL 83–399, June 17	Menominee WI
68 Stat. 718 (1954); PL 83–587, August 13	Klamath OR
68 Stat. 724 (1954); PL 83–588, August 13	Western Oregon (61 tribes & bands)
68 Stat. 768 (1954); PL 83–627, August 23	Alabama and Coushatta TX
68 Stat. 868 (1954); PL 83–671, August 27	"Mixed-Blood" Utes UT
68 Stat. 1099 (1954); PL 83–792, September 1	Southern Paiute UT
70 Stat. 58 (1956); PL 84–443, March 29	Lower Lake Rancheria CA
70 Stat. 893 (1956); PL 84–887, August 1	Wyandotte OK
70 Stat. 937 (1956); PL 84–921, August 2	Peoria OK
70 Stat. 963 (1956); PL 84–943, August 3	Ottawa OK
71 Stat. 283 (1957); PL 85–91, July 10	Coyote Valley Rancheria CA
72 Stat. 619 (1958); PL 85–671, August 18	California Rancheria Act (37–38)
73 Stat. 592 (1959); PL 86–322, September 21	Catawba SC
76 Stat. 429 (1962); PL 87–629, September 5	Ponca NE

Note: Lists compiled from Charles F. Wilkinson and Eric R. Biggs, "The Evolution of the Termination Policy," *American Indian Law Review* 5 (1977): 151; Congressional Records; *Federal Register*; Bureau of Indian Affairs; and NARA sources.

NOTES

ABBREVIATIONS

AAIA	Association on American Indian Affairs
BIA	Bureau of Indian Affairs
CCF	Central Classified Files
CPM	College Park, Maryland
CSRSC-UNML	Center for Southwest Research and Special Collections, University of New Mexico Libraries
CTCLUSI	Confederated Tribes of Coos, Lower Umpqua and Siuslaw Indians
DC	Washington DC
ELWPP	Ernest L. Wilkinson Personal Papers
HSTL	Harry S. Truman Library
IIAC	Interior and Insular Affairs Committee or Committee on Interior and Insular Affairs
LOC	Library of Congress
LR	Letters Received
LTPSC	L. Thom Perry Special Collections
MAC-FSC	McKay Archives Center, Florida Southern College
MADC	Menominee Agency Decimal Correspondence
MHSRCA	Montana Historical Society Research Center Archives
MMMASC-UM	Maureen and Mike Mansfield Archives and Special Collections, University of Montana
NAC	National Archives at Chicago

NARA	National Archives and Records Administration
NCAI	National Congress of American Indians
NCAIR	National Council on American Indians records
NL	Newberry Library
NMAI	National Museum of American Indians
PAO	Portland Area Office
PAR	Pacific Alaska Region
RCIA	Records of the Committee on Indian Affairs
RG	Record Group
SI	Smithsonian Institution
UCLSCRC	University of Chicago Library Special Collections Research Center
UWLSC	University of Washington Libraries, Special Collections
WCBICCR	Wilkinson, Cragun and Barker Indian Claims Commission Records
WCBR	Wilkinson, Cragun & Barker Records

INTRODUCTION

Epigraph: Dorgan, *The Girl in the Photograph*, 173–74.

1. The term *tribe* is an increasingly contested term for American Indian or Indigenous nations. Some groups, such as the Menominee Indian Tribe of Wisconsin, have consciously incorporated it into their legal name. (Author discussions with Carol Dodge over the years.) Others, such as the Seneca Nation of Indians in New York, have long used the term Nation in their official name. In this work I use a variety of terminology, recognizing that some of it will change over time: tribes, tribal nations, Indigenous nations. When referring to specific Indigenous nations I use either their legal name or a shortened version of it. I use the terms *American Indian* and *Indian* to refer to the Indigenous peoples of what is now the United States. The terms are embedded in the names of numerous Indigenous U.S. nations. I also use the terms *Indian country*, which has legal implications, *Indigenous people*, and *Indigenous peoples* throughout this book. Finally, some Indigenous people refer to themselves as tribal members, and some as citizens. I use both these terms in the book.
2. Charles House, "Abandonment or Freedom? 'Great Knife' Cuts Menominee Bonds; Indians Study Cause," *Milwaukee Sentinel*, August 15, 1954.
3. Beck, *Struggle for Self-Determination*, 139–41.
4. Ralph M. Shane, "Superintendent's Comments," *Fort Berthold News Bulletin* 5, no. 7 (July 20, 1954), folder 4, box 11, Robert Rietz Papers, Native American Educational Services Chicago Community Agencies Records (hereafter Rietz

Papers), University of Chicago Library Special Collections Research Center (UCLSCRC). This collection was formerly housed at NAES College in Chicago.

5. Deloria, *Custer Died for Your Sins*, 78–79. Deloria went on to say, "So powerful is Gamble that" Senator Henry Jackson, chair of the Interior and Insular Affairs Committee, "might be characterized as his front man." Journalist Mark Trahant has referred to Gamble as "the 'greatest enemy' of Indian country." *The Last Great Battle*, 48. In 1964 Gamble expressed frustration to the then committee chairman Frank Church that the BIA had not updated its list of tribes that were ready for termination. "You will recall during consideration of several judgment funds disposition bills in the last weeks of the session I suggested it would be desirable to get an up-to-date appraisal of the competence of all Indian tribes to manage their own affairs." The list had not been updated in more than a decade. He added, "If some tribes have reached the place where they can look after their own business, we ought to know about it." Gamble to Church, October 29, 1964, folder General Files (Indians Subcommittee)–to Indian, Bureau of, box 13, Sen 88A-F11, Senate Interior and Insular Affairs Committee (IIAC), Record Group (RG) 46, NARA, Washington DC (NARA-DC).
6. Author interview with George C. Barton, Edgar A. Bowen, Don Whereat, and Eddie Helm, June 28, 2006, Empire, Oregon. CTCLUSI termination is discussed in Beck, *Seeking Recognition*.
7. Lewis to A. L. Miller, April 17, 1953, U.S. Congress, Senate, Committee on Interior and Insular Affairs, *Per Capita Distribution*, 3.
8. On Montana and Idaho see Clow, "Crossing the Divide," 48, 51; U.S. Congress, Senate, *Tax-Exempt Indian Lands*, 3.
9. The BIA was variously known as the Office of Indian Affairs or OIA, the Indian service, the Indian bureau, the bureau, and the Indian department before it was officially named the Bureau of Indian Affairs in the 1940s.
10. 1952 Republican Party Platform; 1952 Democratic Party Platform, both available online at https://www.presidency.ucsb.edu. Governmental efficiency has been an on-again, off-again focus of congressional dreams for more than a hundred years, since the Taft administration. Lederle, "Hoover Commission," 89–90.
11. Sinclair, *Congressional Realignment*, 61, 71–72.
12. 1952 Republican Party Platform. The Republican Party Platform also said, "We shall eliminate the existing shameful waste by the Bureau of Indian Affairs which has obstructed the accomplishment of our national responsibility for improving the condition of our Indian friends."
13. Dudziak, *Cold War Civil Rights*, 9–14; Biondi, *To Stand and Fight*, 143–45, 160; Hall, "Long Civil Rights Movement," 1,249.
14. Dudziak, *Cold War Civil Rights*, 11.
15. Biondi, *To Stand and Fight*, 156.

16. Erdrich, *Night Watchman*, 90. Wazhask's character is modeled on Erdrich's grandfather.
17. Foreword, Silva, *Power of the Steel-Tipped Pen*, ix.
18. This was well articulated in 1832 by Chickasaw leader Levi Colbert when he wondered whether the U.S. notions of "liberality and equality" were simply "an unwillingness to be oppressed themselves" or instead "respect for the rights of others." Quoted in Saunt, *Unworthy Republic*, 110.
19. This tendency inspired the work edited by Sleeper-Smith et al., *Why You Can't Teach*.
20. Hitchcock, *Age of Eisenhower*, chs. 9, 14.
21. Political scientist David Lake, in his comprehensive analysis of U.S. Cold War policy, provides discussion of American imperial ambitions in Micronesia as unique in the decolonizing era, but his focus is outward on big power relations rather than on the people whose islands the country took control over. See Lake, *Entangling Relations*, esp. 147–48, 176, 183–85, 191–92. He also argues that since Micronesians had not established a unified nation-state under four centuries of occupation by Spain, Germany, and Japan, the United States needed to fill the political vacuum created. Lake, *Entangling Relations*, 184. Gaddis, in his sweeping history *The Cold War*, briefly discusses colonialism, but only in the context of U.S. relations with European colonies and former colonies and their role in U.S.-Soviet relations. Immerwahr, *How to Hide an Empire*, is an exception to this rule.
22. For U.S. Cold War policy impacts on Indigenous peoples of the Pacific see Dibblin, *Day of Two Suns*; Immerwahr, *How to Hide an Empire*; Nevin, *American Touch*; Niedenthal, *For the Good of Mankind*; and Saranillio, *Unsustainable Empire*.
23. U.S. Congress, House, *Report with Respect to the House Resolution Authorizing the Committee on Interior and Insular Affairs to Conduct an Investigation of the Bureau of Indian Affairs*, 11. Martha L. Jay of the Institute of Ethnic Affairs alerted a broader public to this report in Jay to American Indians, their friends, and those interested in our national honor, October 19, 1954, folder 13 Indians-Termination, 1948–1955, box 288, James E. Murray Papers, Maureen and Mike Mansfield Archives and Special Collections, University of Montana (MMMASC-UM).
24. Sinclair, *Transformation*, 9–10.
25. Sinclair, *Congressional Realignment*, 73.
26. Sinclair, *Party Wars*, 3–4.
27. Sinclair, *Transformation*, 16–17, 29–30.
28. Schrecker, *No Ivory Tower*, 7.
29. Rosenthal, *Their Day in Court*, 93.
30. The four other subcommittees ranged from nineteen to twenty-four members. House Committee on Interior and Insular Affairs Minutes, January 23, 1951,

Envelope Minutes Committee on Interior and Insular Affairs, 82d Congress, 82nd Congress IIAC, box 706, RG 233, NARA-DC.

31. Arnold, *Bartering*; Beck, *Seeking Recognition*; Daly, "'American Indian Freedom Controversy'"; Haynal, "From Termination through Restoration"; Lewis, "Termination of the Confederated Tribes"; Metcalf, *Termination's Legacy*; Peroff, *Menominee Drums*; Puisto, *This Is My Reservation*; and Valandra, *Not Without Our Consent.* Overviews of termination and the policies surrounding it include Burt, *Tribalism in Crisis*; Fixico, *Termination and Relocation*; Philp, *Termination Revisited*; and Ulrich, *American Indian Nations.*
32. Curley, "Infrastructures," 389.

1. CONGRESSIONAL ABUSE

Epigraph: *United States v. Winans.*

1. Pevar, *Rights of Indians and Tribes*, 32.
2. Schmeckebier, *Office of Indian Affairs*, 1.
3. Anaya, *Indigenous Peoples*, ch. 1. The three cases are *Johnson v. M'Intosh, Cherokee Nation v. Georgia,* and *Worcester v. Georgia.*
4. Wilkins, in *American Indian Sovereignty and the U.S. Supreme Court*, provides a powerful analysis of fifteen cases that he argues are among the most egregious in undermining tribal sovereignty.
5. It also determined that individual Indians were incompetent to manage their own affairs. To this day the BIA has the authority to determine the legal competency of individual American Indian people. Clark, *Lone Wolf.*
6. See, for example, statement of various funds paid for the benefit of "Northern Montana Indians," which distinguishes between money expended in accordance with a legal agreement with the tribes relating to land sales and funds paid "*as an absolute gratuity*" (emphasis in original). House of Representatives, "Reduction of Indian Reservations," 12.
7. Wilkins, *Hollow Justice*, xvii.
8. Rosenthal, *Their Day in Court*, 4. Also cited in Wilkins, *Hollow Justice*, 5. Rosenthal points out that from 1796 to 1820 the price of publicly owned land was actually $2 per acre, so the losses to tribal nations would be even greater. See Rosenthal, *Their Day in Court*, 36n2.
9. Wilkins, *Hollow Justice*, 7–26.
10. Jeffrey Ostler's masterful book *Surviving Genocide* makes a strong evidence-based argument "that [U.S.] government officials consistently used genocidal threats to secure consent" to land and resource dispossession, and "that the United States adopted a policy of exterminating Indians who resisted its demands." Ostler, *Surviving Genocide*, 386.
11. Wallace, *Jefferson and the Indians.*

12. Fritz, *Movement for Indian Assimilation*, 27.
13. Much of the following is taken from Beck, *Siege and Survival*, 165–86.
14. Wisconsin became a state in May 1848, and the Menominee treaty was negotiated in October 1848.
15. Dodge to Ellis, October 18, 1847, in Green Bay and Prairie du Chien Papers, vol. 75, doc. 48, Wisconsin Historical Society Archives. Minnesota Territory would not be established until 1849.
16. Historian Claudio Saunt argues that removal is too "soft" a term, used by those who supported the removal policy, and deportation more accurately reflects actual policy. Saunt, *Unworthy Republic*, xiii–xiv.
17. Articles 2 and 6, Treaty with the Menominee, 1848, Kappler, *Indian Treaties*, 572–73.
18. Beck, *Siege and Survival*, 179–97. In 1856 the Menominee sold a portion of the reservation they had regained to provide a home for the Stockbridge and Munsee tribes. See Treaty with the Menominee, 1856, in Kappler, *Indian Treaties*, 755–56.
19. Beck, *Siege and Survival*, 168–69. The 1853 General Land Office figure was 5,230,240 acres. U.S. Congress, Senate, Ex. Doc. No. 72, 36–39; "Memorandum on Claim of Menominee Tribe with Respect to Unconscionable Aspects of Treaty of October 18, 1848," folder Menominee Indians, box 20, Wilkinson, Cragun & Barker records (WCBR), L. Tom Perry Special Collections (LTPSC).
20. CPI Inflation Calculator (website), accessed November 21, 2022, https://www.in2013dollars.com/.
21. Article 4, Treaty with the Menominee, 1848, in Kappler, *Indian Treaties*, 573; Beck, *Siege and Survival*, 169–86; and Witgen, *Seeing Red*. On the law that Congress passed, which made individual debts the responsibility of tribal nations and led to both increased lending by traders and massive debt payments added to treaties, see Clayton, "Impact of Traders' Claims."
22. Article 4, Treaty with the Menominee, 1848, in Kappler, *Indian Treaties*, 573. The buyout occurred the next year, and the "forty-niners" played a controversial role in Menominee politics for decades to come. Menominee families, including women and children whose white husbands had accepted the buyout money, later petitioned for enrollment back into the tribe. See, for example, "Hearing Before the Committee on Indian Affairs, United States Senate, On the Claims of Certain Menominee Indians to Enrollment as Members of the Tribe, April 15, 1910," in Central Classified Files (CCF) 1907–1939 Keshena 053, RG 75, NARA-DC. These claims all date to the 1849 buyout sanctioned by the 1848 treaty. For more on the Ewing brothers see Trennert, *Indian Traders*.
23. Calculated from Article 4, Treaty with the Chippewa, 1854, Kappler, *Indian Treaties*, 649.

24. Saunt, *Unworthy Republic*, 122, 212–17. Article XIII of Treaty with the Chickasaw, 1834, says, "On the happening of such a contingency, and information thereof being given of an intention of the whole or any portion of the nation to remove; the United States will furnish competent persons, safely to conduct them to their future destination, and also supplies necessary to the same, and for one year after their arrival at the west, provided the Indians shall desire supplies, to be furnished for so long a period; the supplies so afforded, to be chargeable to the general Chickasaw account, provided the funds of said nation shall be adequate to the expenses." Kappler, *Indian Treaties*, 422.
25. LaPier, *Invisible Reality*, 20.
26. Wilkinson, "Indian Tribal Claims," 516.
27. George Boyd to Lewis Cass, August 25, 1834, frame 55; Boyd to Elbert Herring, September 25, 1834, frame 198, both in National Archives and Records Administration, Washington DC, *Letters Received*, M234–316. This incident is described in greater detail in Beck, *Siege and Survival* 133–41.
28. Boyd to Commissioner of Indian Affairs Carey Allen Harris, March 10, 1838, and Harris to Boyd, April 27, 1838, both in Bloom, *Territorial Papers*, vol. 27, 940, 992. See also Beck, *Siege and Surivival*, 138–39.
29. Article 1, Treaty with the Osage, 1865, in Kappler, *Indian Treaties*, 879; *Osage Tribe of Indians v. the United States*; and Wilkinson, "Indian Tribal Claims," 516–17.
30. Wilkinson, "Indian Tribal Claims," 517–18; and Wilkins, *Hollow Justice*, 106–7.
31. "Indians Call for Full Citizenship, Resent Being Wards," *Chicago Daily Tribune*, September 28, 1929, 15; and LaPier and Beck, *City Indian*, 126.
32. *United States v. Cook*; and Beck, *Struggle for Self-Determination*, 52.
33. Grann, *Killers of the Flower Moon*, 45–46.
34. Act to Provide for the Allotment of Lands in Severalty to Indians on the Various Reservations, Chap. 199, 49 Cong., Sess. 2, 24 Stat. 388 (1887), Section 5.
35. See section 7, Act to Provide for Determining the Heirs of Deceased Indians, for the Disposition and Sale of Allotments of Deceased Indians, for the Leasing of Allotments, and for Other Purposes, Pub. L. No. 61–313, 36 Stat. 855 (1910), p. 857. A 1909 law provided for $100,000 to pay some of the costs for the new forestry work being done by the OIA: Act Making Appropriations for the Current and Contingent Expenses of the Indian Department, for Fulfilling Treaty Stipulations with Various Indian Tribes, and for Other Purposes, for the Fiscal Year Ending June Thirtieth, Nineteen Hundred and Ten, Pub. L. No. 60–316, 35 Stat. 781 (1909), 783. However, this was "wholly inadequate" to fund the work. See Kinney, *Indian Forest and Range*, 85.
36. For the Nez Perce, for example, the administrative fee totaled 8 percent of the sales. See Catton, *American Indians and National Forests*, 258–59.

37. Act to Authorize the Cutting of Timber, the Manufacture and Sale of Lumber, and the Preservation of the Forests on the Menominee Indian Reservation in the State of Wisconsin, Pub. L. No. 60–74, 35 Stat. 51 (1908), Section 4.
38. Bonnin, Fabens, and Sniffen, "Oklahoma's Poor Rich Indians"; Act For the Removal of Restrictions from Part of the Lands of Allottees of the Five Civilized Tribes, and for Other Purposes, Pub. L. No. 60–140, 35 Stat. 312 (1908); Grann, *Killers of the Flower Moon*; and Harmon, *Rich Indians*, 171–208.
39. Act for the Removal of Restrictions; Bonnin, Fabens, and Sniffen, "Oklahoma's Poor Rich Indians," 5, 10–11.
40. Bonnin, Fabens, and Sniffen, "Oklahoma's Poor Rich Indians," 11.
41. Bonnin, Fabens, and Sniffen, "Oklahoma's Poor Rich Indians," 7.
42. *Indians, Outlaws, and Angie Debo*. The state of Oklahoma later argued that this theft caused the dissolution of the reservations of the five tribes—essentially comprising much of eastern Oklahoma. In 2020, more than a century later, the U.S. Supreme Court ruled, however, that since Congress itself had never abolished the reservations, they still exist. See *McGirt v. Oklahoma*. Oklahoma continues to contest this, and the Supreme Court has since diminished tribal authority. See *Oklahoma v. Castro-Huerta*.
43. Grann, *Killers of the Flower Moon*, 55–56; and Harmon, *Rich Indians*, 171–208.
44. Bauer, *We Were All*; Beck, *Unfair Labor?*; Harmon, *Rich Indians*; Hosmer, *American Indians*; McNenly, *Native Performers*; Phillips, *Trading Identities*; Raibmon, *Authentic Indians*; Rasenberger, *High Steel*; Warren, *Buffalo Bill's America*; and Warren, "Wage Work."
45. Bauer, "Working for Identity," 244–45.
46. Rosenthal, *Their Day in Court*, 17.

2. RIGHTS AND RESPONSIBILITIES

Epigraph 1: Daly, "'American Indian Freedom Controversy,'" 4.
Epigraph 2: Rosenthal, *Their Day in Court*, 166.

1. Personal and professional interactions with Sol Tax at NAES College, Chicago, in the 1980s and 1990s.
2. U.S. Congress, House, "Hearings before a Subcommittee of the Committee on Indian Affairs, House of Representatives pursuant to H. Res. 166," 8.
3. Richmond L. Clow Termination Lecture, unpublished, in author's possession. For a brief overview of federal Indian policy see Carter, "U.S. Federal Indian Policy."
4. The Montana Committee Against Termination, James J. Flaherty, Chairman, "Obligation of Federal Trust," 66.
5. Antiracism quotes from Kendi, *How to Be an Antiracist*, 31.
6. Meriam, *Problem of Indian Administration*, 1–7, 430–59.

7. Cohen, "Erosion of Indian Rights," 348.
8. This was brought to my attention by David Martínez.
9. Memorandum, Curry to Ickes, n.d., folder Indian Claims and Contracts (James E. Curry) (1 Statements, box 401, Harold L. Ickes Papers, Library of Congress [LOC]).
10. Parts of this section have been influenced by Richmond Clow's unpublished lectures.
11. Schmeckebier, *Office of Indian Affairs*, 509–15.
12. Kelly, "Charles James Rhoads," 264; and DeJong, *Paternalism*, 263.
13. Meriam, *Problem of Indian Administration*, 21, 52–55. On the history of Indian education during this era see Szasz, *Education*. On the role of Indian bureau officials working to change family structure see Cahill, *Federal Fathers and Mothers*.
14. C. S. Rhoads and J. Henry Scattergood, "Indian Administration Since July 1, 1929," March 3, 1933, 4, folder 5 Withdrawal Programs 1:2, new box 36, Sen 83A-F9 Records of the Committee on Indian Affairs (RCIA), RG 46, NARA-DC.
15. "Indian Affairs Service," Jonathan M. Steere, President, Indian Rights Association, letter to the Editor, *New York Times*, May 12, 1933.
16. U.S. Congress, House, "Hearings before a Subcommittee of the Committee on Indian Affairs, House of Representatives pursuant to H. Res. 166," 6–10.
17. Deloria and Lytle, *Nations Within*; and Deloria, *Indian Reorganization Act*.
18. "Statement of Luke Gilbert, Representing the Cheyenne River Sioux Tribe, Cheyenne Agency, S. Dak.," June 18, 1940, U.S. Congress, House, Committee on Indian Affairs, *Hearings on S. 2103*, 339–44.
19. Ickes to Elmer Thomas, March 31, 1939, U.S. Congress, House, Committee on Indian Affairs, *Hearings on S. 2103*, 19.
20. Haynal, "From Termination through Restoration," 64–65.
21. Richmond L. Clow Home Rule lecture, unpublished, manuscript in author's possession.
22. Sady, "The Menominees," 6; Dodge to Collier, August 2, 1935, CCF 1907–1939 Keshena 047, RG 75, NARA-DC; Fredenberg to Collier, January 3, 1938, CCF 1907–1939 Keshena 054, RG 75, NARA-DC. A copy of the "Charter of the Menominee Tribe of Indians" that circulated within the Department of the Interior ca. 1936 is in folder 1566, box 97, Felix S. Cohen Papers, Beinicke Rare Book and Manuscript Library, Yale University Library.
23. "Constitution of the Menominee Tribe of Indians of the State of Wisconsin, 1904," CCF 1907–1939 Keshena 054, RG 75, NARA-DC. Tribal members Mitchell Oshkenaniew and Peter LaMotte had written the tribe's first proposed constitution in 1892, but it never actually became law. It can be found in Letters Received (LR) 1892:32904, RG 75, NARA-DC.

24. Act to Authorize the Cutting of Timber.
25. Act to Authorize the Cutting of Timber, Sections 3, 4, and 5, 51–52; An act to Amend the Law Relating to Timber Operations on the Menominee Indian Reservation, Pub. L. No. 73–357, 48 Stat. 964 (1934), 965; and personal communication with Rich Clow, December 31, 2021.
26. Beck, *Struggle for Self-Determination*, 122–23, 130–31.
27. Richmond L. Clow Home Rule lecture, unpublished, manuscript in author's possession.
28. These included the Navajo in New Mexico, the Eastern Band of Cherokee, and tribes in South Dakota, California, Nevada, and elsewhere. U.S. Congress, House, Committee on Indian Affairs, *Hearings on S. 2103*.
29. S. Rept. No. 1047, 76th Cong., 1st sess., U.S. Congress, House, Committee on Indian Affairs, *Hearings on S. 2103*, 7.
30. U.S. Congress, House, "Hearings before a Subcommittee of the Committee on Indian Affairs, House of Representatives pursuant to H. Res. 166," part 4, 3–6, 16.
31. These efforts extended across the forty-eight states and even into the Territory of Alaska. Legal scholar Felix Cohen excoriated the new Interior department policy in a 1948 article. "Even the Russian czars ordered their subordinate officials to respect the possessory rights of the Alaskan natives, and persuaded the United States to include a promise of such respect in the Alaskan Treaty of Cession. But that promise is also forgotten in the Department of the Interior, which is currently assuring inquirers that it is all right to take away Indian property in Alaska because no treaties are involved." Cohen, "Breaking Faith," 3.
32. Hosmer, "Harry Truman and Native Americans," xx–xxiii; and Hoxie, "Seeing and Not Seeing," 5.
33. Subpoena for January 28, 1947, folder 21, box 2, William Zimmerman Jr. Papers, Center for Southwest Research and Special Collections, University of New Mexico Libraries (CSRSC-UNML).
34. Staff chart, box 3, entry 190, RG 75, NARA-DC; Krug to Mrs. O. A. Rosborough, Chairman, Indian Welfare, General Federation of Women's Clubs, Chicago, February 7, 1947, folder February 1947, box 11, Julius A. Krug Papers, LOC.
35. DeJong, *Paternalism*, 284.
36. Zimmerman to Miss Frances E. Andrews, February 25, 1947, folder 21, box 2, Zimmerman Papers, CSRSC-UNML.
37. Perhaps this was justification for the role he played, or perhaps he was projecting his views onto congressional representatives. Minutes, Menominee Advisory Council Meeting, July 16, 1955, folder 19, box 9, Zimmerman Papers, CSRSC-UNML.
38. Bess Furman, "Bills Aim to Free All Our Indians," *New York Times*, July 22, 1947; "Statement by Senator Hugh Butler (R. Neb.) in Explanation of Bills

Introduced to Remove all Restrictions on Ten Indian Tribes," folder 9, Indian Bureau Liquidation, new box 15, Sen 83A-F9 RCIA, RG 46, NARA-DC; *Congressional Record—Senate*, July 21, 1947, 9632.

39. Krug to John G. Evans, February 7, 1947, folder February 1947, box 11, Krug Papers, LOC.
40. Henry Jackson to [Name restricted], July 7, 1947, folder 15/9 U.S. Indian Affairs Bureau 1945–48, box 15, accession 3560–002, Henry M. Jackson Papers, University of Washington Libraries, Special Collections (UWLSC).
41. Resolution of the Fort Hall Business Council of the Shoshone-Bannock Tribe, November 9, 1948, folder 10333-1946-054, part 2, 2 of 3, box 11, CCF 1940–1957 Uintah & Ouray 054, RG 75, NARA-DC.
42. [Name restricted], Northwestern Federation of American Indians, to Jackson, April 28, 1947; Jackson to [Name restricted], May 2, 1947, both in folder 15/9 U.S. Indian Affairs Bureau 1945–48, box 15, accession 3560–002, Jackson Papers, UWLSC.
43. Rossin statement to House Subcommittee on Indian Affairs, April 11, 1947, folder Association on American Indian Affairs, box 24, Papers of Harry S. Truman, SMOF: Philleo Nash Files, Indian File, 1946–1952 (hereafter Nash Files), Harry S. Truman Library (HSTL).
44. Cohen, "Breaking Faith," 6–7. This was a 1948 publication.
45. Thye to Miss Frances Andrews, February 21, 1947, folder 21, box 2, Zimmerman Papers, CSRSC-UNML.
46. *Annual Report of the Secretary of the Interior*, 1947, 348–49.
47. Quote from Assistant Commissioner Circular 3675, May 28, 1948, in Tyler, *History of Indian Policy*, 166. See also Field Memorandum no. 146, E. Morgan Pryse to all superintendents in Region 3, Regional Director, August 10, 1948, folder 6, box 15, Portland Area Office (PAO) 02, RG 75, NARA-Pacific Alaska Region (PAR). The Navajo and Hopi crises of the late 1940s had caused Truman to view long-term planning as the way to resolve Indian economic problems. Hosmer, "Harry Truman and Native Americans," xxiv–xxv.
48. Felix Cohen, in "The Erosion of Indian Rights," argued that the establishment of area offices had the opposite effect. "According to Bureau theory, the area directors were supposed to be exercising powers delegated by the Washington officials, and the whole process was officially described as 'bringing administration closer to the reservations.' In practice, however, the area directors found it much easier to take over authority from the reservation superintendents they were supposed to supervise than to take over authority from the Commissioner of Indian Affairs or the Secretary of the Interior." Cohen, "Erosion of Indian Rights," 382.

49. Pryse to all Superintendents in Region 3, August 10, 1948; Pryse to Regional Office Staff, August 17, 1948, both in folder 6-Year Reservation Program-Withdrawal, box 15, PAO 02; Pryse, Portland Area Office Narrative Report of February 1949, folder 1948–1949, box 1, PAO 01, all in RG 75, NARA-PAR; and Beck, *Seeking Recognition*, 123–24, 159.
50. Material for Annual Report, Fiscal 1953, folder 19919-1952-031, box 1, CCF 1940–57 Phoenix Area, RG 75, NARA DC. On decentralization plans within Interior, see Secretary of the Interior to Chiefs of Bureau of Reclamation, Bureau of Mines, Bureau of Land Management, Bureau of Indian Affairs, Fish and Wildlife Service, Geological Survey, National Park Service, February 6, 1947, folder February 1947, box 11; and documentation in folder Departmental Organization, box 67, both in Krug Papers, LOC.
51. Collier, "The Beleaguered Indian."
52. "A report to the Commissioner of Indian Affairs, U.S. Department of the Interior, A General Review of Credit Policies and Procedures of the Bureau of Indian Affairs with Recommendations." By Wm. A. Schoenfeld, Consultant. Corvallis OR, January 3, 1953, 7. Folder 11, box 2, Zimmerman Papers, CSRSC-UNML.
53. H. J. Res. 490.
54. Metcalf, *Termination's Legacy*, 76.
55. Ickes to Anderson, August 2, 1949, folder General Correspondence 1946–1952, Indian Bills 1949–1950, 1, box 61, Ickes Papers, LOC.
56. Report of Resources Conference, October 8–10, 1952, Bureau of Indian Affairs, Aberdeen, South Dakota, folder 00 Aberdeen Area 1952 Resource Conf., box 7, CCF 1940–1957 Aberdeen Area Office 054, RG 75, NARA-DC.
57. Commissioner to Secretary of the Interior, March 20, 1953, folder Personal Correspondence File, 1953, box 4, Dillon S. Myer Papers, HSTL.
58. Cohen, "Erosion of Indian Rights," 380–82.
59. Collier, in an effort to protect both his legacy and the rights of tribes, wrote an angry letter to Senator Herbert H. Lehman. Myer, told by Secretary of the Interior Oscar Chapman that he had been hired with a free hand, had quickly cleaned house. He brought in undersecretaries from the War Relocation Authority, which he had previously overseen. The only remaining assistant commissioner, John Province, had been in the BIA for four years but also came from War Relocation Authority and had "learned the mechanics of Indian Service, and its political opportunisms, but of its substance and spirit, little indeed. And it is these perfectly honorable but abysmally ignorant, withal very self-confident, men, who are pushing this Bosone bill and who would administer it." Collier to Lehman, August 21, 1950, folder General Correspondence 1946–1952, Indian Bills 1949–1950 (3, box 61, Ickes Papers, LOC. Chapman defended the bill, writing, "It is my belief that integration of American Indians, and other minority groups, is

taking place within our Nation. The problem is one of determining how best to assist this process." Chapman to J. Hardin Peterson, Committee on Public Lands, House of Representatives, July 25, 1950, folder General Correspondence 1946–1952, Indian Bills 1949–1950, 3, box 61, Ickes Papers, LOC.

60. Ickes to Leahy, August 19, 1950, folder General Correspondence 1946–1952, Indian Bills 1949–1950, 3, box 61, Ickes Papers, LOC.
61. Minutes of Special Meeting with the Commissioner, September 26, 1952, box 2, folder 1950–1953 Commissioner of Indian Affairs, Memoranda and Reports (2 of 4), Myer Papers, HSTL.
62. Robert L. Bennett, Regional Secretary, National Congress of American Indians to Myer, January 5, 1949, folder Personal Correspondence File, 1949 (1 of 2), box 4, Myer Papers, HSTL.
63. *Congressional Record—Senate*, December 15, 1950, 16768–69.
64. The BIA budget in 1950 was estimated at $58,108,746 while the U.S. budget was approximately $41.9 billion. Of the BIA budget, $3,138,300, or slightly more than 5 percent, consisted of tribal funds. BIA budget estimate in "Appropriations, budget estimates, etc., statements, 81st Cong. 1st sess., Jan. 3-Oct. 19, 1949," *U.S. Congressional Serial Set* (1949), 94–102; U.S. budget in Harry S. Truman, Annual Budget Message to the Congress: Fiscal Year 1950, January 10, 1949, Harry S. Truman Library, digital document at Harry S. Truman Library and Museum (website), accessed February 9, 2022, https://www.trumanlibrary.gov/library/public-papers/8/annual-budget-message-congress-fiscal-year-1950.
65. Lesser to Philleo Nash, June 6, 1952, folder Association on American Indian Affairs, box 24, Nash Files, HSTL. The California bill followed a previously introduced bill that purported to give citizenship rights to California Indians—even though those rights had been guaranteed since the 1848 Treaty of Guadalupe Hidalgo. In exchange for this, California Indians would be treated "in the same manner as any other citizen." S. 3197, "A Bill To extend personal rights and duties of the Indians of California," copy in folder Indian Bills 1949–1950, box 401, Ickes Papers, LOC. Critics described the bill as "exorbitant and unconscionable" and "the greatest fraud that has been imposed upon our citizens of California during the present century." Author unnamed, "Downey—The Friend of the Indian?" March 9, 1950, draft of press release, probably either AAIA or NCAI, folder Indian Bills 1949–1950, box 401, Ickes Papers, LOC.
66. John Collier, "Statement of Indian Service and Indian Appropriations," March 31, 1943, folder 15/2 U.S. Indian Affairs Bureau 1943–44, box 15, accession 3560–002, Jackson Papers, UWLSC.
67. John C. Rainer, Executive Secretary, to Chiefs, Governors, Councilmen, and Officers of N.C.A.I., July 20, 1950, folder B5.1 Helen L. Peterson Papers NCAI

Correspondence 1945 to 1950, box 5, Helen Peterson Papers, National Museum of the American Indian Archives (NMAI Archives), Smithsonian Institution (SI).

68. "Indian Bureau appointments," Bureau of Indian Affairs press release, September 14, 1951, folder Indians 1946–1952, 1, box 401, Ickes Papers, LOC; "Indian Bureau Moves to Transfer Functions," DOI Information Service press release n.d., folder 13, box 288, Murray Papers, MMMASC-UM. Latter press release also in folder 5 Withdrawal Programs 2:2, new box 36, Sen 83A-F9 RCIA, RG 46, NARA-DC.
69. Commissioner to All Bureau Officials re Withdrawal programming, August 5, 1952, folder 1950–1953 Commissioner of Indian Affairs, Memoranda and Reports (1 of 4), box 2, Myer Papers, HSTL. Copy also in folder 5 Withdrawal Programs 2:2, new box 36, Sen 83A-F9 RCIA, RG 46, NARA-DC.
70. Commissioner to All Bureau Officials re Withdrawal programming, August 5, 1952, folder 1950–1953 Commissioner of Indian Affairs, Memoranda and Reports (1 of 4), box 2, Myer Papers, HSTL.
71. George to All Tribal Council Chairmen, September 26, 1952, folder 1950–1953 Commissioner of Indian Affairs, Memoranda and Reports (1 of 4), box 2, Myer Papers, HSTL.
72. Myer to All Tribal Council Members, October 10, 1952, folder 1950–1953 Commissioner of Indian Affairs, Memoranda and Reports (1 of 4), box 2, Myer Papers, HSTL.
73. Myer, "Program of the Bureau," 353; reprint pp. 15–16, in folder Indian Claims and Contracts (James E. Curry), 4, Memorandums 1951 July—November, box 401, Ickes Papers, LOC.
74. "Resolutions Adopted by the American Baptist Convention," Minneapolis, May 28, 1954, attached to Donald B. Cloward, Executive Secretary, Council on Christian Social Programs, The American Baptist Convention to Senator Hugh Butler July 13, 1954; "Indian Rights, Resolution adopted unanimously by the General Council of the Congregational Christian Churches at New Haven, Connecticut, on June 30, 1954," attached to Galen R. Weaver, The Council for Social Action of the Congregational Christian Churches to Guy Cordon, Senate Committee on Insular and Interior Affairs, July 30, 1954, both in Folder #32–Indians 2 of 2, box 23, Sen 83A-F9, IIAC, RG 46, NARA-DC.
75. "Address by Commissioner of Indian Affairs Dillon S. Myer, before the Western Governors' Conference at Phoenix, Arizona, December 9, 1952," folder 1950–1953 Commissioner of Indian Affairs, Memoranda and Reports (1 of 4), box 2, Myer Papers, HSTL.
76. Alva A. Simpson Jr., Chairman, "Report to the Western Governors' Conference, December 9, 1952, Phoenix, Arizona, from the Chairman and Executive Committee of the Governors' Interstate Indian Council," folder 3, Governors' Interstate Indian Council, 1954, 2:2, new box 14, Sen 83A-F9 RCIA, RG 46, NARA-DC.

77. John Collier, Institute of Ethnic Affairs, "House Subcommittee Advocates Denying Rights of Other Citizens Groups to American Indians," April 30, 1951, folder 3, box 3, Zimmerman Papers, CSRSC-UNML.
78. "American Indian Development Report of Activities for 1952," 1, 4, folder 173; "Third Annual Report, American Indian Development," 1, folder 174, both in box 21, D'Arcy McNickle Papers, Newberry Library (NL).
79. G. Warren Spaulding, in Area Resources Conference, January 12-13-14, 1953, folder 22217–53 061, box 6, CCF 1940–57 Phoenix Area, RG 75, NARA DC.
80. Minutes of a Meeting of Tribal Council of the Confederated Salish and Kootenai Tribes of the Flathead Reservation, August 16, 1952, folder 1950–1953 Commissioner of Indian Affairs, Memoranda and Reports (2 of 4), box 2, Myer Papers, HSTL.
81. Minutes of a Meeting of Tribal Council of the Confederated Salish and Kootenai Tribes of the Flathead Reservation, August 16, 1952, folder 1950–1953 Commissioner of Indian Affairs, Memoranda and Reports (2 of 4), box 2, Myer Papers, HSTL.
82. Commissioner to Secretary of the Interior, March 20, 1953, folder Personal Correspondence File, 1953, box 4, Myer Papers, HSTL.
83. "Abandonment and Liquidation in a Hurry," *Indian Affairs* (AAIA newsletter), October 20, 1953, folder Association on American Indians File . . . I Termination-General, August 1953–February 1954, box 76, Philleo Nash Papers, HSTL.
84. "Indian opposes end of U.S. Tribal Rule." *New York Times*, February 12, 1954.
85. Oliver La Farge to Board of Directors and Executive Director, AAIA, August 7, 1953, folder Association on American Indians File . . . I Termination-General, August 1953–February 1954, box 76, Nash Papers, HSTL.
86. S. Lyman Tyler, "A Work Paper on Termination: With an Attempt to Show its Antecedents," 71, folder 21, box 21, Sophie D. Aberle Papers, CSRSC-UNML. Lewis wrote the same to congressman William Henry Harrison, March 13, 1953, Klamath Executive Committee, 10, April 13, 1953, folder 15324–1949 Part 1A, box 23, CCF 1940–57 Klamath 054, RG 75, NARA-DC; copy also in folder Termination of Federal Control: Correspondence, 1953–1954 (A), box 154, James A. Haley Papers, McKay Archives Center, Florida Southern College (hereafter Haley Papers, MAC-FSC). Emmons said that Lewis articulated this policy with the help of Secretary of the Interior Douglas McKay. "Future Prospects in Indian Affairs," "An Address by Commissioner of Indian Affairs Glenn L. Emmons before the Annual Meeting of the Indian Rights Association, Philadelphia, Pennsylvania," January 21, 1954, 2, folder 13 1:2 Glenn L. Emmons, new box 11, Sen 83A-F9 RCIA, RG 46, NARA-DC.
87. Watkins to Brethren, First Presidency, Church of Jesus Christ of Latter-Day Saints, April 13, 1954, folder 11, box 11, Arthur V. Watkins papers; "This is Senator Watkins

from Utah," Mailing brochure from Friends for Watkins Committee, folder 17 Watkins, Arthur, box 221, Ernest L. Wilkinson Personal Papers (ELWPP), both in LTPSC.

88. Congressional desire became the BIA mantra. For example, "Mr. Spaulding stated that the withdrawal program is an edict or decree of Congress, not the Bureau of Indian Affairs; that Congress has been pressing the Commissioner to get out of business, especially for those phases where it can be done readily; and that the Commissioner is in the job to carry out the task. He is there to finish up a work that was started 100 years ago." Report of Resources Conference, October 8–10, 1952, Bureau of Indian Affairs, Aberdeen, South Dakota, Folder 00 Aberdeen Area 1952 Resource Conf., Box 7, CCF 1940–1957 054 Aberdeen Area Office, RG 75, NARA-DC.
89. Lesser to Nash, February 1, 1954, folder Association on American Indians File . . . I Termination-General, August 1953–February 1954, box 76, Nash Papers, HSTL.
90. "NCAI 'Atah Danilíníǵí Wááshindoondi 'Ałah," *Adahooníłígíí* (April 1, 1954): 14.
91. Emmons to All Area Directors, except Juneau, May 16, 1955, folder 11, box 2, Zimmerman Papers, CSRSC-UNML.
92. "Indian Ownership of Land," William Zimmerman Jr., letter to the editor, *New York Times*, July 12, 1955; Dorothy Van de Mark, "The Raid on Reservations," *Harpers Magazine*, reprint from March 1956 issue, folder 1, box 289, Murray Papers, MMMASC-UM.
93. Editorial, "How We Can Help the Indians," *Christian Century* 74, no. 7 (February 13 1957), reprinted by the Association on American Indian Affairs, Inc., in folder 214, box 25, McNickle Papers, NL.
94. Rosenthal, *Their Day in Court*, 169.
95. Metcalf, *Termination's Legacy*, 61.
96. Quote in Metcalf, *Termination's Legacy*, 236–37.
97. 1 Nephi 23, 2 Nephi 21–22, *Book of Mormon*.
98. Watkins to Brethren, First Presidency, Church of Jesus Christ of Latter-Day Saints, April 13, 1954, folder 11, box 11, Watkins papers, LTPSC.
99. Memo G. A. W. [Glen Wilkinson] to E. L. W. [Ernest Wilkinson], January 16, 1954, folder Menominee Indians, box 20, WCBR, LTPSC.
100. The Institute on Ethnic Affairs identified just three senators and seven representatives "supporting the rights of Indians" in early 1954, with five more senators and three more representatives who might be persuadable to support Indians. Martha L. Jay to Friend, February 1954, folder 13, box 288, Murray Papers, MMMASC-UM.
101. "Blackmail Charged to Indian Bureau," *New York Times*, September 17, 1958. Also cited in Metcalf, *Termination's Legacy*, 196. Lee Metcalf, "Termination in the 83rd Congress," 57.
102. "U.S. Ignores Indian, Montanan Charges," *New York Times*, January 31, 1958.

3. JUDGMENT MONEYS

Epigraph: Rosenthal, *Their Day in Court*, 8.

1. Barsh, "Indian Land Claims Policy," 9; and A Bill Amending an Act to Establish a Court for the Investigation of Claims Against the United States, chap. 92, 37th Cong., Sess.3, 12 Stat. 765 (1863).
2. "Statement Concerning H. R. 4497," folder 43/13 Legislation HMJ Sponsored 79th H R 4497 Indian Claims Commission—Creation 1945–46, box 43, accession no. 3560-002, Jackson Papers, UWLSC.
3. Rosenthal, *Their Day in Court*, 24. Russel Barsh wrote that almost one hundred tribes filed claims. Barsh, "Indian Land Claims Policy," 10.
4. Sutton, "Part 1: Focus on the Indian Claims Commission," in Sutton, *Irredeemable America*, 17–18.
5. Rosenthal, *Their Day in Court*, xi.
6. Rosenthal, *Their Day in Court*, 19–20.
7. Olson and Wilson, *Native Americans*, 134.
8. Rosenthal, *Their Day in Court*, 16–19.
9. "Address to the Law Faculty and Present and Past Law Review Staffs, University of California Law School," May 19, 1955, 13–14, folder Legal Subjects, 1949–72 (2 of 2), box 123, ELWPP, LTPSC.
10. "Address to the Law Faculty and Present and Past Law Review Staffs, University of California Law School," May 19, 1955, 14–15, folder Legal Subjects, 1949–72 (2 of 2), box 123, ELWPP, LTPSC.
11. "Address to the Law Faculty and Present and Past Law Review Staffs, University of California Law School," May 19, 1955, 15–16, folder Legal Subjects, 1949–72 (2 of 2), box 123, ELWPP, LTPSC. Wilkinson said that tragedy struck Ickes that week as his wife Anna was killed in an automobile accident on the Navajo Reservation. Roosevelt signed the bill, and Wilkinson recalled, "I have always felt that F. D. R. signed the bill more out of sympathy for Secretary Ickes than for any other reason" ("Address to the Law Faculty," 16). But Anna Ickes died August 31, 1935, and the bill became law in June 1938. Wilkinson probably confused this bill with the Menominee jurisdiction act, which became law on September 3, 1935. James, James, and Boyer, *Notable American Women*, vol. 2, 252; Act Conferring Jurisdiction upon the United States Court of Claims to Hear, Examine, Adjudicate, and Render Judgment on Any and All Claims which the Ute Indians or Any Tribe or Band Thereof May Have Against the United States, and For Other Purposes, Pub. L. No. 75-754, 52 Stat. 1209 (1938); Act to Refer the Claim of the Menominee Tribe of Indians to the Court of Claims with the Absolute Right of Appeal to the Supreme Court of the United States, Pub. L. No. 74-413, 49 Stat. 1085 (1935).

12. Rosenthal, *Their Day in Court*, 21–26, 68.
13. Rosenthal, *Their Day in Court*, 21–26.
14. Wilkinson, "Indian Tribal Claims," 517–18.
15. Wilkins, *Hollow Justice*, 23–24; Rosenthal, *Their Day in Court*, 32.
16. Wilkinson, "Indian Tribal Claims," 517–18.
17. William A. Brophy to Henry M. Jackson, May 20, 1946, folder 60/22 U.S. Indian Affairs Committee Indian Claims Commission Bill 1946–47, box 60, accession no. 3560–002, Jackson Papers, UWLSC.
18. "The Blackfeet Tribe of the Blackfeet Indian Reservation," (press release), April 14, 1951, folder Blackfeet [Indian Reservation], box 24, Nash Files, HSTL.
19. Loose form BIA620-4-59, n.d., folder Claims-Indian Claims Commission, box 86, William A. Brophy and Sophie Aberle Brophy Papers, 1923–1973 (Brophy Papers), HSTL.
20. [Name restricted], attorney to Henry M. Jackson, March 8, 1948, folder 15/23 U.S. Indian Claims Commissioner 1947–48, box 15, accession no. 3560–002, Jackson Papers, UWLSC.
21. [Name restricted], Clerk, Indian Claims Commission to Jackson, March 12, 1948, folder 15/23 U.S. Indian Claims Commissioner 1947–48, box 15, accession no. 3560–002, Jackson Papers, UWLSC.
22. One congressman, Charles Robertson of North Dakota, wrote of the role that claims attorney Ernest Wilkinson played in passage of the Indian Claims Commission Act: "I will say . . . in all candor, that Mr. Wilkinson is more responsible for it than any member of Congress." Metcalf, *Termination's Legacy*, 55. Wilkinson viewed the ICC work as critical to the Ute claims case, and to the Menominee claims case as well, as he charged some of the ICC work to the funds used to conduct those cases. See John W. Cragun to Ernest L. Wilkinson, November 29, 1952, folder Ute Fees, Moyle Controversy, box 18, WCBR, LTPSC.
23. Fixico, *Termination and Relocation*, 43. He titled chapter 2 "The Indian Claims Commission and the Zimmerman Plan."
24. Rosenthal, *Their Day in Court*, 50–63; and Meriam, *Problem of Indian Administration*, 48.
25. Meriam, *Problem of Indian Administration*, 19.
26. Bauer, *We Were All*; Beck, *Unfair Labor?*; Black, *Picturing Indians*; Child, *Holding Our World Together*; Child, *My Grandfather's Knocking Sticks*; and LaPier and Beck, *City Indian* are just some recent examples.
27. Hoxie, "Seeing and Not Seeing," 5–6.
28. Statement by the President Upon Signing Bill Creating the Indian Claims Commission, August 13, 1946, Harry S. Truman Library, accessed June 10, 2021, https://www.trumanlibrary.gov/library/public-papers/204/statement-president-upon-signing-bill-creating-indian-claims-commission.

29. Rosenthal, *Their Day in Court*, 92.
30. Statement by the President Upon Signing Bill Creating the Indian Claims Commission.
31. Rosenthal, *Their Day in Court*, 49.
32. "Indian Claims Commission Act," 60 Stat. 1049 (1946), section 2. Also discussed in Philp, *Termination Revisited*, 27. For Ernest Wilkinson's discussion of his role in convincing Congress to limit offsets, see *In the United States Court of Claims, No. 44304, with which are consolidated Nos. 44296, 44298, 44300, 44303, 44305 and 44306, The Menomine Tribe of Indians vs. The United States, Appendix to Statement in Support of Petition and Motion of Attorneys for an Award of Fees, Supplemental Statement on Services of the Attorneys* [1951], in *Menominee Fee Hearing* bound volume, 22–33, WCBR, LTPSC.
33. He told the Uintah and Ouray Tribal Business Committee that the offsets charged at $368,000 in their successful $31.5 million lawsuit would have been $2 million without this provision. Wilkinson to R. O. Curry, March 25, 1949, in Minutes, Uintah and Ouray Tribal Business Committee Special Meeting, March 29, 1949, folder 10333-1946-054, part 2, 2 of 3, box 11, CCF 1940–1957 Uintah & Ouray 054, RG 75, NARA-DC.
34. CAP, Secretary of the Interior to Henry Jackson, July 31, 1946; CAP, Secretary of the Interior to Joseph O'Mahoney, July 31, 1946, folder July 1946, box 10, Krug Papers, LOC.
35. "Indian Claims Commission Act," section 24.
36. Jackson to [Name restricted], January 27, 1948, folder 15/23 U.S. Indian Claims Commissioner 1947–48, box 15, accession no. 3560–002, Jackson Papers, UWLSC.
37. "Statement Concerning H. R. 4497," folder 43/13 Legislation HMJ Sponsored 79th H R 4497 Indian Claims Commission—Creation 1945–46, box 43, accession no. 3560–002, Jackson Papers, UWLSC.
38. "Statement Concerning H. R. 4497," folder 43/13 Legislation HMJ Sponsored 79th H R 4497 Indian Claims Commission—Creation 1945–46, box 43, accession no. 3560–002, Jackson Papers, UWLSC.
39. "Statement Concerning H. R. 4497," folder 43/13 Legislation HMJ Sponsored 79th H R 4497 Indian Claims Commission—Creation 1945–46, box 43, accession no. 3560–002, Jackson Papers, UWLSC.
40. Rosenthal, *Their Day in Court*, 115.
41. "The Overprotected Indian," 1. For an argument that the need for tribes to get approval to hire attorneys from the BIA and secretary of the Interior was both unconstitutional and unnecessary, see Willacy, "Contract Approval."
42. Rosenthal, *Their Day in Court*, 117–18.
43. [Name restricted] to Jackson, June 17, 1946, folder 15/5 U.S. Indian Affairs Bureau 1946–47. He received a similar letter from a Washington woman, saying, "My

Grand mother was born on the Cowlitz Reservation, of Indian blood, and how will I go about collecting money coming from Gov. Stevens treaties with the Indian." [Name restricted] to Jackson, January 16, 1951, folder 15/14 U.S. Indian Affairs Bureau General Correspondence 1950–51. Both in box 15, accession no. 3560-002, Jackson Papers, UWLSC.

44. For a detailed analysis of the confederated tribes' history, see Beck, *Seeking Recognition.*
45. Author interview with George C. Barton, Edgar A. Bowen, Don Whereat, and Eddie Helm, June 28, 2006, Empire, Oregon.
46. Kennedy, "Buying It Back," 17.
47. Rosenthal, *Their Day in Court*, xi, 266–67.
48. Several tribes that won judgments refused the money; they had gone through the process merely to prove that their lands had been illegally taken. The Taos Pueblo in New Mexico eventually had their sacred place of origin returned through a separate congressional bill. Gordon-McCutchan, *Taos Indians*; Lazarus, *Black Hills/White Justice*; and Olson and Wilson, *Native Americans*, 138. Quote from Robert W. Barker, "The Indian Claims Commission—the Conscience of the Nation in its Dealings with the Original American," Remarks given before the Committee on Indian Law, Federal Bar Association Convention, Washington DC, February 26, 1959, folder 3 Indians, box 211, ELWPP, LTPSC.
49. Lawson, *Dammed Indians*, xix.
50. Minutes, Uintah and Ouray Tribal Business Council Meeting, August 14, 1950, folder 1033-1946-054 1 of 3, box 11, CCF 1940–1957 Uintah and Ouray 054, RG 75, NARA-DC.
51. "Indian Tribal Funds," Extension of Remarks of Hon. Hubert H. Humphrey of Minnesota, April 19, 1949. *Congressional Record* offprint, folder General Correspondence 1946–1952, Indian Bills 1949–1950, 1, box 61, Ickes Papers, LOC.
52. U.S. Congress, House, Committee on Indian Affairs, "Hearings on H. Res. 166," 23.

4. MENOMINEE OF WISCONSIN

Epigraph: "The Current Termination Program in Indian Affairs," 55.

1. Some of the narrative in this chapter is from my book *Struggle for Self-Determination.*
2. *United States v. Cook.* A 1938 law changed this. Indian Mineral Leasing Act, Pub. L. No. 75-506, 52 Stat. 347 (1938).
3. The following summary is drawn from Beck, *Siege and Survival*; and Beck, *Struggle for Self-Determination.*
4. Beck, *Struggle for Self-Determination*, xii–xiii, 21.
5. "In the Court of Claims, No. 44302, Menominee Tribe of Indians v. The United States of America, Petition 9, Excess Timber Cutting, Act of 1890, filed December 1, 1938," *Menominee Petitions*, WCBR, LTPSC.

6. "In the Court of Claims, No. 44303, Menominee Tribe of Indians v. The United States of America, Petition 10, 1905 Blow Down, filed December 1, 1938," *Menominee Petitions*, WCBR, LTPSC.
7. The bill limited the cut of timber to 20 million feet per year. Act to Authorize the Cutting of Timber.
8. Senate Report 110, 60th Congress, 1st Session; James Rudolph Garfield to LaFollette, January 21, 1908, both in *Congressional Record* 42 (1908), 1182–83.
9. Beck, *Struggle for Self-Determination*, 79.
10. 1892 proposed constitution, LR 1881–1907, 1892:31904, RG 75, NARA-DC; "Constitution of the Menominee Tribe of Indians of the State of Wisconsin, 1904"; Minutes of Menominee Council Meeting, March 5, 1910; School Superintendent Thomas Wilson to Commissioner of Indian Affairs, March 18, 1910; Commissioner of Indian Affairs Valentine to Secretary of the Interior, April 2, 1910; John Francis Jr., Acting Chief Land Division to Wilson, April 12, 1910, all in CCF 1907–1939 Keshena 054, RG 75, NARA-DC.
11. McQuillan, "American Indian Timber Management Policy," 85–87.
12. H. H. Chapman, "The Menominee Indian Timber Case," 11–13, 18–19, Menominee Indian Papers, Wisconsin Historical Society Archives.
13. Nicholson to Commissioner of Indian Affairs, December 4, 1913, CCF 1907–1939 Keshena 174.1, RG 75, NARA-DC; Hosmer, *American Indians in the Marketplace*, 98–101; Cartwright, "Board of Indian Commissioners," vi; and Ayer, *Report*.
14. Ayer, *Report*, 15–17.
15. Nicholson to Commissioner of Indian Affairs, June 10, 1913; Hauke to Mrs. Jane Jacobs, November 9, 1914; Hauke to Nicholson, April 13, 1915; Assistant Commissioner Merritt to Aug. A. Breuninger, December 8, 1915; and Report of H. M. Creel, Inspector, March 10, 1923, all in CCF 1907–1939 Keshena 313, RG 75, NARA-DC; Merritt to Peter Washinawotoke, April 4, 1914; Minutes of the Council Meeting held by the Menominee Indians, Keshena, January 16, 1915, both in CCF 1907–1939 Keshena 054; Report of E. B. Linnen, October 12, 1915, 111; Minutes of a Conference held at Keshena, 10 September 1915, Exhibit W attached to Linnen Report, both in CCF 1907–1939 Keshena 150, all in RG 75, NARA-DC.
16. Kinney, *Indian Forest and Range*, 122–123; Sterling, *Report of a Forest Survey and Supplemental Investigations of the Menominee Indian Reservation*, February 8, 1935, p. 6, Miscellaneous Records of Forest Supervisor, 1905–1955, Records of the Menominee Indian Mills, 1900–1961, RG 75, National Archives at Chicago (NAC); Herzberg, "From Treaty to Termination," 288, 294; and Chapman, "Menominee Indian Timber Case," 3–4, 19–20.
17. Chapman, "Menominee Indian Timber Case," 19–20, 26.
18. In 1908 Pinchot "secured a cooperative agreement between the secretaries of Agriculture and Interior that 'gave the Forest Service supervision over the

handling of timber on Indian reservations.'" Although management of Indian forests was returned to the Indian Service in 1910, the USDA remained in charge of marking trees for cutting on the Menominee reservation under the LaFollette Act. McQuillan, "American Indian Timber Management," 85–87.

19. Kinney, *Indian Forest and Range*, 132–133, 323; Chapman, "Menominee Indian Timber Case," 13–14, 41, 54.
20. "In the Court of Claims, No. 44304, Menominee Tribe of Indians v. The United States of America, Petition 11, Clear Cutting of Timber, filed December 1, 1938" *Menominee Petitions*, WCBR, LTPSC.
21. Sterling, *Report of a Forest Survey*, 4.
22. Beck, *Struggle for Self-Determination*, 95–102; District Superintendent Peyton Carter, Inspection Report, October 19, 1927, CCF 1907–1939 Keshena 150; Carter to Commissioner of Indian Affairs, CCF 1907–1939 Keshena 313, both in RG 75, NARA-DC; Meriam, *Problem of Indian Administration*, 462.
23. McQuillan, "American Indian Timber Management," 86–87.
24. Meriam, *Problem of Indian Administration*, 42, 462–466, 515–516; Phebe Jewell Nichols, "Stating the Case for the Menominees," Wisconsin Historical Society Library; Carter to Commissioner of Indian Affairs, March 17, 1931, CCF 1907–1939 Keshena 806, RG 75, NARA-DC; Sady, "The Menominees," 5; Report of Delegation, Minutes of Menominee General Council Meeting, August 9, 1930, Menominee Tribal Archives and CCF 1907–1939 Keshena 054, RG 75, NARA-DC; Oral History Interview with Oscar R. Ewing, Harry S. Truman Library; Hughes, Schurman and Dwight, "Tentative Draft of Act to Incorporate the Menominee Tribe of Indians," box 136, Special Committee on Indian Affairs, Committee on Interior and Insular Affairs, Sen. 83 A-F9 RCIA, RG 46, NARA-DC.
25. Beck, *Struggle for Self-Determination*, 112.
26. Beck, *Struggle for Self-Determination*, 114–18.
27. Sterling, *Report of a Forest Survey*; Act to Refer the Claim of the Menominee Tribe of Indians to the Court of Claims with the Absolute Right of Appeal to the Supreme Court of the United States, Pub. L. No. 74–413, 49 Stat. 1085 (1935), p. 1087; and Sady, "The Menominees," 5–7.
28. Minutes of Meeting of Menominee General Council, August 9, 1930, Menominee Tribal Archives and CCF 1907–1939 Keshena 054, RG 75, NARA-DC. This is one of the few council meetings where Menominee language speakers' words were translated and transcribed into the minutes; Oshkosh gave his remarks in Menominee.
29. Beck, *Struggle for Self-Determination*, 124, 127–28.
30. Beck, *Struggle for Self-Determination*, ch. 8; Frechette to Collier, May 7, 1941; Minutes of Council Meeting, May 7, 1941, 24–31, box 136, Special Committee on Indian Affairs, Committee on Interior and Insular Affairs, Sen. 83 A-F9 RCIA, RG

46, NARA-DC; Letter from Zimmerman, July 10, 1941, CCF 1940–1943 Keshena 066, RG 75, NARA-DC; Fredenberg to Ernest Wilkinson, September 24, 1941, subfolder Menominee Personal and Confidential, folder Menominee Indians Reports etc., box 20, WCBR, LTPSC; U.S. Congress, House, Committee on Interior and Insular Affairs, Subcommittee on Indian Affairs, Hearings on H.R. 7104, 4.

31. Zimmerman to Murphy, April 1, 1946, General Correspondence 1935–1961, General Records, Records of the Keshena/Menominee Agency, RG 75, NAC.
32. Sterling, *Report of a Forest Survey*, 5; Kinney, *Indian Forest and Range*, 323; Statements of Al Dodge and Gordon Dickie, U.S. Congress, House, Committee on Interior and Insular Affairs, Subcommittee on Indian Affairs, Hearings on H.R. 7104, 19, 22; and Beck, *Struggle for Self-Determination*, 134.
33. U.S. Congress, Senate, *Officers and Employees*, 547.
34. Herzberg, "From Treaty to Termination," 304.
35. U.S. Congress, Senate, *Officers and Employees*, 560–63.
36. Dickie to Watkins, June 14, 1949, folder 9, box 12, Watkins Papers, LTPSC.
37. Menominee Tribe of Indians v. United States, no. 44304, Memorandum of History of Case in Court of Claims, December 9, 1949, folder Menominee Indians Reports etc., box 20. All thirteen claims as filed are bound into one volume, *Menominee Petitions*. Both in WCBR, LTPSC.
38. "Argument in Menominee Tribe of Indians vs. United States," 1, folder Menominee Indians Reports etc., box 20, WCBR, LTPSC.
39. "Argument in Menominee Tribe of Indians vs. United States," 3, folder Menominee Indians Reports etc., box 20, WCBR, LTPSC.
40. Herzberg, "From Treaty to Termination." 292–95. The bulk of the judgment was for mismanagement of the mill, and the next most significant claim was for clear-cutting. Seven suits were combined in the judgment. "Memorandum for the Commissioner of Indian Affairs on Settlement," folder Menominee Indians, box 20, WCBR, LTPSC.
41. Herzberg, "From Treaty to Termination," 310, 318.
42. Senator Hugh Butler, chair of the Senate Interior and Insular Affairs Committee wrote that the Menominee tribe "makes a profit on its lumber business and pays all its own expenses including governmental costs for education, welfare, etc. out of tribal funds." He believed "that fact demonstrates how completely out of date this wardship program is." Butler to James DeLancey Verplanck, April 11, 1953, folder 32–Indians, box 23, Sen 83A-F9 IIAC, RG 46, NARA-DC.
43. Actually, the tribe first requested $1,000, but it changed to $1,500 by the time it became pertinent to this story.
44. Orme Lewis to Watkins, July 22, 1953, reprinted in *Congressional Record-House*, August 1, 1953, 11198–99, and in *Congressional Record-Senate*, July 24, 1953, 10067–68.

45. Commissioner of Indian Affairs to Senator Hugh Butler, March 16, 1953, folder 1950–1953 Commissioner of Indian Affairs, Memoranda and Reports (3 of 4), box 2, Myer Papers, HSTL.
46. Lewis to Watkins, July 22, 1953.
47. File memo by John B. Keliiaa, Program Officer, May 16, 1952 re Conference with Menominee Delegation, 8 May 1952; "Attitude [of] Delegation—extracts from [memo] to Commissioner." n.d. Both in Menominee Agency Decimal Correspondence (MADC) Files, 1934–1961, RG 75, NAC.
48. G.A.W. [Glen Wilkinson] memorandum for E.L.W. [Ernest Wilkinson], May 13, 1953. Local Shawano attorney Lloyd Andrews wrote to Glen Wilkinson on April 16, 1953, that he thought the Menominee had been interested in extricating themselves from federal supervision in the 1930s, "Today, however, with separation pressure coming from the Congress and, likewise, from the Indian Office, the Tribe, as you know, is resisting the idea of separation." Both in folder Menominee Indians, box 20, WCBR, LTPSC.
49. Keliiaa, Program Officer, Robert Beasley, Acting Director, Division of Program, June 11, 1952; "Notes—Meeting with Members of the South Branch Community. 6/18/52"; Keliiaa to Beasley, June 24, 1952, Neopit. All in MADC Files, 1934–1961, RG 75, NAC.
50. "Notes—Meeting with Members of the South Branch Community. 6/18/52," MADC Files, 1934–1961, RG 75, NAC.
51. Keliiaa to Beasley, June 24, 1952, Neopit, MADC Files, 1934–1961, RG 75, NAC.
52. Mary Dodge interview with Mitchell Al Dodge, February 5, [1976?], box 10; Al Dodge and John Fossum to Douglas McKay, June 11, 1953, box 6, both in Mitchell A. Dodge Papers, LTPSC. The typed transcript of the interview is filled with typographical errors; they have been corrected in this quote. The budget director happened to be named Joseph Dodge, and Al pretended to be a relative, which got him into the office to convince him to sign off on the house version of the bill. Representative Wesley D'Ewart of Montana agreed with the interest figure, stating in a congressional hearing that the $9.5 million in the treasury was costing the federal government about $200,000 annually. The Menominee funds were earning 4 percent interest in the federal treasury. "Menominee Indian Tribe of Wisconsin," *Congressional Record—House*, August 1, 1953, 11197.
53. Testimony of Representative Henry S. Reuss (Wis.) before Subcommittee on Indian Affairs, House Committee on Interior and Insular Affairs, 27 February 1956, folder 20, box 9, Zimmerman Papers, CSRSC-UNML.
54. William Zimmerman Jr., "Menominee Termination Problems—1955," June 1955, folder 20, box 9, Zimmerman Papers, CSRSC-UNML.
55. Herzberg, "From Treaty to Termination," 311. These machinations are also discussed in "Report to Menominee Tribe on Activities of Menominee Tribal

Delegates and Attorneys During Period from June 20, 1953 to August 1, 1953 Regarding H. R. 2828," August 17, 1953, folder Menominee Indians, box 20, WCBR, LTPSC.

56. Minutes, Uintah and Ouray Tribal Business Committee, June 23, 1953, folder 1033-1946-054 Part 3, 1 of 2, box 11, CCF 1940–1957 Uintah & Ouray 054, RG 75, NARA-DC.
57. Herzberg, "From Treaty to Termination," 311.
58. Gordon Keshena, June 20, 1953, quoted in Testimony of Representative Henry S. Reuss (Wis.) before Subcommittee on Indian Affairs, House Committee on Interior and Insular Affairs, February 27, 1956, folder 20, box 9, Zimmerman Papers, CSRSC-UNML.
59. Watkins, June 20, 1953, quoted in Testimony of Representative Henry S. Reuss (Wis.) before Subcommittee on Indian Affairs, House Committee on Interior and Insular Affairs, February 27, 1956, folder 20, box 9, Zimmerman Papers, CSRSC-UNML.
60. Mr. Worden, June 20, 1953, quoted in Testimony of Representative Henry S. Reuss (Wis.) before Subcommittee on Indian Affairs, House Committee on Interior and Insular Affairs, February 27, 1956, folder 20, box 9, Zimmerman Papers, CSRSC-UNML.
61. Deer, et al, "Effects of Termination on the Menominee," 7. In Gordon Dickie Sr., Papers, Menominee Historic Preservation Department.
62. Herzberg, "From Treaty to Termination," 311–16; Lurie, "Menominee Indians," 39; Ray, *Menominee Tribe of Indians*, 14–21; interviews with Menominee people by the author, 1991–1999 (interviewees were granted anonymity); "Resolution, Menominee General Council-June 20, 1953," attached to Exhibit No. 1, Glen Wilkinson to Watkins, June 23, 1953, "Report to Menominee Tribe on Activities of Menominee Tribal Delegates and Attorneys During Period from June 20, 1953 to August 1, 1953 Regarding H. R. 2828," August 17, 1953, folder Menominee Indians, box 20, WCBR, LTPSC.
63. *Shawano Leader*, June 22, 1953. Other area newspaper headlines portrayed the same perspective: "Menominee Indians to Back Three-Year Freedom Plan," *Minneapolis Star*, June 23, 1953; and "Freedom Plan Okayed by Menominee Indians," *Milwaukee Journal* June 23, 1953.
64. "Report to Menominee Tribe on Activities of Menominee Tribal Delegates and Attorneys During Period from June 20, 1953 to August 1, 1953 Regarding H. R. 2828," August 17, 1953, folder Menominee Indians, box 20, WCBR, LTPSC.
65. Herzberg, "From Treaty to Termination," 314–16.
66. See for example Lee Metcalf to Mrs. Eugene E. Wilson, Billings, February 24, 1956; Metcalf to Edward P. Whiteman, February 10, 1956, and other similar correspondence in 240/7 Department of the Interior: Bureau of Indian Affairs,

Termination of Federal Responsibility, 1955–1965. Shortly thereafter Metcalf admitted that he had been fooled by the assurances he received. He told NCAI members, "Later it developed that in at least two instances the consent was obtained by refusal to permit the tribes to withdraw and use their own funds until the termination bills had received the tribe's consent." He referred there to the Klamath and the Menominee. "A Story of Two Congresses" Speech before the 13th Annual Convention, National Congress of American Indians, September 24–28,1956, Salt Lake City, Utah, 661/2 Speeches 1949–1960. All in Lee Metcalf Papers, Montana Historical Society Research Center Archives (MHSRCA).

67. "Report to Menominee Tribe on Activities of Menominee Tribal Delegates and Attorneys During Period from June 20, 1953 to August 1, 1953 Regarding H. R. 2828," August 17, 1953, folder Menominee Indians, box 20, WCBR, LTPSC.
68. Al Dodge, James Frechette, Allie Frechette, Jerome Worden, Menominee Delegates, "Memorandum of the Menominee Indians in Opposition to H.R. 2828," exhibit no. 11, attached to "Report to Menominee Tribe on Activities of Menominee Tribal Delegates and Attorneys During Period from June 20, 1953 to August 1, 1953 Regarding H. R. 2828."
69. Gordon Dickie Sr., Interview, Menominee Historic Preservation Department, March 16, 1993.
70. "Menominee Indian Tribe of Wisconsin," *Congressional Record—House*, August 1, 1953, 11197.
71. *Menominee Termination Act*, act to provide for a per capita distribution of Menominee tribal funds and authorize the withdrawal of the Menominee Tribe from Federal jurisdiction, Pub. L. No. 83–399, 68 Stat. 250 (1954). See also tables 5 and 6, Termination Laws, in appendix.
72. Donald Janson, "Tribesmen Decry U.S. Policy," *New York Times*, June 15, 1961.
73. "Blackmail Charged to Indian Bureau," *New York Times*, September 17, 1958; and "A Story of Two Congresses" Speech before the 13th Annual Convention, National Congress of American Indians, 24–28 September 1956, Salt Lake City, Utah, folder 661/2 Speeches 1949–1960 includes Indians, box 661, Metcalf Papers, MHSRCA.
74. "Indians Came Out Better Than Expected in 83rd Congress," NCAI Report, 1954, originally viewed in 549.22.2–4, Fort Berthold Papers, Robert Rietz Collection, Community Archives of NAES College, now in Robert Rietz Papers 1876–1982, UCLSCRC; Statement of Jonathan M. Steere, President Indian Rights Association, before Subcommittees on Interior and Insular Affairs in the Senate and House re termination bills for Texas Indians, Sac and Fox in Nebraska and Kansas, Klamath, Flathead, Seminole, Turtle Mountain, California Indians, and Menominee, folder Termination of Federal Control: Correspondence, 1953–1954 (B), box 155, Haley Papers, MAC-FSC.

75. *Menominee Termination Act.*
76. Orfield, "Ideology and the Indian"; Beck, *Struggle for Self-Determination*, 129–49.
77. George W. Kenote and Glen A. Wilkinson, Memorandum for Conference Committee on Menominee Termination Bill (H.R. 4130), June 21, 1961, folder Folder Indian Affairs: Menominee Tribe, 1958–1962 (B), box 150, Haley Papers, MAC-FSC.
78. *Menominee Tribe of Indians v. United States.*
79. Peroff, *Menominee Drums*; Herzberg, "Termination to Restoration;" Beck, *Struggle for Self-Determination*, 166–88; and Ulrich, *American Indian Nations*, 143–58.
80. He added, "This legislation does not, of course, provide any such assurance." "The New Indian Law and Its Forestry Implications," speech by Glen A. Wilkinson at Washington Section of the Society of American Foresters, Washington DC, September 22, 1954, folder Menominee Indians, box 20, WCBR, LTPSC.
81. Untitled, undated speech on Indian policy by Lee Metcalf, 661/5 Speeches; Metcalf made the same observation in "A Story of Two Congresses," speech before the 13th Annual Convention, National Congress of American Indians, September 24–28, 1956. Salt Lake City, Utah, 661/2 Speeches 1949–1960, both in Metcalf Papers, MHSRCA.

5. KLAMATH TRIBES OF OREGON

Epigraph 1: Crawford to President Dwight Eisenhower, March 5, 1953, folder 32—Indians, box 23, Sen 83A-F9 IIAC, RG 46, NARA-DC.

Epigraph 2: Proceedings of General Council Meeting, December 17–21, 1953, folder 00–1951, box 24, CCF 1940–1957 Klamath 054, RG 75, NARA-DC.

1. Forrest Cooper to Orme Lewis, December 11, 1953, folder #32–Indians 2 of 2, box 23, Sen 83A-F9 IIAC, RG 46, NARA-DC.
2. For discussion of this effort see Beck, *Seeking Recognition*, ch. 6, 7.
3. Harvey Wright, Report on Interstate Council on Indian Affairs held at Salt Lake City, May 12, 1950, folder "Indian Affairs, Jan 1950-Aug 1950"; Minutes, Governor's Advisory Committee on Indian Affairs, November 29, 1950, folder "Indian Affairs, Sept.-Dec. 1950," both in Office of Governor Douglas McKay Papers, Oregon State Archives.
4. Stephen Dow Beckham testimony, AIPRC Task Force #10 Transcript, March 13, 1976, Salem Oregon, p. 101, Records of the American Indian Policy Review Commission, RG 220, NARA College Park, Maryland (CPM).
5. *Youth Wants to Know*, program transcript, Sunday, March 29, 1953, Frank Blair guest moderator, folder TV and Radio Broadcasts by Secretary McKay-1953, box 65, Douglas McKay Papers, University of Oregon Special Collections and University Archives.
6. Pryse to all Superintendents in Region 3, August 10, 1948; folder 6 Year Reservation Program-Withdrawal folder, box 15, PAO 02, RG 75, NARA-PAR.

7. Act To provide for the termination of Federal supervision over the property of certain tribes and bands of Indians located in western Oregon and the individual members thereof, and for other purposes, Pub. L. No. 83–588, 68 Stat. 724 (1954); *Klamath Termination Act*, Act To provide for the termination of Federal supervision over the property of the Klamath Tribe of Indians located in the State of Oregon and the individual members thereof, and for other purposes, Pub. L. No. 83–587, 68 Stat. 718 (1954).
8. Cooper to Lewis, November 25, 1953, folder #32–Indians 2 of 2, box 23, Sen 83A-F9 IIAC, RG 46, NARA-DC.
9. Bilka, "Remaking," 37; Haynal, "Termination and Tribal Survival," 271–72.
10. Stern, "Livelihood and Tribal Government," 172–73.
11. Bilka, "Klamath's Path after Termination," 21–22.
12. "The New Indian Law and Its Forestry Implications," speech by Glen A. Wilkinson at Washington Section of the Society of American Foresters, Washington DC, September 22, 1954, folder Menominee Indians, box 20, WCBR, LTPSC.
13. Members of Klamath Tribal Council to Secretary of the Interior, February 18, 1914, folder 002122-016-0005, "Major Council Meetings"; 20 Ind. Cl. Comm. 522, Before the Indian Claims Commission, The Klamath and Modoc Tribes and Yahooskin Band of Snake Indians, Plaintiffs v. The United States, Defendant, May 14, 1969, in folder 93, box 9, Erminie Wheeler-Voegelin Papers, NL. The Klamath received $108,750 for the eighty-seven thousand acres, which was valued at $2,980,000. *Klamath & Moadoc v. United States*, 296 U.S. 247–48. Wilkinson, Cragun, and Barker argued that this case was the basis for including an unconscionable clause in the Indian Claims Commission Act. Memorandum on Claim, etc., folder Menominee Indians, box 20, WCBR, LTPSC.
14. Act to Provide for Determining the Heirs of Deceased Indians, for the Disposition and Sale of Allotments of Deceased Indians, for the Leasing of Allotments, and for Other Purposes, Pub. L. No. 61–313, 36 Stat. 855 (1910), Section 7.
15. February 19, 1916, in Proceedings of the Klamath Tribal Council at a series of Meetings at Klamath Agency, Oregon, beginning Feb. 19, 1916, to discuss the Proposed Opening of the Reservation, folder 002122-016-020, "Major Council Meetings."
16. Kirk to Commissioner of Indian Affairs, March 20, 1917, folder Klamath Agency, box 135, Sen 83A-F9 IAAC, RG 46, NARA-DC.
17. "Hearing in the Indian Bureau on December 30, 1927, on the Klamath items in the appropriation acts for the fiscal year ending July 1, 1929," folder Klamath Agency, box 135, Sen 83A-F9 IAAC, RG 46, NARA-DC.
18. "The Melodrama of Klamath Still Incredibly Unrolls"; John Collier, American Indian Defense Association to Lynn Frazier, Chairman, Senate Indian Investigation Committee, December 18, 1930, both in folder Klamath Agency, box 135, Sen 83A-F9 IAAC, RG 46, NARA-DC.

19. Frederic A. Baker to Senator William Langer, February 1, 1947, folder Indians 1946–1952, 1, box 62, Ickes Papers, LOC.
20. Beaird, "Termination of Federal Supervision," 21–22; and Haynal, "Termination and Tribal Survival," 275–76.
21. Ickes to Willoughby Waller, June 19, 1933, folder Harold L. Ickes Secretary of Interior File Indians, 1, 1933–1935, box 168, Ickes Papers, LOC.
22. Personal communication with Rich Clow, June 1, 2019.
23. Act to Provide for Determining the Heirs of Deceased Indians, Section 7. On the budget knowledge of Klamath tribal leaders and their allies see correspondence and data, including Minutes of Meeting of General Tribal Council, March 9,1928, in folder Klamath Agency, box 135, Sen 83A-F9 IAAC, RG 46, NARA-DC.
24. See, for example, the Crawfords to Commissioner, June 23, 1932, folder Crawford, Wade D., box 136, Sen 83A-F9 IAAC, RG 46, NARA-DC.
25. Beaird, "Termination of Federal Supervision," 17.
26. Ickes to Frederic A. Baker, February 9, 1947, folder Indians 1946–1952, 1, box 62, Ickes Papers, LOC.
27. Statement of John Collier, Executive Secretary, American Indian Defense Association, U.S. Congress, Senate, *Incorporation of the Klamath Indian Corporation*, 16.
28. U.S. Congress, Senate, *Dismissal of Wade Crawford.*
29. The OIA moved its headquarters to the Merchandise Mart in Chicago from 1942 to 1947 to make room in DC for federal agencies directly involved with the war effort.
30. Minutes, Business Committee Meeting, November 11, 1943, folder 49796–1942 Klamath Part 4A 054, box 17, CCF 1940–1957 Klamath 054, RG 75, NARA-DC.
31. See for example Minutes, General Council Meeting, 27 December 1945; Minutes, General Council Meeting, January 24, 1946, both in box 17, CCF 1940–1957 Klamath 054, RG 75, NARA-DC.
32. Copy of resolution presented by Jesse L, Kirk, vice chairman of the business committee, and Clayton Kirk to General Council, December 27, 1940; Resolution. No date or signature but prepared at request of December 27, 1940, General Council; Minutes, General Council, December 27, 1940, reconvened from December 19, 1940; Jesse Kirk to Boyd Jackson, January 28, 1941; Collier to B. G. Courtright, Superintendent, Klamath Agency, May 14, 1941; Courtright to Collier, May 28, 1941, all in folder 33974–1941 Klamath 054, box 17, CCF 1940–1957 Klamath 054, RG 75, NARA-DC.
33. Minutes, General Council Meeting, January 24, 1946, folder 49796–1942 Klamath Part 5A 054, box 17; Minutes, General Council Meeting, December 11, 1947, folder 49796–1942 Klamath Part 6A 054, box 18, both in CCF 1940–1957 Klamath 054, RG 75, NARA-DC.

34. Resolution introduced by Dice Crain, defeated 54–60, on October 4, 1946. After dinner break, Boyd Jackson's delegate report was accepted by a vote of 81–0. Jackson had followed business committee instructions. Minutes, General Council Meeting, 3, October 4, 1946, folder 49796–1942 Klamath Part 6C 054, box 18, CCF 1940–1957 Klamath 054, RG 75, NARA-DC.
35. Wade Crawford delegate report, October 4, 1946, in Minutes, General Council Meeting, 3, October 4, 1946, folder 49796–1942 Klamath Part 6C 054, box 18, both in CCF 1940–1957 Klamath 054, RG 75, NARA-DC.
36. Cora M. Crystal, John W. Vaughan, Wilbur Eggeman, Evelyn Cheraldo, Delford Lang, Nettie Smith, Debbon Cook, Wade Crawford to Morse, June 16, 1945, folder 25357–1945 Klamath 054, box 19, CCF 1940–1957 Klamath 054, RG 75, NARA-DC.
37. Text of bill in Minutes, Business Committee Meeting, June 5, 1947, folder 49796–1942 Klamath Part 6B 054, box 18, both in CCF 1940–1957 Klamath 054, RG 75, NARA-DC.
38. U.S. Congress, Senate, *Officers and Employees of the Federal Government*, 547.
39. Seldon Kirk, in Minutes, General Council Meeting, June 26, 1947, folder 49796–1942 Part 6B box 18, CCF 1940–1957 Klamath 054, RG 75. See 1932 letterhead of Indian Citizenship League of Oregon, in folder Wade D. Crawford, box 136, Sen 83A-F9 IAAC, RG 46, NARA-DC. Both in NARA-DC.
40. Minutes, General Council Meeting, June 26, 1947, folder 49796–1942 Klamath Part 6B 054, box 18, both in CCF 1940–1957 Klamath 054, RG 75, NARA-DC.
41. Quoted in Beaird, "Termination of Federal Supervision," 43.
42. Minutes, General Council Meeting, July 29, August 2, 1948, folder 19982–1948 Part 2C, box 20, CCF 1940–1957 Klamath 054, RG 75, NARA-DC.
43. Ray, "Klamath Oppose Liquidation," 16.
44. Ray, "Klamath Oppose Liquidation," 22.
45. Minutes, General Council Meeting, November 11–15, 1948, folder 19982–1948 Klamath Part 1A 054, box 19, CCF 1940–1957 Klamath 054, RG 75, NARA-DC.
46. Proceedings of Special General Council Meeting, 30, August 31, September 6, 1951, folder 19982–1948 Part 4A, box 21, CCF 1940–1957 Klamath 054, RG 75, NARA-DC.
47. Proceedings, General Council Meeting, February 2, 3, 9, 1950, folder 19982–1948 Part 3A, box 20, and folder 19982–1948 Part 3B, box 21, CCF 1940–1957 Klamath 054, RG 75, NARA-DC.
48. Cooper to Kirkley Coulter, January 21, 1954, folder #32–Indians 2 of 2, box 23, Sen 83A-F9 IIAC, RG 46, NARA-DC.
49. Delegate Boyd Jackson report, Minutes, General Council Meeting, June 24–25, 1948, folder 19982–1948 Klamath Part 1B 054, box 19, CCF 1940–1957 Klamath 054, RG 75, NARA-DC.

50. Haynal, "From Termination through Restoration," 102.
51. Proceedings of General Council Meeting, December 17–21, 1953, folder 00–1951, box 24, CCF 1940–1957 Klamath 054, RG 75, NARA-DC.
52. Minutes, Klamath Tribal Executive Committee, 29, September 30, 1953, folder 19982–1948 Part 5A, box 21, CCF 1940–1957 Klamath 054, RG 75, NARA-DC.
53. For analysis of the plenary power doctrine see Wilkins, *American Indian Sovereignty*; and Clark, *Lone Wolf v. Hitchcock.*
54. Minutes, Klamath General Council Meeting, January 14–15, 1954; Resolution of executive committee, February 6, 1954, both in folder 00–1952 Part 2B, box 24, CCF 1940–1957 Klamath 054, RG 75, NARA-DC.
55. Minutes, Klamath Tribal Executive Committee and Special Committee, February 4, 1954, folder 19982–1948 Part 5A, box 21, CCF 1940–1957 Klamath 054, RG 75, NARA-DC.
56. Minutes, Klamath Tribal Executive Committee and Special Committee, February 6, 1954, folder 19982–1948 Part 5A, box 21, CCF 1940–1957 Klamath 054, RG 75, NARA-DC.
57. This observation is based on a reading of correspondence between the Crawfords and Grorud from the early 1930s through 1949 in folder Crawford, Wade D., box 136, and folder Klamath Investigation, box 137, Sen 83A-F9 IAAC, RG 46, NARA-DC.
58. Report of Delegates, Proceedings of General Council Meeting, July 29, 1954, folder 19982–1948 Part 7B, box 22, CCF 1940–1957 Klamath 054, RG 75, NARA-DC.
59. Proceedings of General Council Meeting, July 29, 1954, folder 19982–1948 Part 7B, box 22, CCF 1940–1957 Klamath 054, RG 75, NARA-DC.
60. Myer to All Tribal Councils, June 8, 1950, in Proceedings of General Council Meeting, July 6, 1950, folder 19982–1948 Part 4B, box 21, CCF 1940–1957 Klamath 054, RG 75, NARA-DC.
61. Proceedings of Klamath General Council Meeting, January 17–18, 1955; McKay to Kirk, April 26, 1954; Kirk to McKay, May 14,1954; all in folder 00–1952 Part 2A, box 24, CCF 1940–1957 Klamath 054, RG 75, NARA-DC.
62. Wilkinson to Senator Richard Neuberger, June 30, 1955; Neuberger to Glen A. Wilkinson, July 25, 1955; Zimmerman to Neuberger, July 28, 1955; Memorandum for Mr. Zimmerman Respecting Current Status of Klamath Termination Bill, attached to Wilkinson to Zimmerman, May 9, 1955, all in folder 14, box 9, Zimmerman Papers, CSRSC-UNML.
63. Baker to Langer, February 1, 1947, folder Indians 1946–1952, 1, box 62, Ickes Papers, LOC; Castaneda, "Making News," 81, 84.
64. Zimmerman to Neuberger, July 28, 1955, folder 14, box 9, Zimmerman Papers, CSRSC-UNML.
65. "Possible Lead Paragraph on Releases on 'Indians and Other Americans,'" Draft GAW 5-13-59, folder 15, box 9, Zimmerman Papers, CSRSC-UNML.

66. Lewis to Richard Nixon, President of the Senate, January 4, 1954, in "Termination of Federal Supervision over Property of the Klamath Tribe," folder 14, box 9, Zimmerman Papers, CSRSC-UNML.
67. Green to Fred A. Seaton, July 31, 1956, folder 14, box 9, Zimmerman Papers, CSRSC-UNML.
68. See for example Minutes, Klamath Tribal Executive Committee and Special Committee, February 4, 1954, folder 19982–1948 Part 5A, box 21; Report of Delegates, Proceedings of General Council Meeting, July 29, 1954, folder 19982–1948 Part 7B, box 22; Proceedings of Special Meeting of Klamath General Council, 28 October 1954; Dorothy McAnulty, Seldon Kirk, and Boyd Jackson comments on 17 January in Proceedings of Klamath General Council Meeting, January 17–18, 1955, both in folder 00–1952 Part 2A, box 24, all in CCF 1940–1957 Klamath 054, RG 75, NARA-DC.
69. Ketcham, "Terminating the Klamaths," 17.
70. Report of Delegates, Proceedings of General Council Meeting, July 29, 1954, folder 19982–1948 Part 7B, box 22; Glenn A. Wilkinson to Seldon Kirk, June 30, 1954, Minutes, Klamath General Council Meeting, July 29, 1954, folder 00–1952 Part 2A, box 24; both in CCF 1940–1957 Klamath 054, RG 75, NARA-DC.
71. Haynal, "From termination to Restoration," 102.
72. Orme Lewis to Richard M. Nixon, January 4, 1954; "Background Data Relating to the Klamath and Modoc Tribes and the Yahooskin Band of Snake Indians, Generally Referred to As the Klamath Tribe and Located on the Klamath Reservation in the State of Oregon"; "Statement of Hon. Sam Coon, A Representative in Congress from the Sate of Oregon"; "Statement of E. Morgan Pryse, Area Director, Portland Office, Bureau of Indian Affairs," all in *Joint Hearing before the Subcommittees of the Committees on Interior and Insular Affairs*, part 4.
73. Proceedings of Klamath General Council Meeting, January 17–18 1955, folder 00–1952 Part 2A, box 24, CCF 1940–1957 Klamath 054, RG 75, NARA-DC.
74. *Klamath Termination Act*, 719.
75. Neuberger, "How Oregon Rescued a Forest," 49.
76. "Klamath Tribal Properties Valued at $121,659,618," Department of the Interior Press Release, February 24, 1958, folder 15, box 9, Zimmerman Papers, CSRSC-UNML.
77. "Klamath Indian Forest and Marsh Areas Designated," For Release December 16, 1958, folder Press Releases—B.I.A., 1954–58, box 92, Brophy Papers, HSTL.
78. Stanford Research Institute, *Preliminary Planning for Termination of Federal Control over the Klamath Indian Tribe*, April 1956, 3, folder 1, box 23, Aberle Papers, CSRSC-UNML.
79. Ketcham, "Terminating the Klamaths," 13, 18.

80. Seaton to Neuberger, September 28, 1957, quoted in "Department Stresses Importance of Conserving Klamath Indian Timber Resources," For Release September 28, 1957, folder Press Releases—B.I.A., 1954–58, box 92, Brophy Papers, HSTL. On timber and lumber industry opposition to this bill, see Mortimer B. Doyle, Executive Vice President, National Lumber Manufacturers Association to Neuberger, March 27, 1958, copy, folder Indian Affairs: Klamath Tribe, 1956–1967 (B), box 150, Haley Papers, MAC-FSC.
81. Neuberger, "How Oregon Rescued a Forest," 52.
82. Neuberger, "How Oregon Rescued a Forest," 52.
83. Lawrence E. Davies, "Oregon Indians Split on Future," *New York Times*, June 19, 1955. See also Minutes May 13, 1965, and May 14, 1965, folder Subcom. On Indian Affairs Minutes 1 of 2, box 75, 89th Congress IIAC, RG 233, NARA-DC.
84. Lawrence E. Davies, "Klamath Indians Wary with Funds," *New York Times*, July 2, 1961.
85. Haynal, "Termination and Tribal Survival," 296; *Klamath Indian Tribe Restoration Act*, Pub. L. No. 99–398, 100 Stat. 849 (1986). Haynal discusses the tribal reunification and restoration process in his dissertation, "From Termination through Restoration," 158–218.
86. Emphasis in original. Elnathan Davis Sr. to Seldon Kirk, Personal Report on NCAI Meeting, Omaha, November 17–22, 1954, Minutes, Klamath General Council Meeting, January 14, 1955, folder 00–1952 Part 2A, box 24, CCF 1940–1957 Klamath 054, RG 75, NARA-DC.
87. Text of Resolutions of Governors' Interstate Indian Council Meeting, Sun Valley ID, in Minutes, Klamath Tribal Executive Committee, November 15, 1954, folder 00–1952 Part 2A, box 24, CCF 1940–1957 Klamath 054, RG 75, NARA-DC.
88. "To Repeal the Klamath Tribe Judgment Fund Act," 2; 20 Ind. Cl. Comm. 522, folder 93, box 9, Wheeler-Voegelin Papers, NL.

6. TRIBES OF FORT BERTHOLD

Epigraph: U.S. Congress, House, "Fort Berthold Hearings," 14.

1. Broto and Calvet, "Sacrifice Zones"; Colten, "An Incomplete Solution"; Fox, "Mountaintop Removal"; Henry, "Extractive Fictions" are just a few examples.
2. Colten, "An Incomplete Solution," 91–92.
3. Voyles, *Wastelanding*, 9–10.
4. Broto and Calvet, "Sacrifice Zones," 280.
5. There is a striking similarity to American Cold War policy impacts on Indigenous communities in its Pacific protectorates and territories where nuclear and other military weapons were tested, or where the military simply took control of the places as part of U.S. colonial ambitions. The territory of Hawaii was also used as a military base and testing grounds, making all these places

sacrifice zones under U.S. policy. Arriolas, "Securing Nature," 29–36; Dibblin, *Day of Two Suns*; Kajihiro, "Nation Under the Gun"; Niedenthal, *For the Good of* Mankind; and Trask, "Struggle for Hawaiian Sovereignty."

6. Hauptman, *In the Shadow of Kinzua*, 65.
7. Personal communication with ethnobotanist Rosalyn LaPier, December 12, 2021.
8. Fenn, *Encounters*, 18–20; Jennings, *Founders of America*, 78.
9. Meyer, "Fort Berthold," 225–26.
10. Meyer, "Fort Berthold," 239–41.
11. Meyer, "Fort Berthold," 241–45.
12. Meyer, "Fort Berthold," 244n20.
13. U.S. Congress, Senate, *Protesting the Construction*, 15.
14. "Testimony and Memorial," April 24, 1945, U.S. Congress, Senate, *Protesting the Construction*, 1, 8–11. See also Harper, "Ft. Berthold Indians Hope," 22; VanDevelder, *Coyote Warrior*, 115–19; Meyer, "Fort Berthold," 239–47. VanDevelder interviewed tribal members who recalled collecting suits from local churches and "dimes and quarters in a Bull Durham sack to help the council buy train tickets." *Coyote Warrior*, 113.
15. U.S. Congress, Senate, *Protesting the Construction*, 4–8.
16. Resolution, May 25, 1946; Cross to Senator O'Mahoney, and Cross to Senator Burton K. Wheeler, June 12, 1946, all in folder 2 Garrison Dam 3:3, box 13, Sen 83A-F9 RCIA, RG 46, NARA-DC.
17. "Garrison Dam, N.D., Lieu Lands Offer not Approved," Department of the Interior Press Release, December 30, 1946, folder 3, box 9, Zimmerman Papers, CSRSC-UNML.
18. Ickes to Walter Remmery, July 17, 1948, folder Indians 1946–1952, 2, box 62, Ickes Papers, LOC.
19. VanDevelder, *Coyote Warrior*, 115.
20. Ralph H. Case, Counsel to George Gillette, Chairman, "Report to the Tribal Council," July 28, 1947, folder Garrison Dam 1:3, box 13, Sen 83A-F9 RCIA, RG 46, NARA-DC.
21. Meyer, "Fort Berthold," 243–47.
22. Whitman to Friend, n.d. [ca. December 1949], folder 3 Garrison Dam, N. Dakota 2:2, box 12, Sen 83A-F9 RCIA, RG 46, NARA-DC; VanDevelder, *Coyote Warrior*, 135. For correspondence written to the senate between 1946 and 1950 opposing the dam and supporting compensation and rights for the tribes from non-Indian citizens and Indian individuals and tribes across the nation, clergy and church groups, the Association on American Indian Affairs, NCAI, various local and national representatives of the Daughters of the American Revolution, women's clubs, Indian and non-Indian tribal support organizations, veterans

organizations, NAACP branches, and more, see Garrison Dam folders in box 12, Sen 83A-F9 RCIA, RG 46, NARA-DC.

23. Ruth M. Bronson, NCAI, to Joseph C. O'Mahoney, December 17, 1949; Carl Whitman Jr. to Alden Stevens, December 19, 1949; Stevens to Felix Cohen, January 16, 1950, all in folder 3, box 9, Zimmerman Papers, CSRSC-UNML; Whitman to Albert A. Grorud, December 19, 1949, folder Garrison Dam, Protestations of the Construction, 1:3, box 12, Sen 83A-F9 RCIA, RG 46, NARA-DC.
24. McCool, *Command of the Waters*.
25. Meyer, "Fort Berthold," 256–57.
26. Statement of Carl Whitman Jr., Chairman, Tribal Business Council, Three Affiliated Tribes, Fort Berthold Reservation to Secretary of the Interior, n.d., folder 5 Garrison Dam 5:5, box 14, Sen 83A-F9 RCIA, RG 46, NARA-DC.
27. "Garrison Dam, Fort Berthold Indians, North Dakota" [prepared by staff of Senate IIAC, ca. 1950]; O'Mahoney to Mrs. Franklin D. Roosevelt, January 11, 1950; O'Mahoney to Ruth Bronson, Acting Secretary, NCAI, 14 February 1950, all in folder 3 Garrison Dam, N. Dakota 1:2, box 12, Sen 83A-F9 RCIA, RG 46, NARA-DC.
28. Ralph H. Case, Garrison Reservoir, North Dakota, Before the Congress of the United States, Brief in Support of Senate Joint Resolution 11 and House Joint Resolution 33 for The Three Affiliate Tribes, Fort Berthold Reservation, 5–6, folder 2 Garrison Dam 1:3, box 13, Sen 83A-F9 RCIA, RG 46, NARA-DC.
29. VanDevelder, *Coyote Warrior*, 133. Lawson, *Dammed Indians*, 59–63.
30. VanDevelder, *Coyote Warrior*, 237–41.
31. "Garrison Dam, N.D., Lieu Lands Offer not Approved," Department of the Interior Press Release, December 30, 1946, folder 3, box 9, Zimmerman Papers, CSRSC-UNML.
32. "Secretary Chapman Announces Settlement of Fort Berthold Land Transfer," Press Release, Bureau of Indian Affairs, March 16, 1950, folder General Correspondence, 1946–1952, Chapman, Oscar L., March 5, 1946–September 8, 1950, box 50, Ickes Papers, LOC.
33. Minutes of a Conference Between Representatives of the Fort Berthold Agency and the Aberdeen Area Office, April 11–13, 1951, folder 00 Aberdeen Area 1951, box 7, CCF 1940–1957 Aberdeen Area Office 054, RG 75, NARA-DC.
34. Minutes of the Plains Regional Conference of the National Fellowship of Indian Workers, Yankton College, Yankton SD June 6–9, 1950; Robert L. Bennett, "Field Experiences in Indian Job Placement," presented at National Conference of Social Workers, Atlantic City NJ, April 25, 1950, both in folder 13505 Aberdeen Area 1950, box 7, CCF 1940–1957 Aberdeen Area Office 054, RG 75, NARA-DC. See also Rietz Papers, UCLSCRC. Rietz served as the bureau's relocation officer at Fort Berthold.

35. Minutes of a Conference Between Representatives of the Fort Berthold Agency and the Aberdeen Area Office, April 11–13, 1951, folder 00 Aberdeen Area 1951, box 7, CCF 1940–1957 Aberdeen Area Office 054, RG 75, NARA-DC.
36. Minutes of a Conference Between Representatives of the Fort Berthold Agency and the Aberdeen Area Office, April 11–13, 1951, folder 00 Aberdeen Area 1951, box 7, CCF 1940–1957 Aberdeen Area Office 054, RG 75, NARA-DC.
37. Meyer, "Fort Berthold," 299–301.
38. Curry to Martin Cross, July 5, 1952, folder Berthold, box 108, Sen 83A-F9 IIAC, RG 46, NARA-DC.
39. "Pledge of Candidates for Councilmen," Fort Berthold Agency News Bulletin 3:12 (August 25, 1952), folder Martin Cross, box 108 Sen 83A-F9 IIAC, RG 46, NARA-DC. Emphasis in original.
40. Report of Resources Conference, October 8–10, 1952, Bureau of Indian Affairs, Aberdeen, South Dakota, folder 00 Aberdeen Area 1952 Resource Conf., box 7, CCF 1940–1957 Aberdeen Area Office 054, RG 75, NARA-DC.
41. Meyer, "Fort Berthold," 299–303.
42. "Rough Draft for Discussion Purposes Only of a Bill to provide for the termination of Federal Supervision over the property of the Three Affiliated Tribes, . . ." May 3, 1954; handwritten notes by Robert Rietz on Letter from Commissioner of Indian Affairs Glenn Emmons to [Bureau of Indian Affairs] Area Director [in South Dakota], May 3, 1954; Glenn L. Emmons to William O. Roberts, Area Director, Aberdeen, South Dakota, May 3, 1954, reprinted in Fort Berthold Agency News Bulletin 5:6 (June15, 1954); and Ralph M. Shane, Superintendent: "Superintendent's Comments," Fort Berthold News Bulletin 5:7 (July 20, 1954), all in folder 4, box 11, Rietz Papers, UCLSCRC.
43. "Notes taken by Tribal stenographer, on Conferences held July 16 and 17, relative to Indian Bureaus [*sic*] approval Comprehensive Plan presented by Commissioner's representatives, Homer B. Jenkins and others," Termination Materials—83rd Congress folder 3 of 3, series 1, box 41, National Congress of American Indians Papers, (hereafter NCAI Papers), NMAI-SI.
44. He said this at a meeting with Quakers in response to Montana Representative Lee Metcalf, who argued that termination should not be carried out without Indian consent. George F. Norris, "Trip to Washington," *Papago Indian News*, February 1, 1956.
45. "Notes taken by Tribal stenographer, on Conferences held July 16 and 17, relative to Indian Bureaus [*sic*] approval Comprehensive Plan presented by Commissioner's representatives, Homer B. Jenkins and others," Termination Materials—83rd Congress folder 3 of 3, series 1, box 41, NCAI Papers, NMAI-SI.
46. Ralph Shane, "Brief Resume of the General Council Meetings of July 16 and July 17 Relative to the Commissioner's 'Comprehensive Plan for Fort Berthold,'

Presented by Mr. Homer Jenkins." Termination Materials—83rd Congress folder 3 of 3, series 1, box 4, NCAI Papers, NMAI-SI.

47. Cross to Helen Peterson, August 8, 1954. Termination Materials—83rd Congress folder 3 of 3, series 1, box 41, NCAI Papers, NMAI-SI.
48. "Termination Draft Spurned by Council," *Minot Daily News*, July 19, 1954. Copy in Rietz Papers, UCLSCRC; Minutes of Special Council Meeting, July 17, 1954, folder 837–46 (Part III) (2 of 4), box 12, CCF 1940–1957 Fort Berthold 054, RG 75, NARA-DC.
49. Ralph Shane, "Brief Resume of the General Council Meetings of July 16 and July 17 Relative to the Commissioner's 'Comprehensive Plan for Fort Berthold,' Presented by Mr. Homer Jenkins." Termination Materials—83rd Congress folder 3 of 3, series 1, box 41, NCAI Papers, NMAI-SI.
50. Cowger, *National Congress of American Indians.*
51. Star to W. W. (Bill) Short, President NCAI, November 15, 1953; Ruth M. Bronson to Star, November 18, 1953; Peterson to George N. Adams, November 18, 1953; Peterson to Clarence Wesley, November 18, 1953, all in folder B. 1.2 NCAI Executive Council Correspondence October 1953–1954, box 1, Peterson Papers, NMAI-SI.
52. Helen L. Peterson to Chairman Martin Cross, Secretary Sam Matthews, Tribal Business Committee member William Dean, Three Affiliated Tribes, August 7, 1954. Termination Materials—83rd Congress folder 3 of 3, series 1, box 41, NCAI Papers, NMAI-SI.
53. Helen L. Peterson to Chairman Martin Cross, Secretary Sam Matthews, Tribal Business Committee member William Dean, Three Affiliated Tribes, August 7, 1954. Termination Materials—83rd Congress folder 3 of 3, series 1, box 41, NCAI Papers, NMAI-SI.
54. Copy of bill in *Fort Berthold Agency News Bulletin* 12, no. 5 (December 27, 1954), folder 5, box 11, Rietz Papers, UCLSCRC.
55. "Indian opposes end of U.S. Tribal Rule," *New York Times*, February 12, 1954.
56. Rietz to Agency Superintendent Ralph [Shane], November 29, 1954, Rietz Papers, UCLSCRC.
57. Minutes, General Council Meeting, January 14, 1955. Recorded by Ralph Shane, folder 837–46 (Part III) (1 of 4), box 11, CCF 1940–1957 Fort Berthold 054, RG 75, NARA-DC.
58. Minutes, General Council Meeting, January 14, 1955.
59. Minutes, General Council Meeting, January 14, 1955 and February 16, 1955, both in folder 837–46 (Part III) (1 of 4), box 11, CCF 1940–1957 Fort Berthold 054, RG 75, NARA-DC.
60. Minutes, General Council Meeting, January 14, 1955.
61. Minutes, General Council Meeting, January 14, 1955.

62. Minutes, Special Council Meeting, March 9, 1955, folder 837–46 (Part III) (1 of 4), box 11, CCF 1940–1957 Fort Berthold 054, RG 75, NARA-DC.
63. Minutes Fort Berthold Tribal Business Council, March 21, 1955, in Washington DC, folder 837–46 (Part III) (1 of 4), box 11, CCF 1940–1957 Fort Berthold 054, RG 75, NARA-DC.
64. Minutes Fort Berthold Tribal Business Council, March 21, 1955.
65. Homer Jenkins, Program Coordination Staff, Richard D. Butts, Program Office, Notes on Conference held to discuss terminal programing for the Western Washington groups of Indians, February 10, 1952, box 3, Entry 1014Y, RG 75, NARA-DC.
66. Minutes Fort Berthold Tribal Business Council, March 21, 1955.
67. Report, Conference held in Senator Milton R. Young's office, room 107, Senate Office Building, March 23, 1955, 1:30 PM, signed by Martin Cross, folder 837–46 (Part III) (1 of 4), box 11, CCF 1940–1957 Fort Berthold 054, RG 75, NARA-DC.
68. NCAI Press Release, March 28, 1955, folder B. 1.3 NCAI Executive Council Correspondence 1955, box 1, Peterson Papers, NMAI-SI. NMAI-SI
69. See list of terminated tribes and corresponding legislation in appendix.
70. NCAI Press Release, March 28, 1955.
71. Cross to Peterson, August 8, 1954, Termination Materials—83rd Congress folder 3 of 3, series 1, box 41, NCAI Papers, NMAI-SI.
72. Lawson, Dammed Indians, 125; Meyer, "Fort Berthold," 303–5. Quote from VanDevelder, *Coyote Warrior*, 167.

7. SENECA NATION AND KINZUA DAM

Epigraph 1: Meyer, "Fort Berthold," 220–21.

Epigraph 2: Billy, Seneca Nation of Indians Negotiating Committee to Wayne Aspinall, March 13, 1963, folder 1794 3 of 10, box 8, House IIAC Legislative Files, 88th Congress, RG 233, NARA-DC.

1. Hauptman, *In the Shadow of Kinzua*, 4–6. For a copy of the 1848 constitution, see "Resolutions and Constitution of the Seneca Nation of Indians (Seneca of Allegheny and Cattaraugus, 1848)," in Wilkins, *Documents*, 75–81.
2. Hauptman, "On and Off State Time," 184. See also Mt. Pleasant, "After the Whirlwind."
3. "Treaty with the Six Nations, 1794," in Kappler, *Indian Treaties*, 34–37.
4. Article 3, "Treaty with the Six Nations, 1794," in Kappler, *Indian Treaties*, 35.
5. These treaties include "Agreement with the Seneca, 1797," 1027–30; "Treaty with the Seneca, 1802," 62; "Treaty with the New York Indians, 1838," 502–16; and "Treaty with the Seneca, 1842," 537–42, all in Kappler, *Indian Treaties*. See also Mt. Pleasant, "After the Whirlwind," 100–102.
6. Hauptman, *In the Shadow of Kinzua*, 206–23; *Honorable Nations*.
7. *Honorable Nations*.

8. Kenneth R. Philp provides the complete list. See Philp, *Termination Revisited*, 75.
9. Act to Confer Jurisdiction on the State of New York with Respect to Offenses Committed on Indian Reservations within Such State, Pub. L. No. 80–881, 62 Stat. 1224 (1948); and Act to Confer Jurisdiction on the Courts of the State of New York with Respect to Civil Actions between Indians or to which Indians are Parties, Pub. L. No. 81–785, 64 Stat. 845 (1950).
10. H.C.R. 108.
11. Histories of the dam and its relation to the Seneca Nation include Hauptman, "General John S. Bragdon"; Hauptman, *In the Shadow of Kinzua*, esp. 49–78; Purcell, "Engineering of Forever"; Rosier, "Dam Building"; and Williams, "Kinzua Dam Controversy."
12. Rosier, "Dam Building," 345; Williams, "Kinzua Dam Controversy," 1–3; and Weist, "For the Public Good," 65.
13. Rosier, "Dam Building," 347.
14. Purcell, "Engineering of Forever," 309.
15. Hauptman, *In the Shadow of Kinzua*, 50–56.
16. Walter Taylor, Coordinator, Kinzua Project of the Indian Committee, Philadelphia Yearly Meeting of Friends, to friend, June 22, 1961, folder New York-Kinzua Dam, box 91, Brophy Papers, HSTL.
17. Cornelius V. Seneca, President, Seneca Nation of Indians. The Allegheny Reservoir Project, Statement in Opposition to the Construction of the Proposed Kinzua Dam. Testimony, Public Works Subcommittee of the House Appropriations Committee, May 10, 1957, folder 6, box 11, Zimmerman Papers, CSRSC-UNML.
18. Seneca, Statement in Opposition to the Construction of the Proposed Kinzua Dam.
19. Hauptman, "General John S. Bragdon," 188, 192, 195. Second brackets in original.
20. Haley letter to the editor, *Warren Times-Mirror*, January 29, 1964, folder Indian Affairs: Seneca Indians: Kinzua Dam Correspondence, 1960–1966 (B), box 153, Haley Papers, MAC-FSC.
21. Haley to President John Kennedy, June 20, 1961, folder Indian Affairs: Seneca Indians: Kinzua Dam Correspondence, 1960–1966 (A), box 153, Haley Papers, MAC-FSC.
22. George D. Heron, Treasurer, Seneca Nation of Indians. The Allegheny Reservoir Project, Statement in Opposition to the Construction of the Proposed Kinzua Dam. Testimony, Public Works Subcommittee of the House Appropriations Committee, May 10, 1957, folder 6, box 11, Zimmerman Papers, CSRSC-UNML.
23. Petition [to the U.S. Supreme Court] for a writ of certiorari to the United States Court of Appeals for the District of Columbia Circuit, *Seneca Nation of Indians v. Wilber M. Bruckner*, Secretary of the Army, and Emerson C. Itschner, Major General, United States Army Corps of Engineers, October term, 1958, folder 7, box 11, Zimmerman Papers, CSRSC-UNML.

24. Hauptman, “General John S. Bragdon,” 187–88.
25. *The Seneca Nation of Indians v. Wilber M. Brucker, Secretary of the Army, et al.*, Civ. No. 2202–57.
26. *The Seneca Nation of Indians v. Wilber M. Brucker, Secretary of the Army, et al.*, United States Court of Appeals.
27. “Indians Advance, Undertow Exists,” *Chicago Defender*, September 12, 1959.
28. Draft of Speech by James A Haley. Ca. May-June 1960, folder Indian Affairs: Seneca Indians: Kinzua Dam: Official, May 1960-December 1963, box 154, Haley Papers, MAC-FSA.
29. Illegible, Department of the Interior, Division of Legislation to [Wayne] Aspinall, June 22, 1960, folder Indian Affairs: Seneca Indians: Kinzua Dam: Official, May 1960-December 1963, box 154, Haley Papers, MAC-FSA.
30. Hauptman, *In the Shadow of Kinzua*, 63–64.
31. Quoted in “The Kinzua Dam Controversy: A Practical Solution—Without Shame,” Kinzua Project of the Indian Committee, Philadelphia Yearly Meeting of Friends, n.d., folder 5, box 11, Zimmerman Papers, CSRSC-UNML. Copy also in folder New York-Kinzua Dam, box 91, Brophy Papers, HSTL.
32. Hauptman, *In the Shadow of Kinzua*, 69–70.
33. Haley to Kennedy, June 20, 1961, folder Folder Indian Affairs: Seneca Indians: Kinzua Dam Correspondence, 1960–1966 (A), box 153, Haley Papers, MAC-FSC.
34. Kennedy to Williams, August 9, 1961, folder 29, box 3, Zimmerman Papers, CSRSC-UNML. Copy in Folder 1794 4 of 10, box 8, House IIAC Legislative Files, 88th Congress, RG 233, NARA-DC. Hauptman, *In the Shadow of Kinzua*, 68.
35. Extension of Remarks of Hon. Thaddeus J. Dulski of New York, House of Representatives, August 1, 1961. *Congressional Record–Appendix*, August 18, 1961, p. A6492, folder New York-Kinzua Dam, box 91, Brophy Papers, HSTL.
36. Aubrey Graves, “Seneca Way of Life is Doomed by Dam, Reservation to be Flooded,” *Washington Post*, November 27, 1962.
37. “A Reminder of Our Obligations.” “Speech by Honorable James A. Haley, (Dem-Fla.), Chairman, Indian Affairs Subcommittee, House Committee on Interior and Insular Affairs, May 21, 1966 at the Dedication of the Seneca Indian Nation’s new community building, Jimersontown, Allegany Reservation, Salamanca New York,” folder Indian Affairs: Seneca Indians, 1962–1978 (A), box 153, Haley Papers, MAC-FSC.
38. Walter Taylor, “The Kinzua Dam and H.R. 1794,” offprint from *Indian Truth*, folder 1794 3 of 10, box 8, House IIAC Legislative Files, 88th Congress, RG 233, NARA-DC.
39. Zimmerman, letter to the editor, *Washington Post and Times Herald*, July 3, 1957; Association on American Indian Affairs, Inc., Press release, January 24, 1957, “U.S. Must Honor Seneca Nation’s Treaty Rights New Yorkers and Pennsylvanians

Assert"; both in folder 29 Correspondence Regarding the Kinzua Dam Project (1957–61), box 3; "The Kinzua Dam Controversy: A Practical Solution—Without Shame," Kinzua Project of the Indian Committee, Philadelphia Yearly Meeting of Friends. N.d.; "The 1964 Crisis for Seneca Indians," Kinzua Project of the Indian Committee, Philadelphia Yearly Meeting of Friends, February 1, 1964; "The 1965 Challenge to Seneca Indians and to All Americans," Kinzua Project of the Indian Committee, Philadelphia Yearly Meeting of Friends (Quakers), January 1965, all in folder 5 Materials Regarding the Kinzua Project and the Seneca Indians, box 11; Eleanor Roosevelt, "Moral Issue at Stake, in Seneca's Land-for-Dam Fight," *Philadelphia Daily News*, June 8, 1961, folder 7, box 11, all in Zimmerman Papers, CSRSC-UNML; correspondence between Downs and James Haley, folder Indian Affairs: Seneca Indians, 1962–1978 (C), box 153, Haley Papers, MAC-FSC; "NAACP Endorses Health Plan for Country's Aged," *Minneapolis Spokesman*, February 23, 1962, 6-A.

40. Walter Taylor to Clyde Robbins, Planning Director, Cattaraugus County Planning Board, October 18, 1962, Folder Indian Affairs: Seneca Indians: Kinzua Dam: Official, May 1960–December 1963, box 154, Haley Papers, MAC-FSA.
41. "'Washington's Word Worthless,': Dam to Inundate Part of Indian Reservation," *Townsville Daily Bulletin*, Queensland, Australia, March 13, 1964. Copy in folder Indian Affairs: Seneca Indians: Kinzua Dam Correspondence, 1960–1966 (B), box 153, Haley Papers, MAC-FSC.
42. Myra MacPherson, "Javits Party Buzzes with March Successes," [Washington DC] *Evening Star*, August 29, 1963, 6A.
43. Hauptman, *In the Shadow of Kinzua*, 60.
44. Heron to Aspinall, February 18, 1964, folder 1794 2 of 10, box 8, House IIAC Legislative Files, 88th Congress, RG 233, NARA-DC.
45. At one point in his frustration with the slow movement of the BIA and the Army Corps of Engineers to find homes for those whose land would be flooded, House Indian Affairs Subcommittee chairman Haley threatened to bring legislation "prohibiting the Corps of Engineers from closing the gates of the dam or taking any action that would apply to the Kinzua Dam until such time as suitable settlements had been made with the Tribe." Minutes of November 1, 1963, Subcommittee on Indian Affairs, folder Minutes Subcommittee on Indian Affairs 2 of 2, box 83, 88th Congress House IIAC Minutes, RG 233, NARA-DC.
46. "H.R. 1794 Slashed by Senate Subcommittee," *Kinzua Planning Newsletter*, vol. 3, no. 4 (March 25, 1964). Senator Dominick's papers shed little light on his role in pushing for termination; in relation to the Kinzua Dam affair they largely consist of correspondence from one Seneca Nation member who opposed the dam. Folder Departments-Interior-Bureau of Indian Affairs (BIA)-Seneca Nation, 1963–1964, Peter H. Dominick Papers, University of Denver Special Collections

and Archives. The amendment went to the full senate on March 26, 1964. See U.S. Congress, Senate, "H.R. 1794, Report No. 969," copy in folder 1794 1 of 10, box 8, House IIAC Legislative Files, 88th Congress, RG 233, NARA-DC. For the termination rider see section 18, Public Law 88–533, 78 Stat. 738 (1964).

47. Arthur Lazarus Jr. to Jacob K. Javits "Re: *Seneca Nation of Indians—H.R. 1794*," March 27, 1964, Folder Indian Affairs: Seneca Indians: Kinzua Dam Correspondence: Official, March 1964, box 154, Haley Papers, MAC-FSC.
48. Hauptman writes that the early termination efforts turned from New York to the west—to Wisconsin and Oregon and Oklahoma after the deaths of Senator Hugh Butler and New York Representative Daniel Reed in the late 1950s. Hauptman, *In the Shadow of Kinzua*, 24–30.
49. "Termination," *Kinzua Planning Newsletter*, vol. 3, no. 4 (March 25, 1964).
50. Dominick letter to the editor, *Kinzua Planning Newsletter*, vol. 3, no. 5 (May 29, 1964).
51. Bowen to Dominick, May 27 1964, folder 1794 2 of 10, box 8, House IIAC Legislative Files, 88th Congress, RG 233, NARA-DC. Reprinted in *Kinzua Planning Newsletter*, vol. 3, no. 5 (May 29, 1964).
52. Dominick letter to the editor, *Kinzua Planning Newsletter*.
53. "Termination," *Kinzua Planning Newsletter*.
54. Bowen to Dominick, *Kinzua Planning Newsletter*; "Termination," *Kinzua Planning Newsletter*.
55. Bowen to Dominick, *Kinzua Planning Newsletter*.
56. Walter Taylor, "Some Comments on Senate Report No. 969 to Accompany H.R. 1794," April 17, 1964, folder Indian Affairs: Seneca Indians: Kinzua Dam: Official, February–September 1964, box 154, Haley Papers, MAC-FSA.
57. Arthur Lazarus Jr. to Jacob K. Javits "Re: *Seneca Nation of Indians—H.R. 1794*."
58. Lazarus to Haley, May 7, 1964, folder Indian Affairs: Seneca Indians: Kinzua Dam Correspondence, 1960–1966 (B), box 153, Haley Papers, MAC-FSC.
59. Douglas to Friend, reprinted in *Kinzua Planning Newsletter*, vol. 3, no. 5 (May 29, 1964).
60. "Our Own DP's—The Senecas," editorial, *New York Times*, March 22, 1964, E8.
61. Brooks Atkinson, "Critic at Large: Delay in Senate is Just Another Chapter in Story of Seneca Nation's Troubles" *New York Times*, June 2, 1964.
62. David G. Paul, Presiding Clerk, Religious Society of Friends to Representative Wayne Aspinall, March 31, 1964, Jonathan M. Steer Jr., Acting President, Indian Rights Association to Aspinall, April 2, 1964, both in folder 1794 2 of 10, box 8, House IIAC Legislative Files, 88th Congress, RG 233, NARA-DC.
63. Sections 2, 4, 18, Public Law 88–533. The addition of an extra year to plan for termination was the result of a House amendment to the bill. U.S. Congress, House of Representatives, "Seneca Indian Nation," Report No. 1821, 88th Congress, 2nd

Session, Conference Report to accompany H.R. 1794, August 17, 1964, folder 1794 10 of 10, box 9, House IIAC Legislative Files, 88th Congress, RG 233, NARA-DC.

64. Heron to Haley, October 31, 1964, folder Indian Affairs: Seneca Indians: Kinzua Dam Correspondence, 1960–1966 (B), box 153, Haley Papers, MAC-FSC.
65. Speech by Philleo Nash, Commissioner of Indian Affairs, September 19, 1964 at Salamanca on the Allegany Reservation, published in *Kinzua Planning Newsletter*, vol. 3, no. 6-b (October 1964).
66. Speech by Philleo Nash.
67. Speech by Philleo Nash.
68. *Kinzua Planning Newsletter*, vol. 1, no. 1 (October 11, 1961).
69. Watt to Haley, November 29, 1966, folder Indian Affairs: Seneca Indians, 1962–1978 (B), box 153, Haley Papers, MAC-FSC.
70. "Indians to View Menominee Film," *Bradford (PA) Era*, April 4, 1967; "Senecas Take to TV To Protest Termination," *Bradford (PA) Era*, July 10, 1967; "Seneca Indian Supervision By U.S. Would End Via Bill," Dunkirk-Fredonia NY *Evening Observer*, September 6, 1967; "Senecas Are Opposed to Legislation," *Altoona Mirror*, September 5, 1967; "Council Headlines," June 22, 1967, *Seneca Nation Newsletter* 5, no. 6 (July 1967), folder Indian Affairs: Seneca Indians, 1962–1978 (B), box 153, Haley Papers, MAC-FSC.
71. Message from the President, *Seneca Nation Newsletter* 5, no. 6 (July 1967), 3, folder Indian Affairs: Seneca Indians, 1962–1978 (B), box 153, Haley Papers, MAC-FSC.
72. Seneca Indian Longhouse, Allegany Reservation, Steamburg NY to Udall, August 11, 1967. Reprinted in *Si Wong Geh*, September 26, 1973, 2.
73. Seneca Indian Longhouse, Allegany Reservation, Steamburg NY to Udall.
74. Seneca Indian Longhouse, Allegany Reservation, Steamburg NY to Udall.
75. "Three Tribes Meet in Pow-Wow On Termination of Indians' Status," *Bradford (PA) Era*, August 1, 1967.
76. Message from the President, *Seneca Nation Newsletter* 5, no. 6 (July 1967), 3, folder Indian Affairs: Seneca Indians, 1962–1978 (B), box 153, Haley Papers, MAC-FSC.
77. "Bill Submitted to End Federal Ties with Seneca Indians," Bureau of Indian Affairs Press Release, September 5, 1967, available at U.S. Department of the Interior, Indian Affairs (website), accessed September 1, 2021, https://www.bia.gov/as-ia/opa/online-press-release/bill-submitted-end-federal-ties-seneca-indians#.
78. Bilharz, *Allegany Senecas*, 100, says it died. There is no record of it in the House Interior and Insular Affairs minutes for the 90th Congress. See minutes in folder 1 of 4 Full Committee Minutes 1st Session, 90th Congress and folder 2 of 4 Full Committee Minutes 2nd Session, 90th Congress, box 1, House IIAC Minutes, 90th Congress, RG 233, NARA-DC.

79. "History of Bills and Resolutions," *Congressional Record*, vol. 117 (January 2 to December 17, 1971), available on Congress (website), accessed January 5, 2022, https://www.congress.gov/92/crecb/1971/12/17/gpo-crecb-1971-pt37-2.pdf. See also article in *Si Wong Geh*, February 9, 1972.
80. "Before the Indian Claims Commission."
81. "Indians Held Short Change," *Si Wong Geh*, May 17, 1972; news item, *Si Wong Geh*, September 12, 1973.
82. Untitled stories, *Si Wong Geh*, September 12, 1973, September 19, 1973.
83. "The Nosey Reporter," *Si Wong Geh*, September 19, 1973.
84. Letter from Concerned People from Newtown, *Si Wong Geh*, September 19, 1973.
85. "Sovereignty Question," *Si Wong Geh*, September 26, 1973.
86. Hauptman, "General John S. Bragdon," 183.
87. George D. Heron, President, Seneca Nation to Friend, January 12, 1959, folder 7, box 11, Zimmerman Papers, CSRSC-UNML.

8. "MIXED-BLOOD" UTES

Epigraph 1: Quoted in O'Neil and McKay, "A History," 11.

Epigraph 2: "Ute Indian Attorney Demanding U.S. Pay Over 5 Million on Claims, Government Responsible For Taking Land From Indians Says Wilkinson," *Daily Sentinel* (Grand Junction CO), August 13, 1947. Copy in folder Ute Litigation General-Newspaper, etc. Clippings, carton 138, Wilkinson, Cragun, and Barker Indian Claims Commission records (WCBICCR), LTPSC.

1. Metcalf, *Termination's Legacy*, 4.
2. Ernest L. Wilkinson, Attorney of Record for Plaintiffs, "Petition and Motion of Attorney of Record for the Uintah and White River Bands of Ute Indians for Award of Attorneys' Fee," 14, folder 9 *Uintah and White River Bands of Ute Indians v. The United States*, no. 39–56 Pleading File, box 128, WCBICCR, LTPSC. Wilkinson made sure to tell the business council that he had saved them $2 million in offsets in the Indian Claims Commission Bill. Minutes, Uintah and Ouray Tribal Business Committee, January 10, 1949, folder 10333-1946-054, part 2, 2 of 3, box 11, CCF 1940–1957 Uintah & Ouray 054, RG 75, NARA-DC. Wilkinson also said that without the offset savings and due to his work with Congress to permit interest payments, the judgment would have been diminished by $13 million. "In the Court of Claims of the United States, Nos. 45585, 46640, 47564, 47566, The Confederated Bands of Ute Indians vs. The United States of America, Proposed Findings of Fact by Attorneys for Plaintiffs Respecting Awards of Fees for All of Above Cases," n.d., 86, box 32, WCBR, LTPSC.
3. For an analysis of the modern disenrollments, see Wilkins and Wilkins, *Dismembered*.

4. "History: The Northern Utes," Utah American Indian Digital Archive, 2008. Accessed July 29, 2022. See also the map "Original Lands of the Ute People," in O'Neil and McKay, "A History," 3, 17.
5. "Memorandum of Facts Relating to Ute Claims," folder 3, box 14, NCAIR; W. Ney Evans, Commissioner, "In the United States Court of Claims Nos. 45585, 46640, 47564, and 47566, Filed May 29, 1951, The Confederated Bands of Ute Indians v. The United States," box 32, WCBR, both in LTPSC. The land loss of the northern Utes is well described in detail in O'Neil and McKay, "A History."
6. "Memorandum of Facts Relating to Ute Claims," folder 3, box 14, National Council on American Indians records, 20th Century Western & Mormon Manuscripts, (NCAIR); W. Ney Evans, Commissioner, "In the United States Court of Claims Nos. 45585, 46640, 47564, and 47566, Filed May 29, 1951, The Confederated Bands of Ute Indians v. The United States," box 32, WCBR, both in LTPSC.
7. Jones, *Being and Becoming Ute*, 195–206.
8. O'Neil and McKay, "A History," 13.
9. *Ute Indians v. United States*, 459.
10. Act to Accept and Ratify the Agreement Submitted by the Confederated Bands of Ute Indians in Colorado for the Sale of Their Reservation in Said State, and for Other Purposes, and to Make the Necessary Appropriations for Carrying Out the Same, Chap. 223, 46th Cong., Sess. 2, 21 Stat. 199 (1880), p. 204.
11. *Ute Indians v. United States*, 440.
12. Act Conferring Jurisdiction upon the United States Court of Claims to Hear, Examine, Adjudicate, and Render Judgment on Any and All Claims which the Ute Indians or any Tribe or Band Thereof May Have Against the United States, and for Other Purposes, Pub. L. No. 75–754, 52 Stat. 1209 (1938) p. 1210; *The United States v. Southern Ute Tribe or Band of Indians*, 359; W. Ney Evans, Commissioner, "In the United States Court of Claims Nos. 45585, 46640, 47564, and 47566, Filed May 29, 1951, The Confederated Bands of Ute Indians v. The United States, Report of the Commissioner To the honorable the Chief Judge and Associate Judges of the United States Court of Claims," 17, box 32, WCBR, LTPSC.
13. Wilkinson, "Address to the Law Faculty and Present and Past Law Review Staffs, University of California Law School," May 19, 1955, 17, folder Legal Subjects, 1949–72 (2 of 2), box 123, ELWPP, LTPSC.
14. "In the Court of Claims of the United States, Nos. 45585, 46640, 47564, 47566," 39–56, box 32, WCBR, LTPSC.
15. Nunn, "Quantum Meruit and Contingent Fees," 624n15; *Ute Indians v. United States*, 462–63; "In the Court of Claims of the United States, Nos. 45585, 46640, 47564, 47566," 60, box 32, WCBR, LTPSC; Curry to John Collier, June 24, 1926, folder Claims Vs. U.S. Uintah and Ouray Agency, box 143, Sen 83A-F9 IIAC, RG 46, NARA-DC.

16. "In the Court of Claims of the United States, Nos. 45585, 46640, 47564, 47566," 64–66, box 32, WCBR, LTPSC.
17. Raymond and his wife Gertrude "practically raised [Oran Curry, who] was instrumental in giving Raymond the rights of attorney from the Utes and kept the Bonnins in contact with the Uintah and Ouray Reservation." "Register to the Gertrude and Raymond Bonnin Collection," LTPSC. U.S. Congress, Senate, *Authorizing Certain Bands*, 13.
18. "Indian Claims Fee Awarded," *Deseret News*, November 6, 1951; "In the Court of Claims of the United States, Nos. 45585, 46640, 47564, 47566," 99, box 32, WCBR, LTPSC. See also correspondence between Ernest Wilkinson and the Bonnins in box 10, NCAIR, LTPSC.
19. "Semi-Annual Report and Budget Authorization Request for Uintah and White River Court of Claims Cases Nos. 47568 through 47574," Ernest L. Wilkinson, July 16, 1952, folder 10333-1946-054 Part 3, 1 of 2, box 11, CCF 1940–1957 Uintah & Ouray 054, RG 75, NARA-DC. The idea to combine claims apparently came from the Utes in 1935. Raymond Bonnin wrote to Ernest Wilkinson, on August 29, 1935, "I am invited to accompany some of these Utes to visit the Southern Utes the latter part of September. They tell me that the Southern Utes desire to employ the same attorneys employed by these Northern Utes." Folder 1, box 10, NCAIR, LTPSC.
20. Nunn, "Quantum Meruit and Contingent Fees," 624–25; "Indian Claims Fee Awarded," *Deseret News*. Wilkinson also said the work consisted of some "1100 conferences with members of Congress." Ernest L. Wilkinson Speech File, "Notes for Address to Teachers and Administrators of Indian Service at Brigham City-June 22, 1953," folder 5 Indians, 1953–60, box 123, ELWPP, LTPSC.
21. Nunn, "Quantum Meruit and Contingent Fees," 624n15.
22. "In the Court of Claims of the United States, Nos. 45585, 46640, 47564, 47566," 90; W. Ney Evans, Commissioner, "In the United States Court of Claims," 24, both in box 32, WCBR, LTPSC; Act to Define the Exterior Boundary of the Uintah and Ouray Indian Reservation in the State of Utah, and for Other Purposes, Pub. L. No. 80–440, 62 Stat. 72 (1948).
23. As early as 1941 Raymond Bonnin wrote to Wilkinson, "You may recall that you made some statement to the Utes (about the time you got the contract) that you would have the money for them in two or three years. They have been asking me how long it will be before we get them some money." Bonnin to Wilkinson, October 6, 1941, folder 10, box 10, NCAIR, LTPSC.
24. Minutes, Uintah and Ouray Tribal Business Committee, Special Meeting, October 19, 1949, folder 10333-1946-054, part 2, 2 of 3, box 11, CCF 1940–1957 Uintah & Ouray 054, RG 75, NARA-DC.
25. Metcalf, *Termination's Legacy*, 43–44.

26. Minutes, Uintah and Ouray Tribal Business Committee, Special Meeting, January 16, 1950, folder 10333-1946-054, part 2, 2 of 3, box 11, CCF 1940–1957 Uintah & Ouray 054, RG 75, NARA-DC.
27. Minutes, Uintah and Ouray Tribal Business Committee Special Meeting, October 4, 1948, folder 10333-1946-054, part 2, 2 of 3, box 11, CCF 1940–1957 Uintah & Ouray 054, RG 75, NARA-DC.
28. Metcalf, *Termination's Legacy*, 43–44.
29. Minutes, Uintah and Ouray Tribal Business Committee Special Meeting, October 9, 1948, folder 10333-1946-054, part 2, 2 of 3, box 11, CCF 1940–1957 Uintah & Ouray 054, RG 75, NARA-DC.
30. Minutes, Uintah and Ouray Tribal Business Committee, April 12, 1948, folder 10333-1946-054, part 2, 3 of 3, box 11, CCF 1940–1957 Uintah & Ouray 054, RG 75, NARA-DC.
31. Jones, *Being and Becoming Ute*, 227.
32. Minutes, Uintah and Ouray Tribal Business Committee, September 15, 1949, folder 10333-1946-054, part 2, 2 of 3, box 11, CCF 1940–1957 Uintah & Ouray 054, RG 75, NARA-DC.
33. Minutes, Uintah and Ouray Tribal Business Committee, April 12, 1948.
34. Minutes, Uintah and Ouray Tribal Business Committee, Special Meeting, April 13, 1948, folder 10333-1946-054, part 2, 3 of 3, box 11, CCF 1940–1957 Uintah & Ouray 054, RG 75, NARA-DC.
35. Minutes, Uintah and Ouray Tribal Business Committee, Special Meeting, October 19, 1949, folder 10333-1946-054, part 2, 2 of 3, box 11, CCF 1940–1957 Uintah & Ouray 054, RG 75, NARA-DC.
36. Minutes, Uintah and Ouray Tribal Business Committee Special Meeting, May 17, 1950, folder 10333-1946-054, part 2, 1 of 3, box 11, CCF 1940–1957 Uintah & Ouray 054, RG 75, NARA-DC.
37. Reginald Curry, in Minutes, Uintah and Ouray Tribal Business Committee, September 8, 1954, folder 10333-1946-054, part 4, 1 of 2, box 11, CCF 1940–1957 Uintah & Ouray 054, RG 75, NARA-DC.
38. Elizabeth Curry Bumgarner to Secretary of the Interior, September 25, 1950; Protest, n.d., stamped received 2 October 1950, both in folder 19040-1950-059, CCF 1940–1957 Uintah & Ouray 059, RG 75, NARA-DC.
39. Reginald Curry, in Minutes, Uintah and Ouray Tribal Business Committee, September 8, 1954, folder 10333-1946-054, part 4, 1 of 2, box 11, CCF 1940–1957 Uintah & Ouray 054, RG 75, NARA-DC.
40. *Confederated Bands of Ute Indians v. United States*. When Wilkinson described how he got large recovery judgments when others did not, he said, "In these Indian suits we were always deliberately modest in pleading damages. We never wanted to frighten the Court at the outset. When damages were proved

we merely asked leave to amend the pleadings so as to conform to the proof." "Address to the Law Faculty and Present and Past Law Review Staffs, University of California Law School," May 19, 1955, 11, folder Legal Subjects, 1949–72 (2 of 2), box 123, ELWPP, LTPSC.

41. Metcalf, *Termination's Legacy*, 86–87.
42. Act To Provide for the Use of the Tribal Funds of the Ute Indian Tribe of the Uintah and Ouray Reservation, to Authorize a Per Capita payment Out of Such Funds, to Provide for the Division of Certain Tribal Funds with the Southern Utes, and for Other Purposes, Pub. L. No. 82–120, 65 Stat. 193 (1951).
43. Myer to Watkins, February 27, 1953, transcribed in Minutes, Uintah and Ouray Tribal Business Committee, March 9, 1953, folder 10333-1946-054, part 3, 1 of 2, box 11, CCF 1940–1957 Uintah & Ouray 054, RG 75, NARA-DC.
44. "Material for Annual Report, 1952, Phoenix Area Office, Part 1," folder 00-1952-031, box 1, CCF 1940–1957 Phoenix Area, RG 75, NARA-DC.
45. Material for Annual Report, Fiscal 1953, folder 19919-1953-031, box 1, CCF 1940–1957 Phoenix Area, RG 75, NARA-DC.
46. Minutes, Uintah and Ouray Tribal Business Committee, November 13, 1951. See also Minutes, Uintah and Ouray Tribal Business Committee, February 11, 1952; Minutes, Uintah and Ouray Tribal Business Committee Special Meeting, May 22, 1952, all in folder 10333-1946-054, part 3, 2 of 2, box 11, CCF 1940–1957 Uintah & Ouray 054, RG 75, NARA-DC.
47. Metcalf, "Lambs of Sacrifice," 324.
48. Resolution no. 600, Uintah and Ouray Agency, May 27, 1953, folder 19799-1950-054, box 12, CCF 1940–1957 Uintah & Ouray 054, RG 75, NARA-DC.
49. Resolution 643, Uintah and Ouray Agency, June 24, 1953, folder 19799-1950-054, box 12, CCF 1940–1957 Uintah & Ouray 054, RG 75, NARA-DC.
50. Reed to Arthur Watkins, October 1952; Reed to George Malone, November 16, 1952, folder 32–Indians, box 23, Sen 83A-F9 IIAC, RG 46, NARA-DC.
51. Metcalf, *Termination's Legacy*, 98–99.
52. Minutes, Uintah and Ouray Tribal Business Committee, September 14, 1953, folder 10333-1946-054, part 3, 1 of 2, box 11, CCF 1940–1957 Uintah & Ouray 054, RG 75, NARA-DC.
53. Metcalf, *Termination's Legacy*, 140.
54. Metcalf, *Termination's Legacy*, ch. 3.
55. Metcalf, *Termination's Legacy*, 99, 142–43.
56. Minutes, Uintah and Ouray Tribal Business Committee, July 13, 1953, folder 10333-1946-054, part 3, 1 of 2, box 11, CCF 1940–1957 Uintah & Ouray 054, RG 75, NARA-DC.
57. Minutes, Uintah and Ouray Tribal Business Committee, July 13, 1953. McKinley earned an AB in political science at George Washington University. Governors'

Interstate Indian Council Newsletter No. 2, September 28, 1950, folder 3, Governors' Interstate Indian Council, 1954, 2:2, new box 14, Sen 83A-F9 RCIA, RG 46. Both in NARA-DC.

58. Metcalf, "Lambs of Sacrifice," 327–28.
59. Metcalf, *Termination's Legacy*, 138–47; Metcalf, "Lambs of Sacrifice," 327–33. On college educated tribal members, see Rex Curry statement in Minutes, Uintah and Ouray Tribal Business Committee, May 8, 1950, folder 10333-1946-054, part 2, 1 of 3, box 11, CCF 1940–1957 Uintah & Ouray 054, RG 75, NARA-DC.
60. Metcalf, *Termination's Legacy*, 147, 161–65; and *Federal Register*, 2209–12.
61. *Joint Hearing . . . on S. 2670 and H.R. 7674*, part 1, 41.
62. Metcalf, *Termination's Legacy*, 151–52, 242.
63. Metcalf discusses this in the case of the Pauites, who were also terminated without consent. See Metcalf, *Termination's Legacy*, 263n30.
64. Lazarus to Zimmerman, September 13, 1954, folder 11, box 11, Zimmerman Papers, CSRSC-UNML.
65. Clyde Johnson to Oliver La Farge, September 8, 1954, folder 11, box 11, Zimmerman Papers, CSRSC-UNML.
66. Resolution, passed unanimously April 29, 1955 by the Executive Committee of the Uncompahgre Band of Utes, folder Utes–Affiliated Utes, box 95, Brophy Papers, HSTL.
67. U.S. Congress, House, *Report to Accompany S. 3532*.
68. Peterson to Ruth [Bronson], Florence, Sunday, September 5, [1954]; Peterson to Flo, Sat. AM Salt Lake [August 1954], both in folder B5.2 Helen L. Peterson Papers NCAI Correspondence 1951–1953, box 5, Peterson Papers, NMAI Archives.
69. Metcalf, *Termination's Legacy*, 190–92.
70. "Indian Group in Utah Secedes From the U.S.," *New York Times*, December 16, 1960. Clipping in folder 6 15.0 Uintah Litigation General-Newspaper Clippings, Carton 128, WCBICCR, LTPSC. NOTE: The final two paragraphs of this article, from which the quote is drawn, are in this clip file but do not appear on the *New York Times* historical archive database.
71. "Ute Tribal Council Decision Speeds Release of $7.7 Million" *Ute Bulletin* 1, no. 4 (December 17, 1960); "Jailed Utes Charge Rights Were Violated," *Lewiston (ID) Tribune*, July 10, 1960, both in folder 1, carton 131, WCBICCR. A retired army general, Herbert C. Holdridge, who claimed to be conducting an investigation under direct orders of the president, first attempted to install Twohy as a chief in February 1959. Clipping "Retired Army General, minute men, attempt to take over Indian offices," *Uintah Basin Standard*, February 5, 1959, folder 3 Indians, box 211, ELWPP. All in LTPSC.
72. "Affiliated Utes are Terminated, Mixed Reaction Greets News," *Ute Bulletin* 1, no. 11 (September 16, 1961), folder 9, carton 133, WCBICCR, LTPSC.

73. "General Council Flops As Productive Meeting," *Ute Bulletin* 2, no. 2 (December 30, 1961), folder 9, carton 133, WCBICCR, LTPSC.
74. Metcalf, *Termination's Legacy*, 198–203; and Nielson, *The Dispossessed.*
75. U.S. Congress, House, *Report to Accompany S. 3532.*
76. Section 24, *Ute Partition Act,* Act To provide for the partition and distribution of the assets of the Ute Indian Tribe of the Uintah and Ouray Reservation in Utah between the mixed-blood and full-blood members thereof; and for the termination of Federal supervision over the property of the mixed-blood members of said tribe; to provide a development program for the full-blood members of said tribe; and for other purposes. Pub. L. No. 671, 68 Stat. 868 (1954), p.877.
77. "A Story of Two Congresses," speech before the 13th Annual Convention, National Congress of American Indians, September 24–28, 1956, Salt Lake City UT, 661/2 Speeches 1949–1960. All in Metcalf Papers, MHSRCA.

9. CONFEDERATED TRIBES OF COLVILLE

Epigraph 1: Affiliated Tribes of Northwest Indians Resolution #9 draft, October 1971, folder Indian Affairs: Indian Affairs: Colville Tribe, 1961–1965, box 147, Haley Papers, MAC-FSC.

Epigraph 2: Arnold, *Bartering*, xv.

1. I would not have been able to complete this chapter had not Laurie Arnold generously shared thousands of pages of documents from her personal collection with me.
2. Arnold, *Bartering*, 4–6.
3. Arnold, *Bartering*, 11.
4. "Justification for Restoration of 'Opened' Lands, Diminished Portion Reservation," Colville Indian Reservation, Washington, January 1, 1949, folder 15/11 U.S. Indian Affairs Bureau General Correspondence 1949–50, box 15, accession no. 3560–002 (hereafter "Justification"), Jackson Papers, UWLSC.
5. "Justification," Jackson Papers, UWLSC.
6. Arnold, *Bartering*, 28.
7. "Justification," Jackson Papers, UWLSC.
8. "Justification," Jackson Papers, UWLSC.
9. "Justification," Jackson Papers, UWLSC.
10. Arnold, *Bartering*, 8.
11. Statement of Hon. Don Magnuson, a representative in Congress from the State of Washington, U.S. Congress, House, Subcommittee on Interior and Insular Affairs, *Colville Indian Lands*, 9. Much of the written documentation is ambiguous regarding exactly what land is proposed for restoration. Arnold erroneously referred to the restoration lands as the North Half, in *Bartering*. As she observes, all the conflict discussed in this chapter derives "from the loss of the North

Half and continued attempts to reduce the reservation even more than the first two reductions (changing the initial eastern boundary then the northern one)." Personal communication with the author, June 23, 2022.

12. "Justification," Jackson Papers, UWLSC.
13. "Justification," Jackson Papers, UWLSC.
14. [Name restricted] to House Committee on Indian Affairs, received May 3, 1946, folder 15/5 U.S. Indian Affairs Bureau 1946–47, box 15, accession no. 3560–002, Jackson Papers, UWLSC.
15. [Name Restricted by rule of archives] to House Committee on Indian Affairs, received May 3, 1946, folder 15/5 U.S. Indian Affairs Bureau 1946–47, box 15, accession no. 3560–002, Jackson Papers, UWLSC.
16. Bob Miller, "Outdoor Review—$2 Indian Permit Won't Cost Any Scalps," *Spokesman Review*, April 21, 1946.
17. Assistant Commissioner of Indian Affairs to Jackson, May 27, 1946, folder 15/5 U.S. Indian Affairs Bureau 1946–47, box 15, accession no. 3560–002, Jackson Papers, UWLSC.
18. [Name restricted] to House Committee on Indian Affairs, received May 3, 1946, folder 15/5 U.S. Indian Affairs Bureau 1946–47, box 15, accession no. 3560–002, Jackson Papers, UWLSC.
19. Press Release, Confederated Tribes, Colville Reservation, January 12, [1951], Frank George, Tribal Relations Officer, folder Indian Claims and Contracts (James E. Curry), 3, Memorandums, September 1950–June 1951, box 401, Ickes Papers, LOC.
20. "Dillon Myer Reversed by Secretary Chapman." National Congress of American Indians Washington Bulletin, March 1951, folder Indian Claims and Contracts (James E. Curry), 3, Memorandums September 1950–June 1951, box 401, Ickes Papers, LOC.
21. The Business Council adopted its resolution opposing this on April 13, 1951, after a general council meeting of March 17, 1951, where tribal members "had lodged a strong protest against this bill and the others that we mention in this agenda." "Agenda, Colville Indian Delegation to Washington DC, January 25, 1952," folder 15/18 U.S. Indian Affairs Bureau General Correspondence 1952, box 15, accession no. 3560–002, Jackson Papers, UWLSC.
22. [Name restricted], Colville Indian Commercial Club, to Members of the Appropriations Committees, U.S. House and Senate, September 21, 1951; [Name restricted] to Jackson, October 2, 1951, both in folder 15/14 U.S. Indian Affairs Bureau General Correspondence 1950–51, box 15, accession no. 3560–002, Jackson Papers, UWLSC.
23. Willard Zellmer, Davenport Washington Commercial Club, to Jackson, June 19, 1953; Colville Indian Commercial Club Resolution, January 10, 1952; W. Barton

Greenwood, Acting Commissioner, to Jackson, May 4, 1953, all in folder 12/12 U.S. Indian Affairs Bureau 1953, box 12; [Name restricted] to Jackson, February 4, 1954; [Name restricted], President, Tri-County Mining Association to Jackson, June 2, 1954, both in folder 16/18 U.S. Indian Affairs Bureau 1954, box 16; James D. White to Jackson, January 19, 1954 telegram, folder 107/5 Indian Affairs 1954, box 107, all in accession no. 3560–003, Jackson Papers, UWLSC. See also C.A. Gray, President and W. W. Sharp, Secretary, Tri-County Mining Association, Spokane to Secretary of the Interior Douglas McKay, March 27, 1954, folder #32–Indians 2 of 2, box 23, Sen 83A-F9 IIAC, RG 46, NARA-DC. The debates over mining on the reservation have continued. See Becky Kramer, "Mountain of Controversy," *Spokesman-Review*, February 13, 2006, https://www.spokesman.com/stories/2006/feb/13/mountain-of-controversy/; and Jack McNeel, "Colville to Vote on Mining Referendum," *Indian Country Today*, September 12, 2018, https://indiancountrytoday.com/archive/colville-to-vote-on-mining-referendum.

24. Arnold, *Bartering*, 15.
25. "Constitution and By Laws," of Colville Indian Association, in Minutes, Second Meeting of Colville Indian Association, August 21, 1954, folder 20/15 U.S. Indian Affairs Bureau General 1955, box 20, accession no. 3560–003, Jackson Papers, UWLSC.
26. Preamble, Colville Indian Association, "Categorical Reply to Printed Hearings on Colville Termination Legislation, Sub-Committee on Indian Affairs of the House Committee on Interior and Insular Affairs," May 15, 1962, folder Indian Affairs: Colville Tribe, 1961–1965, box 147, Haley Papers, MAC-FSC.
27. Lucy Swan Secretary and Marcel Arcasa President, Colville Indian Association, to W. Barton Greenwood, January 29, 1955, folder 20/15 U.S. Indian Affairs Bureau General 1955, box 20, accession no. 3560–003, Jackson Papers, UWLSC.
28. Greenwood to Henry Jackson, December 20, 1954, folder 20/15 U.S. Indian Affairs Bureau General 1955, box 20, accession no. 3560–003, Jackson Papers, UWLSC.
29. Emmons to Horan, November 6, 1955, folder 14300–1954 CCF 1940–1957 Colville 054, RG 75; Frank W. Moore, President, Colville Indian Association to Senator James Murray, October 9, 1956, folder Indians Subcommittee (1 of 7), box 883, Sen 84A-F9 IIAC, RG 46, both in NARA-DC.
30. Arnold, *Bartering*, 19–30.
31. Thomas E. Edwards, President, Colville Indian Association to Haley, August 18, 1964, folder Indian Affairs: Colville Tribe, 1961–1965, box 147, Haley Papers, MAC-FSC.
32. Restoration refers here to the return of lost lands. In a broader sense, the term is used to define the change in status when tribal nations were able to reverse the termination policy beginning in the 1970s, but that is not the case here.

33. Untitled, undated speech on Indian policy by Lee Metcalf, 661/5 Speeches, Metcalf Papers, MHSRCA.
34. [Name restricted], attorney for Colville Tribe, to Jackson, February 5, 1954, folder 16/18 U.S. Indian Affairs Bureau 1954, box 16, accession no. 3560–003, Jackson Papers, UWLSC.
35. Arnold, *Bartering*, 22. Grorud is listed as "General Attorney" on Colville Indian Association letterhead in the 1960s. See, for example, Frank W. Moore, Violet Assing, and Alyce P. Hallenius to Haley, February 10, 1964, folder Indian Affairs: Colville Tribe, 1961–1965, box 147, Haley Papers, MAC-FSC.
36. Jackson to [Name restricted], February 12, 1954, folder 16/18 U.S. Indian Affairs Bureau 1954, box 16, accession no. 3560–003, Jackson Papers, UWLSC.
37. Arnold, *Bartering*, 21.
38. Minutes, Colville Business Council in Special Session, August 30, 1954, folder 00–1953, box 21, CCF 1940–1957 Colville 053, RG 75, NARA-DC.
39. *Menominee Tribe of Indians v. United States.*
40. Arnold, *Bartering*, 14, 19, 21.
41. Colville Confederated Tribes, Nespelem, Washington, Portland Area Office Conference with Tribal Delegates Reviews Concerning Restoration, Termination and the Agreement with Okanogan an [F]erry Counties, Portland, Oregon, April 1, 1955, Charles DePoe, Executive Secretary, Business Council, 227/5 Department of the Interior: Bureau of Indian Affairs, Colville Indians, 1955–1966, Metcalf Papers, MHSRCA. Copy also in folder 9, box 103, NCAI Papers, NMAI-SI (hereafter Meeting of April 1, 1955).
42. Minutes, Colville Business Council in Special Session, August 30, 1954, folder 00–1953, box 21, CCF 1940–1957 Colville 053, RG 75, NARA-DC.
43. Summary of Views of Colville Delegates a Conference, Portland Area Office, April 1, 1955, 227/5 Department of the Interior: Bureau of Indian Affairs, Colville Indians, 1955–1966, Metcalf Papers, MHSRCA.
44. Summary of Views of Colville Delegates a Conference.
45. Meeting of April 1, 1955.
46. Meeting of April 1, 1955; and Arnold, *Bartering*, 21.
47. Act Restoring to Tribal Ownership Certain Lands upon the Colville Indian Reservation, Washington, and for Other Purposes, Pub. L. No. 84–772, 70 Stat. 626 (1956) p. 627.
48. Text of H.R. 6154 and H.R. 7190, and Lewis to Engle, July 20, 1955, all in U.S. Congress, House, Committee on Interior and Insular Affairs, *Restoring to Tribal Ownership.*
49. Lewis to Engle, 20 July 1955, in U.S. Congress, House, Committee on Interior and Insular Affairs, *Restoring to Tribal Ownership.*
50. U.S. Congress, House, Committee on Interior and Insular Affairs, *Restoring to Tribal Ownership.*

51. See, for example, Lee Metcalf to Mrs. Eugene E. Wilson, Billings, February 24, 1956; Metcalf to Edward P. Whiteman, February 10, 1956, and other similar correspondence in 240/7 Department of the Interior: Bureau of Indian Affairs, Termination of Federal Responsibility, 1955–1965; "A Story of Two Congresses" Speech before the 13th Annual Convention, National Congress of American Indians, September 24–28, 1956, Salt Lake City, Utah, 661/2 Speeches 1949–1960. All in Metcalf Papers, MHSRCA.
52. U.S. Congress, House, Committee on Interior and Insular Affairs, *Restoring to Tribal Ownership.*
53. Act Restoring to Tribal Ownership Certain Lands; and Arnold, *Bartering*, 23, 25, 55, 145. Sherman was an attorney for the Veteran's Bureau in Washington DC. Laurie Arnold and Paul G. Wapato tell us, "While he never held elected office for the Colville Tribes, his commitment to tribal culture, combined with his experience in the political world of Washington DC, allowed Sherman to influence reservation opinion against termination and successfully argue against the policy at the national level." Arnold and Wapato, "Paschal Sherman," 66.
54. Act Restoring to Tribal Ownership Certain Lands, 627.
55. Peroff, *Menominee Drums*, 132; Minutes of House Subcommittee on Indian Affairs March 15, 1966, folder Subcom. On Indian Affairs Minutes 2 of 2 and Minutes House Committee on Interior and Insular Affairs, August 25, 1966, folder Full Com. Minutes 2nd Sess 2 of 2, both in box 75, 89th Congress IIAC and Subcommittee Minutes, RG 233, NARA-DC.
56. Gamble to Henry Jackson, March 13, 1963, folder General Files (Indians Subcommittee)–to Indian, Bureau of, box 13, IIAC Sen 88A-F11, RG 46, NARA-DC.
57. Arcasa to Frank Church, March 18, 1964, folder General Files I (Indians) 1 of 2, box 13, IIAC Sen 88A-F11, RG 46, NARA-DC.
58. Edwards to Haley, August 18, 1964, telegram, folder Indian Affairs: Colville Tribe, 1961–1965, box 147, Haley Papers, MAC-FSC.
59. "Economic Aspects of Timber Management on the Colville Indian Reservation, Washington," 1962, United States Department of the Interior, Stewart L. Udall, Secretary, Bureau of Indian Affairs, Philleo Nash, Commissioner, Business Council of the Confederated Tribes of the Colville Reservation, Harvey Moses, Chair, folder 1 Warm Springs Timber Management-Colville Material, box 31, series 8 Confederated Tribes of the Colville Reservation, WBCICCR, LTPSC.
60. Udall to Wayne Aspinall, June 16, 1965, U. S. Congress, House, *Colville Termination*, 12. James Gamble expressed his frustration with the 88th Congress's House failure to pass the Colville termination bill, which the Senate had passed, in Gamble to Senator Church, August 12, 1964, folder General Files (Indians Subcommittee)–to Indian, Bureau of, box 13, IIAC, Sen 88A-F11, RG 46, NARA-DC.

61. Minutes of January 27, 1966, folder Subcom. On Indian Affairs Minutes 1 of 2, box 75, 89th Congress IIAC and Subcommittee Minutes, RG 233, NARA-DC
62. Arnold, *Bartering*, 28–30.
63. Arnold, *Bartering*, 15, 27.
64. Arnold, *Bartering*, 10.

CONCLUSION

Epigraph 1: Introduction of Cornel West, Piʻo Summit 2022 Wai Sovereignty & Justice, Honolulu, December 15, 2022.

Epigraph 2: La Farge to Board of Directors and Executive Director, AAIA, August 7, 1953, folder Association on American Indians File . . . I Termination—General, August 1953–February 1954, box 76, Nash Papers, HSTL.

Epigraph 3: *United States v. Jicarilla Apache Nation*, 175.

1. *United States v. Jicarilla Apache Nation*, 175–76.
2. When BIA termination plans were not made quickly enough for him, Senate staffer Gamble believed that "Congress had not been specific in preparing and submitting to the Bureau the manner in which its most recent policy declaration (H. Con. Res. 108, 83d Congress) [was] to be implemented." Gamble to Anderson and Church, July 10, 1961 re Comments on Task Force Report, written with collaboration from Dr. John Taylor, House Interior Committee Indian Affairs Consultant, and Dr. William Gilbert LOC Legislative Reference Service Indian Affairs Analyst, folder Bureau of Indian Affairs, box 10, Sen 87A-F11 IIAC, RG 46, NARA-DC.
3. Lee, *Congress Vs. The Bureaucracy*, xii.
4. "H.R. 1794 Slashed by Senate Subcommittee," *Kinzua Planning Newsletter*, vol. 3, no. 4 (March 25, 1964).
5. On manufacture of consent, see Lippmann, *Public Opinion*, ch. 15. See also Bernays, *Engineering of Consent*.
6. Copy of identical letters from Secretary of the Interior to All Area Directors, except Juneau and Window Rock, February 18, 1953, folder 1950–1953 Commissioner of Indian Affairs, Memoranda and Reports (3 of 4), box 2, Myer Papers, HSTL.
7. Myer to All Area Directors, February 19, 1953, folder 1950–1953 Commissioner of Indian Affairs, Memoranda and Reports (3 of 4), box 2, Myer Papers, HSTL.
8. Secretary of the Interior Wesley d'Ewart to Senator James Murray, June 25, 1956, folder Press Releases–B.I.A., 1954–58, box 92, Brophy Papers, HSTL.
9. Black, "Counsel of Their Own Choosing," 3.
10. Charles F. Jones to La Farge, August 31, 1955, folder 12, box 2, Zimmerman Papers, CSRSC-UNML.
11. "Indian Ownership of Land," William Zimmerman Jr. letter to the editor, *New York Times*, July 12, 1955; Dorothy Van de Mark, "The Raid on Reservations,"

Harpers Magazine, reprint from March 1956 issue, folder 1, box 289, Murray Papers, MMMASC-UM.

12. Their funds were later distributed to a different tribe altogether. Beck, *Seeking Recognition*, 171.
13. Alexander Lesser to Philleo Nash, February 1, 1954, folder Association on American Indians File . . . I Termination-General, August 1953–February 1954; Arthur Lazarus Jr. and Richard Schifter, "Statement on S. 2747 and H.R. 7321," March 12, 1954, folder Association on American Indians File . . . I Termination-Seminole, both in box 76, Nash Papers, HSTL. On the Seminole termination crisis, see Kersey, *Assumption of Sovereignty*; and Kersey, "'Give Us Twenty-Five Years.'"
14. Commissioner to Area Directors, October 28, 1957, folder Paiutes–Termination, box 92, Brophy Papers, HSTL.
15. Commissioner to Area Directors, October 28, 1957.
16. McKay to La Farge, November 30, 1955, folder Press Releases–B.I.A., 1954–58, box 92, Brophy Papers, HSTL.
17. McKay to La Farge, November 30, 1955.
18. Metcalf, *Termination's Legacy*, 15–16, 22; and Beck, *Seeking Recognition*, 156–57.
19. Proceedings of Klamath General Council Meeting, January 17–18, 1955, folder 00–1952 Part 2A, box 24, CCF 1940–1957 Klamath 054, RG 75, NARA-DC.
20. "Frank Parker Makes Indian Goals His Own," *Idaho State Journal*, Pocatello, April 6, 1954. Folder B5.3 Helen L. Peterson Papers NCAI Correspondence 1954, box 5, Peterson Papers, NMAI-SI.
21. This is clear from reading minutes of tribal councils when meeting with bureau officials. For one example, see Minutes of a Meeting of Tribal Council of the Confederated Salish and Kootenai Tribes of the Flathead Reservation, August 16, 1952, folder 1950–1953 Commissioner of Indian Affairs, Memoranda and Reports (2 of 4), box 2, Myer Papers, HSTL.
22. Thiong'o, foreword to Silva, *Power of the Steel-Tipped Pen*, ix.
23. Minutes of the Executive Council Meeting, Hotel Utah, Salt Lake City, December 8–10, 1955, folder B1.16 NCAI Executive Council Meetings September–December 1955, box 1, Peterson Papers, NMAI-SI.
24. "Indian Legislation Pending," May 1, 1954, Competency Bill folder, series 1, box 41, NCAI Papers; "Indians Came Out Better than Expected in 83rd Congress"; folder B3.12 Helen L. Peterson Papers, NCAI Conventions, Tenth Annual Convention, Omaha, NE 1954, box 3, Peterson Papers, both in NMAI-SI.
25. "Official American Indian Leaders Wind Up Week-Long Session; Denounce White House Picketing by Unrepresentative Tribe," NCAI Press Release, March 23, 1959, folder 7, box 11, Zimmerman Papers, CSRSC-UNML.
26. "'Termination Is Genocide,'" *Win Awenen Nisitotung*, September 1983, 12.

27. On the fishing violence see Whaley and Brestte, *Walleye Warriors*; and Nesper, *Walleye War*. See also Durdas, "In the Name"; Anna V. Smith, "Why Don't Anti-Indian Groups Count as Hate Groups?" *High Country News*, October 8, 2018, https://www.hcn.org/issues/50.20/tribal-affairs-why-don't-anti-indian-groups-count-as-hate-groups.
28. "Secretary Zinke Advocates 'Off-Ramp' for Taking Lands Out of Trust," Indianz.com, May 3, 2017, https://indianz.com/news/2017/05/03/secretary-zinke-advocates-offramp-for-ta.asp.
29. Beck, *Struggle for Self-Determination*, 187.

BIBLIOGRAPHY

ARCHIVAL SOURCES

Beinicke Rare Book and Manuscript Library, Yale University Library

Felix S. Cohen Papers, 1916–1992. WA MSS S-1325.

Center for Southwest Research and Special Collections, University of New Mexico Libraries

Sophie D. Aberle Papers. MSS 509 BC

William Zimmerman Jr. Papers, 1933–1965. MSS 517 BC

Community Archives of NAES College: See University of Chicago Library Special Collections Research Center

Harry S. Truman Library, Independence MO

Dillon S. Myer Papers, 1934–1966

Oral History Interview with Oscar R. Ewing. Available at http://www.trumanlibrary.org/oralhist/ewing1.htm

Papers of Harry S. Truman

SMOF Philleo Nash Files

Philleo Nash Papers, 1925–1998

William A. Brophy and Sophie Aberle Brophy Papers, 1923–1973

Library of Congress

Harold L. Ickes Papers, MSS 27011

Julius A. Krug Papers, MSS 009302

L. Thom Perry Special Collections, Harold B. Lee Library, Brigham Young University, Provo UT

Arthur V. Watkins (1886–1973) Papers, MSS 146
Ernest L. Wilkinson Personal Papers, UA 1000
Mitchell A. Dodge papers on the Menominee Indian Tribe, MSS 1538. Formerly known as Mary Dodge Papers, A-80-60
National Council of American Indians Collection, MSS 1704
"Register to the Gertrude and Raymond Bonnin Collection, MSS 1704"
Wilkinson, Cragun, and Barker Indian Claims Commission Records, MSS 2291
Wilkinson, Cragun, and Barker Records, MSS 2382

Maureen and Mike Mansfield Archives and Special Collections, University of Montana, Missoula

James E. Murray Papers 1918–1969, MSS 091
Series I: General Correspondence

McKay Archives Center, Florida Southern College, Lakeland

James A. Haley Papers, 1948–1977

Menominee Historic Preservation Department, Keshena WI

Gordon Dickie Sr. Papers
Interviews with tribal members. VHS taped, used with permission

Menominee Tribal Archives, Keshena

Minutes of Menominee General Council and Advisory Council Meetings. 1920–1933

Montana Historical Society Research Center Archives, Helena

Lee Metcalf Papers, 1934–1995

National Archives and Records Administration, College Park MD

Record Group 220: Records of Temporary Committees, Commissions, and Boards
Records of the American Indian Policy Review Commission, 1975–1977

National Archives and Records Administration, Pacific Alaska Region (Seattle)

Record Groups 75: Records of the Bureau of Indian Affairs: Portland Area Office Records
Portland Area Office Records
PAO 01: Subject Files of the Area Director, 1946–1957
PAO 02: Desk Files for the Assistant Area Director for Administration

National Archives and Records Administration, Washington DC

Record Group 46: Records of the United States Senate
Sen 83A-F9: Interior and Insular Affairs Committee

Sen 83A-F9: Records of the Committee on Indian Affairs
(70th–82nd Congress) (1928–54), part 1
Sen 84A-F9: Interior and Insular Affairs Committee
Sen 87A-F11: Interior and Insular Affairs General Files
Sen 88A-F11: Committee on Interior and Insular Affairs

Record Group 75: Records of the Bureau of Indian Affairs
Central Classified Files 1907–1939
Central Classified Files 1940–1943
Central Classified Files 1940–1957, entry E-121
Entry 190: Memoranda of Assistant Commissioner
William Zimmerman, 1935–48
Entry 1014Y: Organization Charts and Related Records, 1936–1968
Letters Received, 1881–1907: Entry 91

Record Group 233: Records of the United States House of Representatives
82nd Congress IIAC
88th Congress House IIAC Legislative Files
89th Congress IIAC
89th Congress and IIAC and Subcommittee Minutes
90th Congress House IIAC Minutes

National Archives at Chicago

Record Group 75: Records of the Bureau of Indian Affairs
Menominee Agency Decimal Correspondence Files, 1934–1961
Records of the Keshena/Menominee Agency, 1892–1961
Records of the Menominee Indian Mills, 1900–1961

National Museum of the American Indian Archives, Suitland MD

Helen Peterson Papers
National Congress of American Indian Papers

The Newberry Library, Chicago

D'Arcy McNickle Papers, 1913–1986
Erminie Wheeler-Voegelin Papers, 1934–1985

Oregon State Archives

Office of Governor Douglas McKay Papers, 1948–1952

University of Chicago Library Special Collections Research Center

Native American Educational Services Chicago Community Agencies
Records, 1892–2001
Robert Rietz Papers 1876–1982

University of Denver Special Collections and Archives

Peter H. Dominick Papers, MS 085

University of Oregon Special Collections and University Archives

Douglas McKay Papers, 1925–1958, Collection Number Ax 063

University of Washington Libraries, Special Collections

Henry M. Jackson Papers

Accession 3560-002: House papers, 1940–1952

Accession 3560-003: Senate papers, 1952–1963

Wisconsin Historical Society Archives

Green Bay and Prairie du Chien Papers, Wis/Mss/C

Menominee Indian Papers, Wis/Mss/BU

Wisconsin Historical Society Library

Phebe Jewell Nichols, "Stating the Case for the Menominees." (Pamphlet Studies of Wisconsin Indian Problems, No. 1. Copyright Phebe Jewell Nichols, 1931).

PUBLISHED PRIMARY AND SECONDARY SOURCES

Anaya, S. James. *Indigenous Peoples and International Law*. 2nd ed. New York: Oxford University Press, 2004.

Annual Report of the Secretary of the Interior, 1947.

Arnold, Laurie. *Bartering with the Bones of Their Dead: The Colville Confederated Tribes and Termination*. Seattle: University of Washington Press, 2012.

Arnold, Laurie, and Paul G. Wapato. "Paschal Sherman: Blue Jay, Ph.D." In *"Our Cause Will Ultimately Triumph": The Men and Women Who Preserved and Revitalized American Indian Sovereignty*, edited by Tim Alan Garrison, 65–75. Durham NC: Carolina Academic Press, 2014.

Arriolas, Theresa Hill. "Securing Nature: Militarism, Indigeneity and the Environment in the Northern Mariana Islands." Ph.D. diss. University of California, Los Angeles, 2020.

Ayer, Edward E. *Report on Menominee Indian Reservation*. United States Board of Indian Commissioners: 1914.

Barsh, Russel L. "Indian Land Claims Policy in the United States." *North Dakota Law Review* 58, no. 1 (1982): 7–82.

Bauer, William. "Working for Identity: Race, Ethnicity, and the Market Economy in Northern California, 1875–1936." In *Native Pathways: American Indian Culture and Economic Development in the Twentieth Century*, edited by Brian Hosmer and Colleen O'Neill, 238–57. Boulder: University Press of Colorado, 2004.

Bauer, William J., Jr. *We Were All Like Migrant Workers Here: Work, Community, and Memory on California's Round Valley Reservation, 1850–1941*. Chapel Hill: University of North Carolina Press, 2009.

Beaird, William Lynn. "Termination of Federal Supervision over the Kalamath Tribe of Indians, Oregon, 1928–1961." Master's thesis, Montana State University, 1974.

Beck, David R. M. *Seeking Recognition: The Termination and Restoration of the Coos, Lower Umpqua, and Siuslaw Indians, 1855–1984*. Lincoln: University of Nebraska Press, 2009.

——. *Siege and Survival: History of the Menominee Indians, 1634–1856*. Lincoln: University of Nebraska Press, 2002.

——. *The Struggle for Self-Determination: History of the Menominee Indians since 1854*. Lincoln: University of Nebraska Press, 2005.

——. *Unfair Labor? American Indians and the 1893 World's Columbian Exposition in Chicago*. Lincoln: University of Nebraska Press, 2019.

"Before the Indian Claims Commission," *The Seneca Nation of Indians, Plaintiff, the Tonawanda Band of Seneca Indians, Plaintiff, v. The United States of America, Defendant*. Docket Nos. 342-A, B, C, E, F and I; Dockets 368 and 368-A. 28 Ind. Cl. Comm. 12 (May 3, 1972).

Bernays, Edward L., ed. *Engineering of Consent*. Norman: University of Oklahoma Press, 1955.

Bilharz, Joy. *The Allegany Senecas and Kinzua Dam: Forced Relocation through Two Generations*. Lincoln: University of Nebraska Press, 2002.

Bilka, Monika. "The Klamath's Path after Termination." Master's thesis, University of Montana, 2008.

——. "Remaking a People, Restoring a Watershed: Klamath Tribal Empowerment through Natural Resource Activism, 1960–2014." Ph.D. diss. University of Arizona, 2015.

Biondi, Marsha. *To Stand and Fight: The Struggle for Civil Rights in Postwar New York City*. Cambridge: Harvard University Press, 2003.

Black, Charles L., Jr. "Counsel of Their Own Choosing." *American Indian* 6, no. 2 (Fall 1951): 3–17.

Black, Liza. *Picturing Indians: Native Americans in Film, 1941–1960*. Lincoln: University of Nebraska Press, 2020.

Bloom, John Porter, ed. *Territorial Papers of the United States*. Vol. 27, *Wisconsin*. Washington DC: National Archives and Records Service, General Services Administration, 1975.

Bonnin, Gertrude (Zitkala Sa), Charles H. Fabens, and Matthew K. Sniffen. "Oklahoma's Poor Rich Indians, An Orgy of Graft and Exploitation of the Five Civilized Tribes—Legalized Robbery." Philadelphia: Indian Rights Association, 1924.

Broto, Vanesa Castán, and Martín Sanzana Calvet. "Sacrifice Zones of Urban Energy Landscapes in Concepcíon, Chile." *Journal of Political Ecology* 27 (2020): 279–99.

Burt, Larry W. *Tribalism in Crisis: Federal Indian Policy, 1953–1961*. Albuquerque: University of New Mexico Press, 1982.

Cahill, Cathleen. *Federal Fathers and Mothers: A Social History of the United States Indian Service, 1869–1933*. Chapel Hill: University of North Carolina Press, 2013.

Carter, Nancy Carol. "U.S. Federal Indian Policy: An Essay and Annotated Bibliography." *Legal Reference Services Quarterly* 30 (2011): 210–30.

Cartwright, Charles Edward. "The Board of Indian Commissioners: Hope, Failure and Abandonment 1869–1887." Master's Thesis, University of Arizona, 1980.

Castaneda, Terri. "Making News: Marie Potts and the *Smoke Signal* of the Federated Indians of California." In *Women in Print: Essays on the Print Culture of American Women from the Nineteenth and Twentieth Centuries*, edited by James P. Danky and Wayne A. Weigand, 77–125. Madison: University of Wisconsin Press, 2006.

Catton, Theodore. *American Indians and National Forests*. Tucson: University of Arizona Press, 2016.

Cherokee Nation v. Georgia, 30 U.S. 1 (1831).

Child, Brenda J. *Holding Our World Together: Ojibwe Women and the Survival of Community*. New York: Penguin Books, 2012.

——— . *My Grandfather's Knocking Sticks: Ojibwe Family Life and Labor on the Reservation*. St. Paul: Minnesota Historical Society Press, 2014.

Clark, Blue. *Lone Wolf v. Hitchcock: Treaty Rights and Indian Law at the End of the Nineteenth Century*. Lincoln: University of Nebraska Press, 1994.

Clayton, James L. "The Impact of Traders' Claims on the American Fur Trade." In *The Frontier in American Development, Essays in Honor of Paul Wallace Gates* edited by David M. Ellis, 301–9. Ithaca: Cornell University Press, 1969.

Clow, Richmond L. "Crossing the Divide from Citizen to Voter: Tribal Suffrage in Montana, 1880–2016." *Montana: The Magazine of History* 69, no. 1 (Spring 2019): 35–64.

Cohen, Felix S. "Breaking Faith with Our First Americans." *Indian Truth* 25, no. 2 (March–April 1948): 1–8.

——— . "The Erosion of Indian Rights, 1950–1953: A Case Study in Bureaucracy." *Yale Law Journal* 62, no. 3 (February 1953): 348–90.

Collier, John. "The Beleaguered Indian." *The Nation*, September 17, 1949, 276.

Colten, Craig E. "An Incomplete Solution: Oil and Water in Louisiana." *Journal of American History* 99, no. 1 (June 2012): 91–99.

Confederated Bands of Ute Indians v. United States, 117 Ct. Cl. 433 (1950).

Congressional Record.

Cowger, Thomas W. *The National Congress of American Indians: The Founding Years*. Lincoln: University of Nebraska Press, 1999.

Curley, Andrew. "Infrastructures as Colonial Beachheads: The Central Arizona Project and the Taking of Navajo Resources." *Environment and Planning D: Society and Space* 39, no. 3 (2021): 387–404.

"The Current Termination Program in Indian Affairs, A Statement of Policy Adopted November 1954 by the Board of Directors." *American Indian* 7, no. 2 (Spring 1955), 55–56.

Daly, Heather Marie. "'American Indian Freedom Controversy:' Political and Social Activism by Southern California Mission Indians, 1934–1958." Ph.D. diss, UCLA, 2013.

DeJong, David H. *Paternalism to Partnership: The Administration of Indian Affairs, 1786–2021*. Lincoln: University of Nebraska Press, 2022.

Deloria, Vine, Jr. *Custer Died for Your Sins, an Indian Manifesto*. New York: Avon Books, 1969.

Deloria, Vine Jr., ed. *The Indian Reorganization Act Congresses and Bills*. Norman: University of Oklahoma Press, 2002.

Deloria, Vine, Jr., and Clifford M. Lytle. *The Nations Within: The Past and Future of American Indian Sovereignty*. 2nd ed. Austin: University of Texas Press, 1988.

Dibblin, Jane. *Day of Two Suns: U.S. Nuclear Testing and the Pacific Islanders*. London: Virago, 1988.

Dorgan, Byron L. *The Girl in the Photograph: The True Story of a Native American Child, Lost and Found in America*. New York: Thomas Dunne Books, 2019.

Dudziak, Mary L. *Cold War Civil Rights: Race and the Image of American Democracy*. Princeton: Princeton University Press, 2000.

Durdas, Jeffrey R. "In the Name of Equal Rights: 'Special' Rights and the Politics of Resentment in Post-Civil Rights America." *Law and Society Review* 39, no. 4 (December 2005): 723–57.

Erdrich, Louise. *The Night Watchman*. New York: Harper Perennial, 2020.

Federal Register 21:66 (5 April 1956).

Fenn, Elizabeth A. *Encounters at the Heart of the World: A History of the Mandan People*. New York: Hill and Wang, 2014.

Fixico, Donald L. *Termination and Relocation: Federal Indian Policy, 1945–1960*. Albuquerque: University of New Mexico Press, 1986.

Fox, Julia. "Mountaintop Removal in West Virginia: An Environmental Sacrifice Zone." *Organization and Environment* 12, no. 2 (June 1999): 163–83.

Fritz, Henry E. *The Movement for Indian Assimilation, 1860–1890*. Philadelphia: University of Pennsylvania Press, 1963.

Gaddis, John Lewis. *The Cold War*. New York: Penguin Press, 2005.

Gordon-McCutchan, R. C., and Frank Waters. *Taos Indians and the Battle for Blue Lake*. Santa Fe: Red Crane Books, 1995.

Grann, David. *Killers of the Flower Moon: The Osage Murders and the Birth of the* FBI. New York: Vintage Books, 2017.

Hall, Jacquelyn Dowd. "The Long Civil Rights Movement and the Political Uses of the Past." *Journal of American History* 91, no. 4 (March 2005): 1233–63.

Harmon, Alexandra. *Rich Indians: Native People and the Problem of Wealth in American History*. Chapel Hill: University of North Carolina Press, 2010.

Harper, Allan G. "Ft. Berthold Indians Hope for Justice." *American Indian* 5, no. 1 (1949): 22–30.

Hauptman, Laurence M. "General John S. Bragdon, the Office of Public Works Planning, and the Decision to Build Pennsylvania's Kinzua Dam." *Pennsylvania History: A Journal of Mid-Atlantic Studies* 53, no. 3 (July 1986): 181–200.

———. *In the Shadow of Kinzua Dam: The Seneca Nation of Indians Since World War II*. Syracuse: Syracuse University Press, 2014.

———. "On and Off State Time: William N. Fenton and the Seneca Nation of Indians in Crisis, 1954—1968." *New York History* 93, no. 2 (Spring 2012): 182–232.

Haynal, Patrick. "Termination and Tribal Survival: The Klamath Tribes of Oregon." *Oregon Historical Quarterly* 101, no. 3 (Fall 2000): 270–301.

Haynal, Patrick Mann. "From Termination through Restoration and Beyond: Modern Klamath Cultural Identity." Ph.D. Diss., University of Oregon, 1994.

H.C.R. 108, Indians, 83rd Congress, 1st Session, August 1, 1953, 67 Stat. 132B.

Henry, Matthew S. "Extractive Fictions and Postextractive Futurisms: Energy and Environmental Injustice in Appalachia." *Environmental Humanities* 11, no. 2 (2019): 402–26.

Herzberg, Stephen J. "The Menominee Indians, From Treaty to Termination." *Wisconsin Magazine of History* 60, no. 4 (Summer 1977): 267–329.

———. "The Menominee Indians: Termination to Restoration." *American Indian Law Review* 6, no. 1 (Summer 1978): 143–86.

Hitchcock, William I. *The Age of Eisenhower: America and the World in the 1950s*. New York: Simon and Schuster, 2018.

H. J. Res. 490, 81st Congress, 2d Session, June 21, 1950.

Honorable Nations. POV Season 4, PBS (2 July 1991).

Hosmer, Brian. *American Indians in the Marketplace: Persistence and Innovations among the Menominees and Metlakatlans, 1870–1920*. Lawrence: University Press of Kansas, 1999.

———. "Harry Truman and Native Americans." In *Native Americans and the Legacy of Harry S. Truman*, edited by Brian Hosmer, xiii–xl. Kirksville MO: Truman State University Press, 2010.

House Committee on Interior and Insular Affairs. Report to accompany H.R. 444, *Per Capita Distribution—Shoshone and Arapaho Tribes, Wyoming*. 83d Congress, 1st Session. April 1953. S. Rep. 263.

House of Representatives. "Reduction of Indian Reservations." 50th Congress, 1st Session. 9 January 1888. Ex. Doc. No. 63.

Hoxie, Frederick E. "Seeing and Not Seeing, American Indians in the Truman Era." In *Native Americans and the Legacy of Harry S. Truman*, edited by Brian Hosmer, 3–21. Kirksville MO: Truman State University Press, 2010.

Immerwahr, Daniel. *How to Hide an Empire: A History of the Greater United States.* New York: Farrar, Straus and Giroux, 2019.

Indians, Outlaws, and Angie Debo. The American Experience. PBS, 1988.

James, Edward T., Janet Wilson James, and Paul S. Boyer, eds. *Notable American Women, 1607–1950: A Biographical Dictionary*. Vol. 2. Cambridge: Belknap Press of Harvard University Press, 1971.

Jennings, Francis. *The Founders of America: How Indians Discovered the Land, Pioneered in It, and Created Great Classical Civilizations; How They Were Plunged into a Dark Age by Invasion and Conquest; and How They Are Now Reviving*. New York: W. W. Norton & Company, 1993.

Johnson v. M'Intosh, 21 U.S. 543 (1823).

Joint Hearing before the Subcommittees of the Committees on Interior and Insular Affairs, Congress of the United States, 83rd Congress, 2nd Session on S. 2670 and H.R. 7674, Part 1 Utah, February 15, 1954.

Joint Hearing before the Subcommittees of the Committees on Interior and Insular Affairs, Congress of the United States, 83rd Congress, 2nd Session on S. 2670 and H.R. 7674, Part 4 Klamath Indians, Oregon, February 23 and 24, 1954.

Jones, Sondra G. *Being and Becoming Ute: The Story of an American Indian People.* Salt Lake City: University of Utah Press, 2019.

Kajihiro, Kyle. "Nation Under the Gun: Militarism and Resistence in Hawai'i." *Cultural Survival Quarterly* 24, no. 1 (2000): 28–33.

Kappler, Charles J., ed. *Indian Treaties, 1778–1871*. New York: Interland Publishing, 1972 [orig. 1904].

Kelly, Lawrence C. "Charles James Rhoads (1929–1933)." In *The Commissioners of Indian Affairs, 1824–1977*, edited by Robert M. Kvasnicka and Herman J. Viola, 263–71. Lincoln: University of Nebraska Press, 1979.

Kendi, Ibram X. *How to Be an Antiracist*. New York: One World, 2019.

Kennedy, Robert F. "Buying It Back from the Indians, Surprised Attorney General finds we must still pay for U.S." *Life* 52, no. 12 (March 23, 1962): 17, 19.

Kersey, Harry A., Jr. *Assumption of Sovereignty: Social and Political Transformation among the Florida Seminoles, 1953–1979*. Lincoln: University of Nebraska Press, 1996.

———. "'Give Us Twenty-Five Years': Florida Seminoles from Near Termination to Self-Determination, 1953–1957." *Florida Historical Quarterly* 67, no. 3 (January 1989): 290–309.

Ketcham, Frank S. "Terminating the Klamaths." *American Indian* 8, no. 1 (Spring 1958): 10–19.

Kinney, J. P. *Indian Forest and Range: A History of the Administration and Conservation of the Redman's Heritage*. Washington DC: Forestry Enterprises, 1950.

Klamath & Moadoc Tribes of Indians v. United States. 296 U.S. 244 (1935).

Lake, David A. *Entangling Relations: American Foreign Policy in its Century*. Princeton: Princeton University Press, 1999.

LaPier, Rosalyn R. *Invisible Reality: Storytellers, Storytakers, and the Supernatural World of the Blackfeet*. Lincoln: University of Nebraska Press, 2017.

LaPier, Rosalyn R., and David R. M. Beck. *City Indian: Native American Activism in Chicago, 1893–1934*. Lincoln: University of Nebraska Press, 2015.

Lawson, Michael L. *Dammed Indians: The Pick-Sloan Plan and the Missouri River Sioux, 1944–1980*. Norman: University of Oklahoma Press, 1994.

Lazarus, Edward. *Black Hills/White Justice: The Sioux Nation Versus the United States, 1775 to the Present*. New York: HarperCollins, 1991.

Lederle, John W. "The Hoover Commission Reports on Federal Reorganization." *Marquette Law Review* 33, no. 2 (Fall 1949): 89–98.

Lee, Mordecai. *Congress Vs. the Bureaucracy: Muzzling Agency Public Relations*. Norman: University of Oklahoma Press, 2012.

Letters Received by the Office of Indian Affairs, 1824–81. Microcopy 234. Washington DC: National Archives and Record Service, General Services Administration, 1959.

Lewis, David Gene. "Termination of the Confederated Tribes of the Grand Ronde Community of Oregon: Politics, Community, Identity." Ph.D. diss., University of Oregon, 2009.

Lippmann, Walter. *Public Opinion*. New York: Harcourt, Brace, 1922.

Lurie, Nancy Oestreich. "The Menominee Indians, Menominee Termination: Or, Can the White Man Ever Overcome a Cultural Lag to Progress with the Indians?" *Indian Historian* 4, no. 4 (Winter 1971): 28–40, 52.

"Major Council Meetings of American Indian Tribes, Part 1, Section 2: Chippewa, Klamath, and Sioux (Standing Rock, Rosebud, Pine Ridge, and Cheyenne River), 1911–1956." History Vault: American Indians and the American West 1809–1971. Proquest database.

McCool, Daniel. *Command of the Waters: Iron Triangles, Federal Water Development, and Indian Waters*. Tucson: University of Arizona Press, 1994.

McGirt v. Oklahoma. 591 U.S. __ (2020)

McNenly, Linda Scarangella. *Native Performers in Wild West Shows: From Buffalo Bill to Euro Disney*. Norman: University of Oklahoma Press, 2012.

McQuillan, Alan G. "American Indian Timber Management Policy: Its Evolution in the Context of U.S. Forest History." In *Trusteeship in Change: Toward Tribal*

Autonomy in Resource Management, edited by Richmond L. Clow and Imre Sutton, 73–102. Boulder: University Press of Colorado, 2001.

Menominee Tribe of Indians v. United States. 391 U.S. 404 (1968).

Meriam, Lewis. *The Problem of Indian Administration*. New York: Johnson Reprint, 1971 [orig. 1928].

Metcalf, Lee, M.C. [Member of Congress]. "Termination in the 83rd Congress." *Social Order* 5, no. 2 (February 1955): 57–59.

Metcalf, R. Warren. "Lambs of Sacrifice: Termination, Mixed-blood Utes, and the Problem of Indian Identity." *Utah Historical Review* 64, no. 4 (1996): 322–43.

———. *Termination's Legacy: The Discarded Indians of Utah*. Lincoln: University of Nebraska Press, 2002.

Meyer, Roy W. "Fort Berthold and the Garrison Dam," *North Dakota History* 35 (1968): 217–355.

The Montana Committee Against Termination, James J. Flaherty, Chairman. "Obligation of Federal Trust." *Social Order* 5, no. 2 (February 1955): 66–68.

Mt. Pleasant, Alyssa. "After the Whirlwind: Maintaining a Haudenosaunee Place at Buffalo Creek, 1780–1825." Ph.D. diss., Cornell University, 2007.

Myer, Dillon S. "The Program of the Bureau." *Journal of Negro Education* 20, no. 3 (Summer 1951): 346–53.

Nesper, Larry. *The Walleye War: The Struggle for Ojibwe Spearing and Fishing Rights*. Lincoln: University of Nebraska Press, 2002.

Neuberger, Richard L. "How Oregon Rescued a Forest." *Harpers* (April 1959): 48–52.

Nevin, David. *The American Touch in Micronesia*. New York: W. W. Norton, 1977.

Niedenthal, Jack. *For the Good of Mankind: A History of the People of Bikini and Their Islands*. Majuro, Marshall Islands: Micronitor, 2001.

Nielson, Parker M. *The Dispossessed: Cultural Genocide of the Mixed-Blood Utes: An Advocate's Chronicle*. Norman: University of Oklahoma Press, 1998.

Nunn, Frances L. "Quantum Meruit and Contingent Fees in Indian Claims Cases." *George Washington Law Review* 20, no. 5 (April 1952): 621–30.

Oklahoma v. Castro-Huerta. 597 U.S. __ (2022).

Olson, James S., and Raymond Wilson. *Native Americans in the Twentieth Century*. Urbana: University of Illinois Press, 1984.

O'Neil, Floyd A., and Kathryn L. McKay. "A History of the Uintah-Ouray Ute Lands." American West Center Occasional Papers 10. Salt Lake City: University of Utah, 1978.

Orfield, Gary. "Ideology and the Indian, A Study of the Termination Policy." Master's thesis: University of Chicago, 1965.

Osage Tribe of Indians v. the United States. 66 Ct. Cl. 64 No. B-38 (May 28, 1928).

Ostler, Jeffrey. *Surviving Genocide: Native Nations and the United States from the American Revolution to Bleeding Kansas*. New Haven: Yale University Press, 2020.

"The Overprotected Indian." Editorial. *American Indian* 6, no. 1 (Summer 1951): 1–2.

Peroff, Nicholas. *Menominee Drums, Tribal Termination and Restoration, 1954–1974*. Norman: University of Oklahoma Press, 1982.

Pevar, Stephen L. *The Rights of Indians and Tribes*. 4th ed. New York: Oxford University Press, 2012.

Phillips, Ruth B. *Trading Identities: The Souvenir in Native North American Art from the Northeast, 1700–1900*. Seattle: University of Washington Press, 1998.

Philp, Kenneth R. *Termination Revisited: American Indians on the Trail of Self-Determination*. Lincoln: University of Nebraska Press, 1999.

Puisto, Jaako. *This Is My Reservation, I Belong Here: The Salish Kootenai Indian Struggle Against Termination*. Lincoln NE: Salish Kootenai College Press, 2016.

Purcell, Aaron D. "The Engineering of Forever: Arthur E. Morgan, the Seneca Indians, and the Kinzua Dam." *New York History* 78, no. 3 (July 1997): 309–36.

Raibmon, Paige. *Authentic Indians: Episodes of Encounter from the Late-Nineteenth-Century Northwest Coast*. Durham: Duke University Press, 2005.

Rasenberger, Jim. *High Steel: The Daring Men Who Built the World's Greatest Skyline*. New York: HarperCollins: 2004.

Ray, Verne F. "The Klamath Oppose Liquidation." *American Indian* 4, no. 4 (1948): 15–22.

———. *The Menominee Tribe of Indians, 1940–1970*. United States Court of Claims Docket No. 134-167, . . . Plaintiff's Exhibit R-1. Escanaba, Michigan: Photo Offset Company, 1972.

Rosenthal, Harvey D. *Their Day in Court: A History of the Indian Claims Commission*. New York: Garland, 1990.

Rosier, Paul C. "Dam Building and Treaty Breaking: The Kinzua Dam Controversy, 1936–1958." *Pennsylvania Magazine of History and Biography* 119, no. 4 (October 1995): 345–68.

Sady, Rachel Reese. "The Menominees: Transition from Trusteeship." *Applied Anthropology, Problems in Human Organization* 6, no. 2 (Spring, 1947): 1–14.

Saranillio, Dean Itsuji. *Unsustainable Empire: Alternative Histories of Hawai'i Statehood*. Durham: Duke University Press, 2018.

Saunt, Claudio. *Unworthy Republic: The Dispossession of Native Americans and the Road to Indian Territory*. New York: W. W. Norton & Company, 2020.

Schmeckebier, Laurence. *The Office of Indian Affairs: Its History, Activities, and Organization*. Baltimore: Johns Hopkins University Press, 1927.

Schrecker, Ellen W. *No Ivory Tower: McCarthyism and the Universities*. New York: Oxford University Press, 1986.

The Seneca Nation of Indians v. Wilber M. Brucker, Secretary of the Army, et al. Civ. No. 2202-57. United States District Court District of Columbia. 162 F. Supp. 580 (1958).

The Seneca Nation of Indians v. Wilber M. Brucker, Secretary of the Army, et al. United States Court of Appeals for the District of Columbia Circuit. 262 F.2d 27 (1958).

Silva, Noenoe. *The Power of the Steel-Tipped Pen: Reconstructing Native Hawaiian Intellectual History*. Durham: Duke University Press, 2017.

Sinclair, Barbara. *Congressional Realignment, 1925–1978*. Austin: University of Texas Press, 1982.

———. *Party Wars: Polarization and the Politics of National Policy Making*. Norman: University of Oklahoma Press, 2006.

———. *The Transformation of the U.S. Senate*. Baltimore: Johns Hopkins University Press, 1989.

Sleeper-Smith, Susan, Juliana Barr, Jean M. O'Brien, Nancy Shoemaker, and Scott Stevens, eds., *Why You Can't Teach United States History without American Indians*. Chapel Hill: University of North Carolina Press, 2015.

Stern, Theodore. "Livelihood and Tribal Government on the Klamath Indian Reservation." *Human Organization* 20, no. 4 (1961): 172–80.

Sutton, Imre, ed. *Irredeemable America: The Indians' Estate and Land Claims*. Albuquerque: University of New Mexico Press, 1985.

Szasz, Margaret Connell. *Education and the American Indian: The Road to Self-Determination Since 1928*. 3d ed. Albuquerque: University of New Mexico Press, 1999.

"Termination of Federal Supervision over Property of the Klamath Tribe, Oregon, Report to accompany S. 2745." 82nd Congress, 2nd Session, Senate Report No. 1631. Calendar No. 1644.

"To Repeal the Klamath Tribe Judgment Fund Act," Report to Accompany S. 46, March 13, 2019. Calendar No. 37, 116th Cong. 1st Sess. Senate Report 116–6.

Trahant, Mark N. *The Last Great Battle of the Indian Wars: Henry M. Jackson, Forrest J. Gerard and the Campaign for the Self-Determination of America's Indian Tribes*. Ft. Hall ID: Cedars Group, 2010.

Trask, Haunani-Kay. "The Struggle for Hawaiian Sovereignty—Introduction." *Cultural Survival Quarterly* 24, no.1 (2000): 8–11.

Trennert, Robert A. *Indian Traders on the Middle Border, The House of Ewing, 1827–1854*. Lincoln: University of Nebraska Press, 1981.

Tyler, S. Lyman. *A History of Indian Policy*. Washington DC: Bureau of Indian Affairs, 1973.

Ulrich, Roberta. *American Indian Nations from Termination to Restoration, 1953–2006*. Lincoln: University of Nebraska Press, 2010.

United States v. Cook. 86 U.S. 591 (1873).

United States v. Jicarilla Apache Nation. 564 U.S. 162 (2011).

The United States v. Southern Ute Tribe or Band of Indians. 423 F.2d 346 (Ct. Cl. 1970).

United States Statutes at Large.

United States v. Winans. 198 U.S. 371 (1905).

U. S. Congress. House. *Colville Termination*. Hearings before the Subcommittee on Indian Affairs of the Committee on Interior and Insular Affairs, House of Representatives, 89th Cong. 1st Sess., on H.R. 5925 and S. 1413 and H.R. 6331. Washington DC. June 18 and August 13, 1965, Spokane WA November 3, 1965, and Nespelem WA, November 4 and 5, 1965.

U.S. Congress. House. Committee on Indian Affairs. "Hearings on H. Res. 166, A Bill to Authorize and Direct and Conduct an Investigation to Determine whether the changed Status of the Indians Requires a Revision of the Laws and Regulations Affecting the American Indian." March 23, 1943. Washington: United States Government Printing Office, 1943.

U.S. Congress. House. Committee on Indian Affairs. *Hearings on S. 2103, An Act to Exempt Certain Indians and Indian Tribes for the Provisions of the Act of June 18, 1934* (48 Stat. 984), as Amended. June 10–14 and 17–20, 1940. Washington: United States Government Printing Office, 1940.

U.S. Congress. House. Committee on Interior and Insular Affairs. *Restoring to Tribal Ownership Certain Lands upon the Colville Indian Reservation, and for other Purposes*. 84th Cong., 2nd Sess., March 13, 1956.

U.S. Congress. House. Committee on Interior and Insular Affairs, Subcommittee on Indian Affairs. Hearings on H.R. 7104, March 20, 1952.

U.S. Congress. House. "Fort Berthold Hearings." Hearings before the Committee on Indian Affairs, House of Representatives. Seventy-Seventh Congress, First Session on H.R. 46. April 23, 1946.

U.S. Congress. House. "Hearings before a Subcommittee of the Committee on Indian Affairs, House of Representatives pursuant to H. Res. 166, A Bill to Authorize and Direct and Conduct an Investigation to Determine whether the changed Status of the Indians Requires a Revision of the Laws and Regulations Affecting the American Indian." Part 4 (Final Volume): December 4, 5, 6, 7, 8, and 13, 1944. Washington: Government Printing Office, 1945.

U.S. Congress. House. *Report to Accompany S. 3532, Providing for the Partition and Distribution of the Assets of the Indian Tribe of the Uintah and Ouray Reservation in Utah Between Mixed-Blood and Fullblood Members thereof; and for the Termination of Federal Supervision over the Property of the Mixed-Blood Members of Said Tribe; to Provide a Development Program for the Fullblood Members of Said Tribe*. House Report No. 2493. 83rd Cong., 2nd Sess., July 26, 1954.

U.S. Congress. House. *Report with Respect to the House Resolution Authorizing the Committee on Interior and Insular Affairs to Conduct an Investigation of the Bureau of Indian Affairs: Pursuant to House Resolution 89*. House Report No. 2680. 83rd Cong., 2nd Sess., 1954.

U.S. Congress. House. Subcommittee on Interior and Insular Affairs. *Colville Indian Lands, Washington*. Hearings. 84th Cong., 1st Sess., July 21 and 22, 1955.

U.S. Congress. Senate. *Authorizing Certain Bands of Ute Indians to Sue in the United States Court of Claims*. Hearing before a Subcommittee of the Committee on Indian Affairs, United States Senate, 71st Cong. 2nd Sess. On S. 615, May 1, 1930.

U.S. Congress. Senate. Committee on Interior and Insular Affairs. *Per Capita Distribution—Shoshone and Arapaho Tribes, Wyoming*. 83d Cong., 1st Sess., May 12, 1953. Report No. 263 to Accompany H.R. 444.

U.S. Congress. Senate. *Dismissal of Wade Crawford, Superintendent, Klamath Indian Reservation, Oreg*. Hearings before the Committee on Indian Affairs, United States Senate, 75th Cong. 1st Sess., July1, 2, and 8, 1937.

U.S. Congress. Senate. Ex. Doc. No. 72. "Report of Senate Committee on Indian Affairs." February 14, 1853.

U.S. Congress. Senate. "H.R. 1794, Report No. 969." Calendar No. 935. 88th Cong., 2nd Sess., February 10, 1964 and March 26, 1964. Reported with amendments.

U.S. Congress. Senate. *Incorporation of the Klamath Indian Corporation*. Hearings before the Committee on Indian Affairs, United States Senate, 71st Cong., 2nd Sess. on S. 4165, 25 and 29, 1930.

U.S. Congress. Senate. *Officers and Employees of the Federal Government*. Hearings before the Committee on Civil Service on S. Res. 41. 80th Cong., 1st Sess., Part 3. 4, 6, 8, 11, 13, February 15 and 18, 1947.

U.S. Congress. Senate. *Protesting the Construction of Garrison Dam, North Dakota, By the Fort Berhold Indians*. Hearing before the Committee on Indian Affairs, 79th Cong., 1st Sess. On S. J. Res. 79, October 9, 1945.

U.S. Congress. Senate. *Tax-Exempt Indian Lands: Report of the Subcommittee on Indian Affairs, February 1933*. 72nd Congress, 2nd Session. Washington: Government Printing Office, 1933.

U.S. Congressional Serial Set.

Ute Indians v. United States. 45 Ct. Cl. 440 (1910).

Valandra, Edward Charles. *Not Without Our Consent: Lakota Resistance to Termination, 1950–1959*. Champaign: University of Illinois Press, 2006.

VanDevelder, Paul. *Coyote Warrior: One Man, Three Tribes, and the Trial that Forged a Nation*. New York: Little Brown and Company, 2004.

Voyles, Traci Brynne. *Wastelanding: Legacies of Uranium Mining in Navajo Country*. Minneapolis: University of Minnesota Press, 2015.

Wallace, Anthony F. C. *Jefferson and the Indians: The Tragic Fate of the First Americans*. Cambridge MA: Belknap Press, 2001.

Warren, Louis S. *Buffalo Bill's America: William Cody and the Wild West Show*. New York: Alfred A. Knopf, 2005.

Warren, Louis S. "Wage Work in the Sacred Circle: The Ghost Dance as Modern Religion." *Western Historical Quarterly* 46, no. 2 (2015): 141–68.

Weist, Katherine. "For the Public Good: Native Americans, Hydroelectric Dams, and the Iron Triangle." In *Irredeemable America: The Indians' Estate and Land Claims*, edited by Imre Sutton, 55–72. Albuquerque: University of New Mexico Press, 1985.

Whaley, Rick, and Walter Bresette. *Walleye Warriors: An Effective Alliance Against Racism and for the Earth.* Philadelphia PA: New Society Publishers, 1993.

Wilkins, David E. *American Indian Sovereignty and the U.S. Supreme Court: The Masking of Justice.* Austin: University of Texas Press, 1997.

———. *Documents of Native American Political Development, 1500s to 1933.* New York: Oxford University Press, 2009.

———. *Hollow Justice: A History of Indigenous Claims in the United States.* New Haven: Yale University Press, 2013.

Wilkins, David E., and Shelly Hulse Wilkins. *Dismembered: Native Disenrollment and the Battle for Human Rights.* Seattle: University of Washington Press, 2017.

Wilkinson, Glen A. "Indian Tribal Claims Before the Court of Claims." *Georgetown Law Review* 55 (1966): 511–28.

Willacy, Aubrey B. "Contract Approval: Attorneys and Indians." *Howard Law Review* 15, no. 1 (Fall 1968): 149–63.

Williams, Vicky. "The Kinzua Dam Controversy." Master's thesis, State University of New York at Buffalo, 2007.

Witgen, Michael John. *Seeing Red: Indigenous Land, American Expansion, and the Political Economy of Plunder.* Chapel Hill: Omohundro Institute and University of North Carolina Press, 2022.

Worcester v. Georgia, 31 U.S. 515 (1832).

INDEX

Page numbers in italics refer to illustrations

In the New Visions in Native American and Indigenous Studies series

Bribed with Our Own Money: Federal Abuse of American Indian Funds in the Termination Era
David R. M. Beck

Ojibwe Stories from the Upper Berens River: A. Irving Hallowell and Adam Bigmouth in Conversation
Edited and with an introduction by Jennifer S. H. Brown

Resisting Oklahoma's Reign of Terror: The Society of Oklahoma Indians and the Fight for Native Rights, 1923–1928
Joshua Clough

The Incarceration of Native American Women: Creating Pathways to Wellness and Recovery through Gentle Action Theory
Carma Corcoran

Ute Land Religion in the American West, 1879–2009
Brandi Denison

Blood Will Tell: Native Americans and Assimilation Policy
Katherine Ellinghaus

Ecology and Ethnogenesis: An Environmental History of the Wind River Shoshones, 1000–1868
Adam R. Hodge

Wardship and the Welfare State: Native Americans and the Formation of First-Class Citizenship in Mid-Twentieth-Century America
Mary Klann

Of One Mind and Of One Government: The Rise and Fall of the Creek Nation in the Early Republic
Kevin Kokomoor

Invisible Reality: Storytellers, Storytakers, and the Supernatural World of the Blackfeet
Rosalyn R. LaPier

Indigenous Languages and the Promise of Archives
Edited by Adrianna Link, Abigail Shelton, and Patrick Spero

Life of the Indigenous Mind: Vine Deloria Jr. and the Birth of the Red Power Movement
David Martínez

Everywhen: Australia and the Language of Deep History
Ann McGrath, Laura Rademaker, and Jakelin Troy

All My Relatives: Exploring Lakota Ontology, Belief, and Ritual
David C. Posthumus

Standing Up to Colonial Power: The Lives of Henry Roe and Elizabeth Bender Cloud
Renya K. Ramirez

Walking to Magdalena: Personhood and Place in Tohono O'odham Songs, Sticks, and Stories
Seth Schermerhorn

To order or obtain more information on these or other University of Nebraska Press titles, visit nebraskapress.unl.edu.

Printed in the USA
CPSIA information can be obtained
at www.ICGtesting.com
CBHW032305190324
5518CB00013B/31/J